this page has been intentinally left blank

The Life of a Blue Collar Actor

From Tobacco Road to Buckingham Palace by way of New York Theatre, and Hollywood Films

Written by
Jordan Rhodes

Comments

"Jordan, I'm proud to call you my friend."
-- Scott Brady

"In the world of acting and theatre, Jordan Rhodes is your guy. He is an actors actor, he has seen and done it all, and is uniquely qualified to tell the real story of the life of a professional actor."
-- John Dempsey President of Sandhills College

"I am pleased to endorse "A Blue Collar Actor" by veteran actor Jordan Rhodes. He has spent a lifetime appearing in theatre, television and motion pictures, and he has a realistic sense of the true life of a professional actor."
-- James Nagel, Ph.D.
Edison Distinguished Professor of American Literature - UGA

"Jordan first came to my attention as a gifted actor on "Marcus Welby, M.D.11", a series I was producing for Universal Studios. Impressed by his talent, we cast him in other episodes and recommended him to other producers."
-- David J. O'Connell
Producer

"The outstanding performance of Jordan Rhodes makes for a wonderful evening of Theatre."
-- Frank Capra, Jr.
Screen Gems Studios

"Brilliant actor."
-- Sam L. Garner
The Thalian Association

"Jordan is clearly in command of his subject, but presents his insights in a friendly and engaging manner."
-- Philip Furia,
Professor Creative Writing - UNCW

The Life of a Blue Collar Actor

From Tobacco Road to Buckingham Palace by way of New York Theatre, and Hollywood Films

Written by
Jordan Rhodes

Copyright © 2020 by Jordan Rhodes www.jordanrhodes.com

All rights reserved under International and Pan-American Copyright Conventions. Published in the United States by Rhodes Productions.

Book Cover Design - Mike Schnorr, Art Center Graphics

No part of this book may be reproduced in any form or by any electronic or mechanical means including information storage and retrieval systems, without permission in writing from the author. The only exception is by a reviewer, who may quote short excerpts in a review.

ISBN-13 978-1-66781-970-9
Rhodes Productions.

www.artcentergraphics.com
Printed in the United States of America, July 2021

Dedication

I dedicate this book to my mother, Edith, who always gave me her love and support, to my daughter, Cheyenne, who believes I'm the greatest dad in the world, and to my friend, Leo Penn, who said to me years ago, "You should write these stories down kid, they're gold."

Table of Contents

Comments	IV
Dedication	VII
Foreword	XII
Introduction	XIII
Chapter One	1
The Early Years	
Chapter Two	9
Chapter Three	22
Chapter Four	32
The Baltimore Years	
Chapter Five	43
Chapter Six	52
New York - The First Tour	
Chapter Seven	65
Chapter Eight	74
Chapter Nine	87
Chapter Ten	100
Chapter Eleven	112
Chapter Twelve	126
Chapter Thirteen	139
Chapter Fourteen	149
Chapter Fifteen	160
Moving to California	
Chapter Sixteen	177

Chapter Seventeen	188
Chapter Eighteen	202
Chapter Nineteen	215
Chapter Twenty	228
Chapter Twenty-One	249
Wedding-Europe-Daughter	
Chapter Twenty-Two	259
Chapter Twenty-Three	272
Chapter Twenty-Four	280
Mountain Move Mistake	
Chapter Twenty-Five	292
Buckingham Palace and Return	
Chapter Twenty-Six	299
New York – Second Tour	
Chapter Twenty-Seven	310
Chapter Twenty-Eight	321
Chapter Twenty-Nine	333
Radio – Wilmington – Hurricane	
Chapter Thirty	350
Marriage and Becoming Hemingway	
Chapter Thirty-One	362
Chapter Thirty-Two	375
Chapter Thirty-Three	383
Return to New York – Present Tour	
Acknowledgments & Notes	393

Foreword

What a wonderful ride this book describes, following a young man from his summers working on his Uncles sharecropper tobacco farm, to the gold and glitter of an invitation to Buckingham Palace by Prince Philip. You'll learn about the people, the actors, and the stars he met along the way, through the theatrical world of New York City, to the film capital of the world, Hollywood. The obstacles he overcame including desertion by an alcoholic father, his triumphs, his mistakes and disappointments. It's all revealed here written in a joyous, sad and devastatingly honest manner with positive thoughts. We have worked with Jordan, and have known him for many years, and consider him a remarkable friend. Throughout his career he has acquired the respect of his co-workers in the theatre, television, and film world, the old fashion way – he earned it.

We admire Jordan tremendously, and after reading his book – we believe you will too!

--- Jill St. John & Robert Wagner

Introduction

When someone first said to me, "You should write a book, man," my reaction was, "Who would want to read a book about me?" Then someone said that I was probably the only person from my background that had not only become a "working actor", but through my trials and travels along this road, was most certainly the only person from my background that had ever been invited to a cocktail reception at Buckingham Palace, hosted by Prince Phillip, along with the likes of Ernest Borgnine, Robert Stack, Telly Savalas, Hal Linden, Richard Crenna, Glen Campbell and Fred MacMurray

Along the way, I managed to work in over two hundred combined television shows, films and theatrical plays, met and even became friends with a few movie stars. So perhaps this is a way to give some hope and encouragement to others from different walks of life. If a "shitkicker" (a term laid on me by one of my best friends) from a lower-than-middle-class family in North Carolina could get to Buckingham Palace, there should be hope for almost anyone, in any field of endeavor.

Hence this book. No holds barred. The entire trip. From the beginning in North Carolina, with my summers spent working on my uncles tobacco farm. Moving to my grandmother's boarding room house when I was 14, and leaving school to journey on to Baltimore, Maryland, to hook up with my dad, who was an alcoholic, and move in with him on "skid row". After lying about my age to get a job selling shoes, I got an apartment for old Dad and me. I managed to get involved with the theatre, did some summer stock and, due to a strange set of circumstances, made the move to the Big Apple - New York City. Trying and failing a number of times to get into the Actors Studio (years later I was invited to join Actors Studio West and worked there a couple of times), a place where any young actor worth his salt wanted to study. Marlon Brando and James Dean had come from the Actors Studio, and, if accepted, you didn't have to pay if you couldn't afford it. I couldn't afford it. But I had seen James Dean in a film and I knew that I wanted to do "that" - acting - whatever it was, whatever it took. Dean was killed in a car crash in September 1955. Five months later, in February, 1956, I was on my way to Baltimore, the first stopping-off point for New York City, where I landed in 1958. Seven years later, Hollywood followed.

    But let's start in Baltimore, Maryland, in 1956, when I arrived by Greyhound Bus to meet up with my dad. I hadn't seen him for over three years, and boy, it was a shock to see him as a shell of his former self when I stepped off the bus.

    I was lucky enough to arrive in California in 1965, in time to catch some of the "old-school" Hollywood. The studio system still existed, which included contract players. I was able to meet and work with some of the "Hollywood elite" like John Wayne, James Garner, Gene Hackman, Gregory Peck and Robert Wagner. I became friends with Scott Brady, Chuck Connors, Robert Wagner, and, from a younger generation, Sean Penn, whom I was actually able to lend a helping hand to very early in his career. One of the highlights of my career was spending an evening at the party for the premier of the first big film I did, MAROONED, meeting and talking with Robert Mitchum and Scott Brady, and listening to the stories told by Bob Mitchum about studio heads like Harry Cohen and his encounter with Shelley Winters. I was even working on the series, Peyton Place, when Mia Farrow got her "famous" haircut, and I know the "real story". As for stories, I've got enough of them to fill a book (no pun intended).

    I was lucky enough along the way to work with some big name directors of the day. Directors like Richard Fleisher, whom I didn't have the best rapport with, John Sturges and Andrew McLaughlin, both of whom I admired and respected, and two of the best directors I ever had both the privilege and pleasure to work for, Leo Penn and his son, actor/director Sean Penn.

    Of course, along the way, there was a "drug period". Hell, it was the 60's when I was getting started and most of my friends were all doing some kind of dope. There was a marriage, followed by another marriage that produced a daughter, and a third marriage that continues today. Some of the other "names" I worked with include Charles Bronson, Karl Malden, Barbara Rush, Fess Parker, Jack Klugman, Sal Mineo, Nick Nolte, Leslie Nielsen, Dennis Hopper, Viggo Mortensen, E.G. Marshall, Michael Landon, Brian Dennehy, Howard DaSilva, Lee J. Cobb, Linda Cristal, Dyan Cannon, Tyne Daly, Lorne Greene, Melissa Gilbert, Pamela Franklin, Walter Brennan, Buddy Ebsen and Jodie Foster, to mention a few. Before you finish this book, you will find out how, when and where I met these people, worked with these people and became friends with many of them, and some interesting "behind the scenes" stories. Amazingly I'M STILL AT IT, some 50 plus years later.

    I Hope You Enjoy The Ride, At Least Half As Much As I Enjoyed Taking It!

-- Jordan Rhodes

Written By Jordan Rhodes

Chapter One
The Early Years

According to my mom and early records from "old" Rex Hospital in Raleigh, North Carolina, I was born on a Sunday morning June 11 at 1:57 a.m.

I learned later from people into astronomy that my sun sign was Gemini, the twins, my rising sign was Aries, and my moon was in Leo. I still don't know what all that means, but a very famous astrological reader, George Darious (Elizabeth Taylor used to go see him), told me that Aries and Leo saved my life.

I was the son of Garland Julian and Edith Mae. Now Mae was not my mother's "given" middle name - she never liked her given middle name, so she changed it to Mae. Since I believe anyone should have the right to change their name, I shall respect her wishes. After all, what is truly in a name? "A rose by any other name would smell as sweet," etc. I doubt that Marion Morrison would have struck the fear in all those bad guys in the movies that the name John Wayne did. Big John certainly carries more weight than Big Marion.

I never cared for my given name, so all through school I was known as C.J. Even my father, to quote Johnny Cash from the song, "A Boy Named Sue", "who gave me that awful name," hardly ever called me anything but "Bo" in my early years, and later he took to calling me Kim, which he said was an Indian name of affection. So, I chose to use the family name, Jordan, which has become quite a popular name these days.

My life growing up in North Carolina wasn't much different than most of my cousins with the exception that they lived on farms and we were "city dwellers". We were poor but I didn't really know it. All of my cousins that lived in the country seemed to be in the same condition that we were. Food on the table, a roof over your head, a comfortable bed to sleep in, and clean clothes to wear. I didn't discover that we didn't have any money until I got to Carr Junior High, and later Durham High School in the city of Durham, a more cosmopolitan city than I was used to. My peers wore Bass Weejun loafers, shirts with the little alligator or polo player on the upper left breast area while all my shirt had was a pocket. For pants, they wore the khaki cotton slacks with the little buckle in the back (which I never understood what the function was) or Levi Jeans, and they had the all-white low cut tennis shoes for gym. Now those tennis shoes I envied. My tennis shoes (or "sneakers" as they are called today) were the black and white high tops from J.C. Penney, and my shoes were lace-up jobs that came from Thom McCann. I got a new pair at the beginning of the school year, and that was usually because I had outgrown the old ones.

My so-called slacks were blue jeans from Sears and Roebucks. They were called "Roebucks". I thought they were pretty neat. They had a raised flap on the front pockets that made it easy to get your hand in even if you were sitting down. I would never have had the nerve to ask for a pair of Levis. I thought I was lucky to have the Roebucks. After all, they weren't overalls, which is what most of my male cousins that lived on the farm wore.

Now I've referred to my peer group, but I don't want to leave out the "beautiful people". Of course they wore all those fashion duds I've described, but they also lived in the big houses, which their parents actually owned. And some, like Nello L. Teer, Jr. (he was really the Third, but they called him Junior), were given a car on their sixteenth birthday. Of course, Nello, Jr., was treated like shit by his father, Nello, Sr., in front of the school crowd, so I don't know if the trade-off was worth it. He did date the prettiest girl in school, Janet Couch. Her father owned the local furniture stores. I discovered later that Nello, Jr., and Janet got married. Of course Junior took over the family business (which, oddly enough, my second stepfather went to work for).

We moved a lot. My dad, in addition to being quite a character, was also something of a vagabond. Growing up, one of my grade schools was in Roxboro, North Carolina, where my dad and mom had a small business, Jordan's Bar-B-Que. Dad cooked pork on the pit, real North Carolina Bar-B-Que. Mom worked in the restaurant and I was a car-hop taking the orders when I could just see above the window on the driver's side. Of course, Dad grew tired of that after a while and let a nephew of his take over the business, which he quickly ran into the ground. There was one encounter that took place between my dad and four local "toughs" on our opening night, which was a Saturday. This episode cemented the view I had of my dad as John Wayne in my kid's mind.

Prior to our opening, two of the local police paid a visit to meet my dad at our little drive-in restaurant. I remember the police officers explaining to my mom and dad that the previous owners had some problems with a local group of young trouble makers, and they had actually caused the owner to close down and move on.

My dad could be a bit of a hot-head. Being Cherokee Indian and Irish, the Irish part might be hot, but the Cherokee part would remain very cool. This made him a pretty dangerous combination to mess with. He was also a tough country boy that had worked hard all his life.

Standing over six feet tall and weighing a hard 240 lbs., he was nobody's push-over. After listening to these two police officers "explaining" how they "might" not be able to be around if these guys did show up to cause trouble, my dad replied that he wasn't worried. He took a meat clever and planted it in a block of wood, then thanked them for the "warning". There was some protesting by the police, and a comment that my dad shouldn't do anything crazy that could get him in trouble. Dad replied, "This was his property and he had every right to defend it, and his family working there against anybody that threatened him." He thanked the police for dropping by and went back to work. After they left, still grumbling about "being careful", Dad told Mom, "Those guys were looking for a pay-off for protection, and I'm not interested."

Well, Saturday night rolled around and we opened. And we were busy. Mom and dad's nephew, Dan, were working in the restaurant, which consisted of a long counter with about fourteen stools, and two booths down on the left. It had one door opening into the restaurant right in the middle, with a screen door closed, keeping flies and other airborne critters outside. The screen door was just a wood frame covered by a mesh screen, with a wood cross section in the middle and a little wire spring attached so it would slam shut. Constructed to the right of the restaurant was a large open cooking pit where my dad cooked the pig and chopped the Bar-B-Que. There was a window section cut out behind the counter between the restaurant and the pit area, so Mom could talk to Dad and he could talk to her if needed. Dad worked in a shirt with the sleeves rolled up, and a pair of dungarees with a big white apron tied around his waist. It was always hot in the pit, and even hotter in the summer – and it was summer.

    Sure enough, the trouble-makers showed up. They arrived in a black four-door Chevy. One of the bigger young guys got out of the right rear door, and before I could get to their car and attempt to take their food order, he walked into the restaurant. About four of the stools were empty at the counter and he took the center one. I came in to give Dan an order I had taken from another car. I was too young to understand the comments this guy was making to my mom, but she didn't appreciate it. Mom was a very attractive lady, and some men would make an effort to flirt a bit, but this was in the late 40's, so it never bordered on anything nasty or obscene. Obviously this guy was going over the line. So Dan told Mom to call Garland, and as she walked toward the window, this guy said, "Hell yeah, go on and call ole Garland, let's get ole Garland in here." Mom called out to my dad about there being trouble inside. Now to see my dad, hot, with sweat running down his face, his dark eyes narrow – as a kid I had seen this look when he was mad, and it was scary! Dad stepped through the door, the guy wheeled around on his stool, with his elbows on the counter, facing my dad, and said, "Well, hell, you must be Garland." Dad, in one quick move as he replied, "Yeah – I'm Garland!" He grabbed this guy by the front collar and jerked him up off his stool, turned him around and grabbed the back of his belt on his pants and the back of his shirt collar - keeping his feet off the floor - and literally ran him through the screen door tearing the screen mesh off, and busting the center wooden piece out. As Dad continued carrying this guy into the gravel parking lot, one of the other guys in the black four-door Chevy started out, and Dad headed straight to the car, slammed the guy into the side of the car, opened the back door and threw the guy head-first into the car. The guy was cussing at my dad, with a lot of, "Let me out - let me get 'em," and when he started out, Dad grabbed him in the face and shoved him back in the car. Then Dad took one step back and said, "The next time you try to come out of there boy, I'm gonna let you!" He said it with such a calm, clear, dangerous tone that the guy just froze. The other guy that had started out on the other side of the car just kind of slithered back into the car. The two guys in the front never made a move. My dad stood there glaring at these guys – no weapons, just all of him. They started the car and slowly drove off. We were never bothered again. Like I said, my dad WAS John Wayne!

Chapter Two

My grade schools continued in North Carolina at Raleigh, Garner, Hope Valley, and Durham, then up to Portsmouth, Virginia, back to North Carolina, then back to Virginia. While living in Portsmouth, I did have the advantage of floating on a truck tire inner tube in Chesapeake Bay. We lived about four blocks from one of the piers that extended out into the Chesapeake Bay, so when the water was warm enough I'd drag an old used truck tire tube down to the Bay, jump in and float around (usually until I was sunburned). I've paid for that later in life by having to have a number of Mohs surgeries. So remember to put on your sunscreen!

But no matter where we were living, each summer from the ages of about nine to twelve years old I'd get to go live and work with one of my dad's brothers. I'd work at my Uncle Paul's, and, for the most part, just visit my Uncle Hubert and Uncle Purvis to spend time with my cousins. We'd get to swim in the creek, where we dug out a large hole and sealed it up like beavers, making a dam and voila! – the old swimming hole! We would enjoy it until the occasional water moccasin snake came floating down the creek bed and made it into the swimming hole. Then it was every man for himself! I'd work and live at my Uncle Paul's with his family on the farm. Uncle Paul had five girls: Evelyn, Gladys, Ruth, Maddie and Betsy; and two boys: Shorty and Bradley. Maddie, Betsy, Ruth and Shorty lived and worked on the farm, but the others had moved away and were on their own. Uncle Paul lived close to another brother - Uncle Hubert - and he had a farm and kids, too. I had a lot of cousins and I was always called the "city kid cousin". I got a fair amount of teasing about living in the city, and even picked on sometimes, but Betsy (she was my favorite, and still is today, I call her "Sis"), she always stuck up for me and looked out for me. I've never forgotten that.

Uncle Paul was a tobacco farmer - a sharecropper (he never owned the farm) - and everybody in the family worked in tobacco. I learned to do everything from "hand tobacco" to "tying" tobacco to the real fun of driving the tobacco sleds. That is, of course, if you consider getting up at 6 a.m. every morning when you're a kid out from school on summer vacation and working until dark - "fun". – then it was fun. Actually it was fun! Driving those sleds. Uncle Paul only had one tractor, so the tobacco sleds were pulled by mules. The sleds were about six feet long and two and a half feet wide with wood slats on the bottom making a floor. There would be six one by three (1 inch X 3 inch) pieces of wood, three to a side, nailed to the bottom slats and extending a little over three feet tall. Gunny sacks would be attached to the one by three pieces of boards on the side of the sled, forming or creating a "holding bin" for the tobacco leaves to be placed into. Running on both sides of the bottom of the sleds and attached to the slats would be the "runners", pieces of wood two inches wide and about four inches high that had been rounded off both front and back so they would traverse the dirt road and paths that led to the tobacco fields. The mule would be hitched up at the front of the sled and the driver would stand on a little platform extending about a foot from the bottom back of the sled. You'd stand back there with the reins in your hands leading to the mule and drive the sled. The commands for the mule were a kind of clicking sound you'd make with your tongue and cheek followed by a loud "git-up mule" to go forward, a firm "gee" and a pull on the right rein to go right and a firm "haw" and pull on the left rein to go left. To stop, you pulled back on both reins and called out "whoa". You'd do a lot of starting and stopping as you drove your sled perpendicular to the rows of tobacco, out in the field where the workers, called "primers", snapped the large tobacco leaves from the bottom of the stalk, moving from stalk to stalk until they reached the end of the row, then they would deposit the leaves in your sled. When the sled was full to the top of the gunny sacks, you would head back to the barn. This is when you'd get a chance to let your imagination run wild.

I'd be a stagecoach driver in the old west transporting a valuable load of cargo and people through hostile Indian Territory. Of course you had to be careful not to run the mule too fast and take the risk of turning over the sled or tiring out the mule. In those days, almost everyone had a bunch of kids but maybe only two or three mules, and you only had to feed and water the mules in order for them to work all day, every day, never complain or want to go into town. You didn't even have to buy them clothes. So, in many ways, the mule was more valuable than the kids. Anyway, that's the impression the adults gave us kids, after all they'd say, "You could have more kids, but a good mule was hard to come by." Back at the barn, there would be a group of people hard at work tying the tobacco leaves to long sticks that would later be hung in the barn to cure before they would take it to the market to sell. You would drive up, help unload your tobacco and head back out to the field. Obviously, another opportunity to drive your "coach" through hostile Indian Territory. Later in my life as a published poet, I wrote a poem about those days, entitled, "A Kid's Delight". Here it is.

Written By Jordan Rhodes

A Kid's Delight

Summers at my Uncle Paul's were always looked forward
To. Early June, school almost out, no more trips
          Down to Chesapeake Bay, where I'd
Jump off the pier and float on the inner tube
          For another lazy day.
Soon I'd be packed off to Uncle Paul's - spend the summer
Working on the tobacco farm. It was a chance to visit
          with the cousins, mostly work
But some play, and this summer I would get to drive the
          Tobacco sleigh! It was really a sled.
But for me and my imagination it was a transport back in
          Time. Standing on the back of the sled.
With the reins going to my trusty steed - a mule - that
Pulled me, a load of tobacco leaves and my imagination
          Through treacherous territory - I was
John Wayne driving the stagecoach and outrunning the
          Indians, making the delivery at the way
Station, then back to the fields for another load, and
          This time I'd have to avoid the outlaws
In order to deliver the tobacco leaves. Yes, it was work,
          Usually taking all day from early morning
Light - but for a kid that lived in the city, spending
summers

At Uncle Paul's was a kid's delight.

-- Jordan Rhdoes

3/26/12

Sometimes, on Saturday, if the work was all caught up, which wasn't often, we'd all pile into the pick-up truck, travel into Raleigh and go to the Capital movie theatre. We'd get to see a western picture show, an episode of a serial (I remember Rocket Man), a comedy (usually the Three Stooges) and two cartoons. Each of us kids would get twenty-five cents. It cost nine cents to get into the movie. Popcorn, a drink and a box of candy would cost five cents each. Me, I was always kinda partial to Good & Plenty. And you'd have a whole penny left over. One Sunday, after having seen a Lash LaRue western on Saturday, I had ventured over to my Uncle Hubert's. Uncle Hubert also had a farm, but I always enjoyed staying and working at my Uncle Paul's house. I got along better with his kids and loved Uncle Paul a lot. Uncle Hubert always amazed us kids because he was a big round man that had these little feet. We could never figure out how he was able to balance himself on those little feet and stay upright. He was also the only person we ever knew or saw that could drink a full six ounce bottle of Coca-Cola with one turn up from start to finish! Sometimes one of us kids would try it and our eyes would practically burst out of the sockets flooded with tears before we could get more than a few swallows down.

On this Sunday, I was off playing by myself, which I would do often. Being an only child, I had learned how to occupy myself and let my imagination take me wherever I wanted to go. Having just seen Lash LaRue round up a gang of bad guys, I was now helping him clean up Tombstone and getting ready to hang one of these guys. I was out behind one of the sheds and of course I was playing all the parts. In preparation to hang the bad guy, I tossed a rope up on the roof of the shed. Unknown to me the rope had managed to wind its way around two large ten-penny nail heads that were extending above the roof. I had one of Uncle Hubert's wooden Coca-Cola crates, he bought Coke by the case, and I stood it up on one end, stepped up on the other end and placed the noose, which I had skillfully created, around my neck. Of course in my role as Black Bart I pleaded with the townspeople not to hang me, all to no avail. While holding the noose with both hands around my neck, I kicked out away from the Coca-Cola crate fully expecting to land on the ground where I would pretend to hang. Imagine my surprise when the rope, held by the two nails on the roof of the shed, tightened and kept my feet about two inches from touching the ground! And there I hung, with both hands inside the noose pressed against my neck. As fate would have it, Uncle Hubert was walking to the shed and came around the corner to see me dangling in mid-air making strange gurgling sounds. Then, in what seemed to take place in absolute slow motion, Uncle Hubert looked up at me hanging there and without any panic whatsoever, proceeded to say the following while methodically reaching for his pocket knife (which he always carried in the breast pocket of his overalls), "Well damn, boy, what in the hell are you trying to do?" as he cut the rope. I fell to the ground grasping for breath as he closed the knife and carefully replaced it back in his breast pocket of the overalls and left me with these parting words, "Damned if you ain't the craziest young'un I've ever seen in my life." And he continued on his way. He never asked me how was I, or what was I doing.

The next weekend, when Mom and Dad came out to see everybody and see how I was getting along, they came to Uncle Hubert's where we all had gathered for the visit, when Dad saw the rope burns on my neck (which were still visible). He asked how I got them. To which Uncle Hubert replied, "You know how that boy is, he was playing some damn cowboy game and almost hung hisself." Needless to say, I haven't lived that story down to this day. Cousins have incredible memories.

Written By Jordan Rhodes

Even though it was hard work, I enjoyed those summers. The last year I remember working on the farm, I had been hinting about getting a bicycle. Hinting is what you did, you didn't have the nerve to ask for a bike – anyway, my dad told me if I saved all my money from working on the farm that summer, he'd put up the rest and buy me a bike. I saved everything I made that summer, a whopping $18, which I had all in one dollar bills. When I came home on a Sunday morning from the country, I gave my hard earned cash, all $18 of it, to my dad. He took the money and told me we'd go into town on Monday and get me a bike. $18 wasn't enough to buy any bike, but Dad kept his word, took me into town to the Montgomery Ward store and bought me a Columbia bicycle.

Like I mentioned before, my dad was a bit of a vagabond. Even though he had that little drive-in restaurant in Roxboro, by trade he was a first-class electrician. All self-taught, learned the basics out of books and the rest by trial and error. When we lived in Portsmouth, Virginia, he worked at the Norfolk Naval Shipyard and was one of the head electricians that helped wire one of the great battleships. I believe it was the USS Missouri. Not bad for a guy that had to leave school in the fourth grade in order to stay home and take care of his mom and dad.

He was the youngest of eight siblings. In those days, the baby of the family stayed behind to take care of the parents. But, to me, my dad was never a baby of anything. As I described him before, standing just over 6 feet 2 inches tall and weighing a lean hard 240 pounds, he was a big man by the standards of the day. To me, as a kid, and long before the booze got the best of him, he was John Wayne. With his craggy face good looks, part Cherokee and part Irish, he had his code of conduct, which was a code I heard much later in life from John Wayne himself in his last film. It went, "I won't be wronged, I won't be insulted, and I won't be laid a hand on. I don't do these things to others and I require the same of them." This fit my dad right down to a T.

He also had a good deal of natural musical talent. He could tap dance and he could play almost any string instrument by ear - the guitar, banjo, fiddle and mandolin. My mom told me how he once won first and third place in the same traveling talent show – part of the final era of traveling vaudeville-type shows. A very early American Idol. It was at the Capital Theatre in Raleigh, North Carolina, the same theatre I would attend on Saturdays in later years to see those westerns. He entered in two categories, tap dancing, playing the banjo and singing. He won first place in the competition by tap dancing in a pair of hobnail work boots, then went backstage, changed into overalls, put on blackface make-up and a straw hat, and won third place singing and playing the banjo in black-face, (which was not politically incorrect at the time).

The lady who ran the traveling show wanted him to join the company and go with them, but my dad said no, he couldn't because he had to stay home to take care of his folks. In addition to the prize money he won (a whopping twenty-five dollars), the lady gave him a pair of real tap shoes, so he didn't have to keep dancing in his hobnail work boots. He told me the story of how he went home with those dancing shoes, he put them on and went out to the barn to give 'em a try. He said those shoes were so light that when he jumped up to click his heels together, he flew clear up and hit his head on the rafters in the ceiling of the barn! Said it took him a year to get used to those damn tap shoes.

As I said, my dad was a character. I remember my dad was a decent and fair man, until alcohol got a hold on him and it all went to shit.

Even though we moved around a lot, never owned a house and I was always the "new kid" in school, we got by OK. In fact, it was due to the new kid "defenses" that I was first bitten by the acting bug. We had just moved again and I was a few days late signing up as a student for the seventh grade at Hope Valley School, located in Hope Valley, North Carolina, just on the outskirts of Durham. Upon entering the classroom, the teacher, Mrs. Valentine, welcomed me and introduced me to the class. She then assigned me a seat in the back of the classroom saying it was all that was available. As I journeyed toward my seat I remarked, "It'll be all right, I'll be able to talk back here." This immediately earned me the title of the "smart ass". Toward the middle of the school year, I was now trying to fit in by playing basketball on the team (and not very well, I might add, as I never excelled in sports in school), some guy came to the classroom one day with an Operetta of Tom Sawyer. It seems this guy traveled all over the country getting seventh graders to perform this show. Mrs. Valentine was thrilled, and agreed that her class would be happy and proud to do Tom Sawyer. And she added that she had the perfect Tom – yours truly. Well I replied in a low growl, as low as I had in the seventh grade, "I'm not doing no dumb play." Mrs. Valentine had other ideas. She knew I was smitten by Rebecca Leigh, a very pretty sandy blonde girl that Mrs. Valentine had picked to play Becky, Tom's girlfriend in the show. She also sweetened the pot by saying if I did the part and rehearsed with Rebecca and the music teacher each day, she would not assign me any homework for the duration of the show! The girl I was sweet on to act with – and no homework! DEAL! I was now in show business.

That show was the most fun I had ever experienced in school. For the three weekends we performed the show, I was King! I quickly learned that I could make the audience laugh, listen quietly, and even gasp. I had now been bitten by the acting bug! Without any doubt, that experience remains a highlight of my academic years. The only negative that lingers is the fact that neither my mom nor my dad ever came to see the show. To say it bothered me would be an understatement. Here it is over fifty years later and I still remember the feeling.

Chapter Three

I believe I would have been a happy kid at Hope Valley. I had a girlfriend and I was kind of a "big man on campus" with the success of Tom Sawyer. But we moved again inside the city limits of Durham and I had to start another new school, Carr Junior High. But this would be the last "school" move until I went to Durham High. Three years in the same schools! Carr Junior and Durham High were sister schools. You would go to Carr Junior for 7th, 8th & 9th grades, then on to Durham High. I was at Carr Junior for the 8th & 9th grades and then I went to Durham High. They were within walking distance of each other.

I don't recall the exact time frame, but during this next period, my dad started drinking pretty heavy. He was now working for Long Dairy Farms, keeping the electrical equipment running properly. As he would put it, "Showing them college educated boys how to put the wires together."

Mom and Dad loved to go out dancing at the various spots around the county. They had a lot of friends at all these country clubs (not to be confused with "country clubs" of today, I'm talking about clubs in the country). Most of them were on some back dirt roads where a band would play country music and almost everyone had a bottle of booze on them or in the glove box of their car. These were not country clubs where you played golf, tennis, had dinner or talked business, these were just clubs – dives, in the country.

    Dad was always popular because he would occasionally sit in with the band and play guitar or banjo during the breaks. One of the more popular things Mom and Dad did together was to dance with each other while Dad played the guitar. He would hang the guitar over Mom's back and play while they danced together. It presented a comical image, but they were good and the crowds loved it. A lot of us kids would be allowed to go with our parents to these clubs, listen to the music and watch the grown-ups having fun. Sometimes you'd get to see a fight. Dad would pitch in and help the bouncer, a good friend of his named Clarence Newton, on the occasion when a group of individuals would start getting rowdy or rude. I saw my dad and Clarence throw as many as five guys out of a club on more than one occasion. Like I said about my dad, in my eyes he was John Wayne. Then the damndest thing you'd ever see - three or four days later, they'd all be buying each other a drink! In those days hardly anyone ever pulled out a gun or a knife, just old-fashioned fisticuffs.

    Everything started to change when Dad began to really drink to excess. He started becoming jealous about Mom for no justifiable reason. Mom was attractive and some of their male friends would kid around within the proper bounds (you have to remember this was around 1952 and people were much more respectful). The kidding was the same good natured fun it had been before, but now Dad observed it through hazy eyes. The verbal fighting kept getting worse, even turning physical on one occasion. I'll never forget pulling my dad off my mom during that altercation. Me, a twelve year old boy grabbing what seemed like a mountain of a man, and pulling him off my mom, then yelling for her to run out the backdoor.

    When he tore free and turned on me, I thought he was going to kill me, but he gathered himself up and just told me to get away. What caused this explosion between them was a poor choice of words my mother used during a very heated verbal fight. She had called him a son-of-a-bitch, which my dad took as a personal affront, and an attack on his mother. If you wanted my dad to fight, all you had to do was use that term. After that "family moment" and exchange, the verbal fighting and bickering was driving me crazy. He was going to leave! She was going to leave! Finally when I couldn't take it anymore – I left! I went to live at my grandmother's boarding house. It's so strange to refer to her as my grandmother, she was my grandma. Her name was

Burra Parham. She was my grandma on my mom's side and she was the only grandparent I ever knew. My dad's parents had died before I ever had a memory of them. Grandma had remarried after her husband, my mom's dad, had passed away – another term for died. Grandma had remarried a man named Mr. Parham, and to this day I don't know the man's first name. We always had to call him Mr. Parham and that was it. Shortly after I moved into Grandma's boarding house, Mr. Parham moved out. No one ever talked about it. Not too long after I moved in with Grandma, Mom also moved in. Dad left the area and went to Baltimore, Maryland, where I would hook up with him some years later.

There were a number of Air Force servicemen that were boarders at Grandma's along with another group that worked at the tobacco barns and factories in Durham. At the time, Durham was quite a tobacco haven. Leggett Meyers, Reynolds and other companies had their headquarters there.

At that time the Air Force had the National Air Observer Corps which I joined. Their headquarters was right across the street from Grandma's boarding house, and I learned how to track and plot airline flights. It was 1954, and America was still on guard to keep from being bombed. We received that wonderfully useless training in the event of being attacked and bombed with an atomic bomb. Once we heard the alarm, we were told to take cover under our wooden desk. Now, you have to remember, this was after being shown a film of an atomic bomb blast which had leveled an entire town! So, hiding under a wooden desk didn't seem to make much sense, but that was our "survival training" at the time.

I had settled into school at Durham High, which was within walking distance (albeit a good walk) from Grandma's. Or, if you were running late, you could take the city bus. I joined the school band hoping to play drums, but being late to register, I couldn't be a first line drummer. I had to be a substitute drummer and join the color guard. That's where I met my only long time-keep-in-touch-with friend from my school years, Bill Hall. He was the captain of the color guard, which was taken very seriously at that time, and was a very important part of the band.

When I was younger, I used to pal around with my cousin Earl. He and his family were city dwellers like us and he was the son of my favorite aunt, Aunt Pauline. She was my mom's favorite sister, and I never missed a chance to go visit her when I would return to North Carolina in later years to see my mom. Earl and I were like brothers for a time as we were growing up. Earl had one sister, Virginia, and I was an only child, so we hung out all the time during the school year. We did all the goofy things kids did in those days. Sneaking into movies, sometimes getting caught, sneaking into the Armory to see real live wrestling, and never getting caught. Of course, this was when we believed professional wrestling was real. We saw wrestlers like Gorgeous George and Antonino Rocca. Earl and I had a lot of fun but when he failed a school year, he lost interest, eventually dropped out and joined the Air Force. That's when Bill Hall became my new buddy and we remained friends until his death. Bill and I did a lot of crazy things, but we never got into any serious trouble. He used to tell his kids that I always got him into trouble when I'd get him to cut school with me. We'd go down to the local pool hall where the owner would let us in to shoot pool for most of the day, then we would go and try to sneak into the Centre Theatre in Durham so we could see the first show and make it out in time to get home as though we had just gotten out of school. One day, Bill came by Grandma's house to meet me so we could go to school together. It was raining really hard. I talked Bill into walking to school in the rain very slowly so we would get soaked. When we arrived at school drenched to the skin, the principal sent us back home to change clothes. We went back to Grandma's where I lent Bill a change of clothes, we got out of our wet clothes and headed directly for the local pool hall, cutting the rest of the school day. That turned out not to be a very smart thing to do as we got caught, which ended our cutting classes for the rest of the school year.

My sophomore year at Durham High was a pretty good year. My home life was okay. Mom had moved into Grandma's and I had adjusted pretty well.

I was able to make trips with the band. I was a substitute drummer, so I served in the color guard carrying a fake rifle as our football team traveled to various cities to play Friday night games. I was dating Rachel Crutchfield, one of the majorettes, and we traveled in the same bus. So we'd sneak into the back of the bus for "making out," which in my day was a lot of kissing, a little fondling (very little) and trying to cop as many "feels" as possible. It was very exciting even if it was hard on your body and your hormones.

In those days, there were really no state funds in North Carolina for a lot of supplies in school. You were responsible for book fees, all your school supplies and, obviously, your clothes. With money being so tight, by my junior year I had to ask to be enrolled in the D.E. or D.O. plan. This was called Diversified Education or Diversified Occupation. You would attend school classes from 8 a.m. until noon, then you would be released so you could go to your job. I had to drop out of the band and didn't have much time to goof off, so some of the "shine" came off the school days. I was never part of the "in-crowd" in high school, much more of a loner, and having to work gave me a different mindset. I decided if I was going to work, I'd really work in order to have more money. I took on a bunch of jobs. My schedule was up at 6 a.m., go do deliveries for my newspaper route, get back to Grandma's, shower, get dressed, grab a bite of breakfast and go to school. I would get out at noon, go to Grandma's, have lunch and change clothes, then head off to the department store, Belk-Leggett in downtown Durham, at one o'clock to sell shoes until 5. I'd go back to Grandma's for dinner, change clothes again and head out to the Carolina Theatre by six o'clock where I was an usher and took tickets until 10 p.m. Then home to bed and do it all over again the next day. There was no school on Saturday or Sunday and Belk-Leggett was closed on Sunday. I'd go to work at Belk-Leggett at 10 a.m. on Saturday and work through closing at 5. I would get one day a week off from the Carolina Theatre, but I always worked the weekends. Unfortunately, the paper route was seven days a week. Once I accumulated a little cash, the paper route was the first job to go. This was my junior year for six months.

My mom was dating a guy in the Air Force at the time and he was nice enough to let me borrow his car on the rare occasion when I was off and could muster up a date of my own. Mom eventually married this guy but he turned out to be such a son-of-a-bitch I'd rather he remain nameless.

Well, with the school and work schedule I had, it didn't take too long for me to completely lose interest in school. My dad had finally resurfaced and let me know he was living in Baltimore, Maryland. I knew my mom was going to be okay, she was always a strong woman with a lot of resolve and the Air Force guy hadn't begun to show his true stripes yet. So, with the misguided thought that my dad could use my help, and since I was already fed up with my life in Durham, I announced to my mom and grandma that I was heading out to Baltimore to join my dad. The only person that really tried to get me to stay in school was Mrs. Sorrells. She was my English teacher (one of my favorites) and a very pretty lady, and she also headed up the Drama Department. She was always trying to get me to join the Drama Club but I just didn't have the time with my work schedule. Like I said, school was not a lot of fun for me in those days. Funny, but years later, when I was enjoying some success in film and television and came back to visit. I ran into Mrs. Sorrells one day. . We said hi, and she remarked how she could never get me into the Drama Club, yet I went off and became a professional actor of some note!

On my leaving, there was a little discussion and some tears. After the packing of one suitcase, I was on a Greyhound Bus bound for Baltimore. I had absolutely no idea where my life was going to take me. I had seen James Dean in "East of Eden," and it shocked me to learn that he had been killed in a car wreck just shortly after the release of that film. But somehow it gave me thoughts of being able to do "that" – whatever "that" - "acting" - was, to make people feel the kind of emotions I felt while watching Dean. It brought back memories of me doing Tom Sawyer in the seventh grade, and the reaction of the audience. Maybe it was something I needed, maybe I was a ham seeking acceptance! I didn't know if I could achieve any of that in my life, and I certainly never imagined a career in the theatre, New York, Hollywood, movies and television, at that time in my young life. One thing I did know for certain - I was getting the hell out of Durham, and a new adventure was beginning.

Chapter Four
The Baltimore Years

Arriving by Greyhound Bus in Baltimore to meet my dad after not seeing him for about three years, I experienced the disappointment of seeing my mountain-of-a-man dad, with all the past images of his six-foot two-inch 240 pound frame, greeting me at the station dressed in a used, blue/gray double breasted suit and old fedora hat, weighing about 160 pounds. Basically a shadow of his former self. It was one hell of a shock! He was now a full-fledged alcoholic. He escorted me to his hotel, a flop house on skid row in the heart of 1956 downtown Baltimore. Our room had two single beds, a dresser, a nightstand table and a small closet, all settled on a hardwood floor. There were six to eight rooms on our floor, with a large community bathroom that served both our floor and the floor below. It had three shower stalls, a line of sinks with a mirror above, and four toilet stalls with doors.

The numerous nights we spent in this flea bag hotel, I hid my tears behind a made-up story of leaving a girlfriend behind. Not wanting to show my dad the disappointment, shock and sadness I had from finding him in such a state, and not wanting the old man to think I was a sissy because of these living conditions. I remember seeing various neighbors go into the "D T's" from drinking. One of them was from a very wealthy family. He was a nice guy, my dad liked him and he was always good to me. One night we heard him screaming, we lived on the same floor, so we both got up from our sleep and ran into his room. He was up on his bed pointing and screaming about the red hot coals on his floor. On a number of occasions he was taken from the flop house to the hospital while suffering from one of these spells. One day his sister showed up. Seems she had been searching for him and finally discovered him in Baltimore. She got him to agree to go back home with her. The family was very wealthy and lived out on Long Island in New York. She convinced him the family loved him and wanted him to come home. He seemed pretty happy on the day he left. He told me and my dad how much he liked us, and thanked us for helping him through a couple of "rough times", and promised to stay in touch as he left in a very nice car with his sister. I never heard from him again.

  I had saved a few bucks from my jobs in Durham, thank God, because my dad was living on some type of welfare. We'd go get our weekly meal ticket from the local hash house. You would buy a ticket for fifteen bucks and they'd punch out the proper amount on the ticket as you picked out your food from the cafeteria-type line-up. My dad used to always tell me to get the navy bean soup, "cause it'd stick to your ribs." So, with my bankroll, we could get a least a couple of meals a day.

    I knew I had to do something to get us out of this hell hole, so I started looking for a job by the second week. I put on my one good suit and started out. I don't remember if I took a bus or walked, but I found myself in this little neighborhood of shops and stores, in a completely different area from the skid row area in Baltimore "proper" where we were living. It was called Dundalk, founded back in the early nineteen hundreds. I was walking down the main street, and right next to a small jewelry store was a Canon Company Shoe Store with a help-wanted sign sitting in the window. I walked in and introduced myself to the only man in the store. His name was Mr. Lacy and he was the manager. I told him I wanted to apply for the job. He asked me if I had any experience selling shoes, and of course since I had been a shoe salesman at Belk-Leggetts in Durham, I enlarged my degree of experience from a part-time employee working after school to a full-fledged full-time shoe salesman. I also lied about my age, telling him I was nineteen and just out of school. Well, the "just out of school" part wasn't a lie, I was "just out of school". Only a bit earlier, and without the proper graduation certificate.

    Mr. Lacy told me to go out and look in the window, pick a number from a couple of pairs of ladies shoes and come back into the store. Then he told me to go find each pair in a size 7B from the wall where the shoes were kept. The boxes were all numbered to match up with the numbers and models of the shoes on display in the window. I went and found the two pairs of shoes and brought them up to him. He must have liked me, because he gave me the job right on the spot. He gave me an application to fill out, which I did, adding in the additional years for the birth date to confirm my age of nineteen. It was 1956, they didn't ask for a lot of identification in those days, plus I looked as middle American as anyone on the planet. Mr. Lacy was a bit surprised by the address I gave him on the application, because he was familiar with Baltimore and knew what a shitty area I was living in. I assured him it was only temporary. He asked me when I could start, I replied immediately, and I started the next day.

    During the week, the store was open from 9 a.m. to 5 p.m., Monday to Friday, and from 9 a.m. to 6 p.m. on Saturday, and the store was closed on Sundays. Mr. Lacy gave me a half-day off on Wednesday, so I could leave by 1 p.m. On Fridays and Saturdays, another man came in to help out with sales. His name was Walter Tushinski. Both he and Mr. Lacy were Polish. Walter introduced me to the Catholic faith, eventually introducing me to the Catholic religion, and he became my godfather.

Within less than a month of having this job, I moved my dad and me out of the skid row flop house into a large one-room furnished apartment in a decent part of town that was in walking distance of the shoe store. It was a large room with two beds, an open sitting area with a sofa, two chairs, a couple of end tables and a coffee table, plus a nice private bath. The furniture was more than decent, and after living in the flop house, it was like moving into a small mansion. It had a step-down area into the kitchen with a nice stove and refrigerator, plus some decent cooking utensils, a small counter and little eating area. My dad was a really good cook when sober, or not completely blitzed – he could sure as hell cook! It was situated on one of those streets in Baltimore where all the row or tract houses (they were connected) had these white marble or stone steps. As far as the eye could see down the street, they all had these white steps. Our building was on a corner.

It was at this address where I lost my virginity. By the standards of today, I was certainly a "late-bloomer". Our apartment was on the first floor of the building, even though you used the steps to walk up to the first floor. There was a basement apartment, with the entrance on the side of the building looking out into a somewhat busy street, but it still had those white steps for the entrance, even though the entrance was on the side of the building. We could enter our apartment from the front or side entrance, but the basement apartment could only enter from the side.

    An attractive young lady (certainly older than me) - she was about twenty-seven and lived alone in the basement apartment. It was a one-bedroom apartment and she had it furnished very nicely. To this day I have no idea what she did for a living, but she went to work each day. In the evenings, especially when it was light, after I'd get home from work, I would go out and sit on the stoop and watch the traffic whiz by. One day she came out to join me. We started talking about different things. She asked me some questions about me and my dad. I was a bit guarded but gave her a little info about where we had lived when I first came up to Baltimore, and about my job over at the shoe store. I don't remember how it happened, but one day she invited me into her apartment, offered me a soda, and soon we were in her double bed. Hence the loss of my virginity. This became a kind of regular meeting for a few weeks. Then one day she stated if I was only coming down to see her for sex, she didn't think I should come down anymore. . So the relationship ended.

    I was doing well at the shoe store, Mr. Lacy had even given me a raise. I got my dad into AA - Alcoholics Anonymous. After a short while he was staying sober for weeks at a time, with an occasional slip off the wagon. I had met this very attractive young lady at the shoe store where she would come to buy her shoes. Her name was Doris, and I swear she looked like Elizabeth Taylor. She was about 5 feet four, had black shoulder length hair, an hour glass figure, and was very well endowed. She always wore tight sweaters and the highest heels we sold. She was a secretary for some company whose office was three blocks past the shoe store, and she walked to work each day. I never missed her walking by, usually for lunch. Once she came in to buy shoes, I quickly asked her out, and to put it lightly, we really hit it off. I started seeing her on a regular basis and we spent a lot of time together when we were not working. I was always going over to her house, having dinner with her and her mom and dad. Doris had one older sister but she didn't live at home. Many evenings after a movie we would find ourselves in the basement, either on the couch or the floor on blankets making love. This was to last a few months, but then I guess, looking back, fate (if you believe in that) stepped in and started me on the trip that I was really looking for when I left Durham, even though I didn't know it at the time.

Doris and I had gotten pretty serious. Well, as serious as a kid pretending to be an older guy could get. People now thought I was a 20 year old guy, going on 21, but I was just going on eighteen. I had been lying about my age for well over a year and actually believed it. Regardless, Doris and I had a big fight over something, I don't even remember what – we had been talking about marriage. I do remember that, but everything came to a head and we split up.

Just a few days later, literally, a few days, I found myself walking past a building that had this large heading: The Hilltop School of Dramatic Art. They taught drama, music, dance and musical comedy. I walked in and asked the receptionist at the desk if I could talk to someone, or if she had a brochure about the school. She called a gentleman, Leslie Irons, not only the head of the drama department, but head of the entire school. After a brief introduction, he invited me to come into his office where he interviewed me for a short while. Then he asked me if I would read something from a play. At this time in my life the only play I could ever remember reading was the Tom Sawyer operetta where I had played the role of Tom, and also did the singing back in the seventh grade at Hope Valley. I looked over the part that he wanted me to read. I couldn't tell you what it was to save my life. After looking it over, I read it with him doing the other role. Afterwards, he asked me if I would come back on Thursday evening when they had some classes. I agreed, we shook hands and I left. I remember thinking as I walked away from the Hilltop School of Dramatic Art, maybe I can do this "acting thing".

    The two days went very quickly, and after work on Thursday, I shot home to the apartment, made a quick change of clothes (I had to save my dress clothes to work in), and headed over to the Hilltop School. When I arrived there were already a few young people in the lobby area talking with each other. I assumed they were students, so I went over to the desk and told the lady I was there to meet with Mr. Irons. She called him, and the students started going into different class rooms. Mr. Irons came out, said hi, and asked me to call him Leslie and to follow him into one of the class rooms. It was a musical study class where you did these musical numbers from shows or films. They played the musical score which was on a record (not sure the young people of today even know what a "record" is, it was played on a phonograph). The teacher, a nice looking lady in her thirties, obviously a former dancer, I believe her name was Susan, explained the number she wanted us to do. It was the Trolley number from a Judy Garland musical.

Susan showed us the steps she wanted us to do to the music. We were each asked to try and repeat the steps she showed us by ourselves, and to the music.

After we each had tried it, she put us all together and had us do it as a group - called the chorus as I later learned. After this workout, and believe me it was a workout Susan had us take a break. Leslie, who had been watching this mess of flailing arms and legs trying to do the dance routine, asked me to come with him. The other kids in the class all had leotards and dance shoes, but I was dressed in my casual street clothes and regular shoes. Plus I was not a member of the school. Mr. Irons (Leslie as he insisted I call him), took me into the office, asked me to sit down, and then asked me if I was serious about attending this dramatic school. I told him I was 100 percent serious, but needed to know how much classes would cost so I could figure out how many, if any, I could take. He told me not to worry about that, they would like to offer me a full scholarship to the school and all the courses, which included speech, drama, dance, movement and musical comedy. I was awarded a scholarship to The Hilltop Theatre School of Drama, which later, if my memory serves me, became the Baltimore College of Dramatic Art. I can only believe that the school was in desperate need of a young all-American looking guy, and I fit the profile. Hard to imagine my artistic talent at that time of my life was impressive enough to garner a scholarship.

So, by a stroke of fate, I became involved with my first dramatic theatre school. I started by attending classes twice a week, both days in the evenings. Wednesday and Friday classes started at 6 p.m. which for Wednesdays never presented a problem because I only worked until 1 p.m., so I had time to go to the apartment, grab a bite to eat and change my clothes. Fridays were a little tighter because I worked until 5:30 p.m., so I had to rush just to make it to the classes on time. I took all the classes they offered to me. In speech class they worked to get me to lose my southern accent, which, looking back, was quite ironic, because the first important roles I wound up getting in films and television years later were always of southern or western characters. I loved the movement classes, and the drama classes taught by Leslie Irons, where we would work on scenes that he picked for us. . I also enjoyed the musical comedy class where we would learn musical singing and dancing routines, which always gave you a good workout.

Written By Jordan Rhodes

Chapter Five

The Hilltop School also owned and operated a summer stock theatre in Harpers Ferry, West Virginia - The Hilltop Theatre. It was situated on a hilltop where you could stand outside and view three states at the same time - West Virginia, Virginia and Maryland. Leslie Irons directed the plays performed at the Hilltop Theatre. When they were casting shows for the upcoming season, I was asked if I wanted to audition for their opening play It was the original play of Dracula that was performed on Broadway in 1934 and starred Bella Lugosi as Dracula. Later Lugosi did the same role for the film and became a huge star in Hollywood, where he would be known as Dracula for the rest of his movie career. I read for the role of young Jonathan Harper, the young man who is in love with the young beautiful Lucy that becomes the victim of Dracula, and has to be rescued by the Professor and young Harper. I got the role!

Now I had to figure out a way to get two weeks off from my job selling shoes at the Canon Shoe store, so I could do the play. We would rehearse at night in Baltimore, which didn't present a problem, but I would need a full week's rehearsal prior to being transported to Harper's Ferry, West Virginia, by van for a few days of dress rehearsals, and then we would perform for a week. We got our room and board plus a small stipend. My dad had been doing pretty well, laying off the booze since being in AA. I had come up with the money to get his tools out of the pawn shop, where he had deposited them long before I arrived from North Carolina. Fortunately, he had hung on to the ticket and I redeemed them so he could pick up some free-lance electrical work. I had also decided to buy a car from one of those places where you made a small down payment, and then paid them every two weeks. If you missed one payment, they would repossess the car. Naturally I was thinking about some nice little used two door sedan, but the dealer that was willing to accept my credit rating (which was absolutely nil) had a Ford Ranch Wagon on the lot, and dad started pitching me about how much more work he could get if I bought the Ranch Wagon. He'd have room for his tools in the back and would be able to load fans and small items that needed repair. So I bought the Ford Ranch Wagon. Little did I know what a short time I'd have that vehicle.

  Well, I worked out my work schedule with Mr. Lacy at the shoe store. I would take a week's vacation and be docked one week without pay so I could take care of some "personal business". I didn't want to tell Mr. Lacy that I was now trying to become an actor and I needed that extra week to go perform in a play. Plus I wanted to hold on to a paying job as long as I could, having no idea if I could actually make a living as an actor.

    Now here's a segment in my relationship with my dad that I never understood, even though his sponsor at AA made a great effort to give me an explanation. On a Saturday evening when I was packing for my trip to Harper's Ferry W. Va., to be picked up early the next morning, Dad asked me if it would be okay if he took the Ranch Wagon for a night out. He had met this waitress at the White Coffee Pot, a local diner chain, and he was going to take her out after work. Since one time before he had left on an "outing", had a couple of drinks, got into a little scrap, and didn't return for two days, I made a joke, and asked him if he planned on being back within the week while I was in West Virginia doing the play. He laughed and said, "Oh hell yeah Bo, I'll be back before you." The next time I saw my dad was over four years later in a TB sanatorium. He knew I was getting ready to leave my steady job, go off and work for little or no pay in the theatre, had spent all my savings getting us into an apartment, buying the vehicle and getting his tools out of hock, yet he took off with the Ranch Wagon leaving me basically high and dry. Yes, I was given an explanation by his sponsor at AA, all filled with the excuses of how he probably fell off the wagon, went on a bender, and when he finally came out of it, was too embarrassed to come back, or get in touch with me. Alcoholism was a disease, and even though it was hard for me to understand, I should try to forgive him. Interesting words at the time, but it took me the four years before I saw him again in the TB Sanatorium, to forgive him. I still never truly understood how he could just leave. However, years later, I did discover that the explanation his sponsor had made in theory, was absolutely correct. Dad went on a bender, the bottle got him again, and when he finally came out of it, weeks or months later, a finance company had located him and the Ranch Wagon in Portsmouth, Virginia, and repossessed it. Dad had been living in it. But he still never called or checked on me. Hard to understand.

    The actor they hired to play Dracula, a very difficult part to pull off in those years - especially in a stage production - was a man named Joseph Bandiera. He was absolutely terrific in the role. He became a very good friend to me, and we did a number of plays together in the Baltimore area. He became my mentor, and did a few small roles in some of the plays I appeared in, just so he could help me learn, and discover my "acting legs".

He was a very good actor and in demand in the theatre circles in Baltimore.

He taught me a lot, both on the stage, and off about how to conduct oneself, and be a professional.

As I said, Joe was terrific in the part of Dracula. The Hilltop Theatre had this large three-quarter stage where the audience sat on the sides and in the front. Unlike theatre-in-the-round where the audience surrounds the stage, the three-quarter stage had an entire wooden wall upstage complete with windows and doors where the actors made their entrances and exits. Obviously Dracula in this time was more of a melodrama than a full-fledged drama, so the audience would begin to snicker just a bit when Joe appeared as Count Dracula with his cape held across his face. On opening night when the audience started to snicker, Joe, as Dracula, wheeled on the audience and stared right at them. It was amazing, an immediate hush fell over the audience, and not a snicker could be heard. Dracula then turned his attention back to the play and his attack on Lucy. Dracula continued to do that "audience stare down" at every performance for the run of the play – and it always worked. The snickers would stop! Years later I discovered that Bella Lugosi, as Dracula on Broadway, had encountered the same situation of nervous laughter from the audience, and he turned directly to the audience, stared at them as he walked downstage, and they also fell silent! I never knew if Joe had this knowledge about Lugosi, or just did it on his own during our production, but I'll tell you, it worked every time! After we had performed the play for the week, all of the actors that were not hired for the following play were taken back to Baltimore in the van. I had just performed my first play in a real theatre, but was now on my way back to Baltimore.

    Joe was an Italian, and he had a look that could make him Italian, Slavic, Russian, even Mexican, and it worked for him. Both his mother and his father were from the "old country", and they didn't speak a lot of English. His mother fed me a good number of Italian meals at their house. She would serve me these huge plates of spaghetti with her homemade sauce, it was delicious, and even though I was as skinny as a rail, I could never finish the plate. I would also ask for milk to drink, which they never understood. Italians drink wine with their spaghetti, and they can all finish what's on their plate. Therefore, I became known as "Jordono, delicato" in the Bandiera household.

    Back in Baltimore, and returning to my job selling shoes, I continued to take my classes at The Hilltop School.

    This time also began my sexual encounters with both younger and older women. I was dating my first and only stripper. She went by the name of "Tequila" and worked at the Gaiety Burlesque Theatre on State Street in downtown Baltimore. Boy, she took me for a ride in more ways than one. The Burlesque Theatre was a place I attended more than a few times. I met and was exposed to the nightlife and backstage stories of the strippers and comics, a most interesting slice of life.

I survived my dad deserting me and in the process taking the car I was still making payments on, while he took off on a "bender" with his tools I had retrieved from the pawn shop, along with most of our funds. As I've stated, it would be four years before I would locate him again in a TB Sanatorium.

I was getting a foothold in the theatre, becoming a new "hot young actor" in the theatre circles of Baltimore, working with the various theatrical companies like The Players Company, The Vagabond Players, and making my first appearance on live TV, even though it was local. Meeting and making a great friend, Joe Banderia, who began tutoring me with my acting ability, educational vocabulary and introducing me to his immigrant mother and father that supplied me with many wonderful Italian meals. This was all an incredible education and learning experience for me!

While becoming successful in the theatre in Baltimore,

I became a "big fish" in a "small pond". I met Hugh Hefner's brother, Keith, who was also pursing an acting career. We would meet again years later in Hollywood as we both continued to ply the acting trade, but from vastly different financial backgrounds.

I met and hung out in a popular watering hole for the elite of the professional football team, the Baltimore Colts. I had the opportunity to meet many of the players that would become famous in the first "Sudden Death" overtime game in playoff history, the Colts versus the New York Giants (the Colts won).

I worked with a director, Bill Parnell, that really pushed me to get out of Baltimore and make the move to New York. He insisted that I had the talent to make a "go of it" in the theatre. He told me he had tried it once, and New York scared the hell out of him, but he thought I could do it. A set of strange occurrences led to Bill's premature death, and, for whatever reason, I was motivated to try New York. So, with the help of my Italian friend, Joe Banderia, I made the move. Joe was kind enough to take me to New York for a weekend so I could see the city and get prepared. Unfortunately one weekend visit would never prepare you for living in the Big Apple. So, leaving the security of my acclaimed success in the theatre in Baltimore, and with $70 in my pocket after bus fare, I arrived in New York City to seek my fame and fortune.

Chapter Six
New York - The First Tour

Fortunately, I had made a good friend, Ed Beres, in drama school and the theatre in Baltimore. Ed had moved to New York a few months earlier and he invited me to become the fourth roommate with him and two friends in a two-room furnished apartment on the second floor of a walk-up in a building on West 76th Street. My share of the rent and utilities was 30 bucks a month. We had two large rooms featuring an oversized pullout couch, two single beds, a few lamps, about four chairs of varying sizes and colors, plus a very small kitchenette and a bathroom with a sink, and a shower in the tub. The kitchenette was hidden by a closed door which gave the illusion of another room, but, in reality, once the door was opened you faced the stove with the small refrigerator on the left and the sink on the right. So, you almost stood in the living room while cooking on the stove. Today that apartment, if available, probably rents for over $2500 a month.

    I arrived in New York by bus in November, 1958, and joined Ed and his two roommates, Don and Tony (can't recall their last names). They were both aspiring actors. Tony spent the first part of his career auditioning for "Westside Story" each time they were seeking replacements, and managed to perform in productions of that show in summer stock and touring companies over the years until we lost touch. Don did summer stock and landed a few jobs off-Broadway.

After settling in at the apartment, which was easy – I arrived with just two suitcases, and with only forty bucks left in my pocket after paying my share of the rent (that was my entire savings from working in the theatre in Baltimore, certainly not a wealthy profession by any means), I knew I had to find a job. A regular job that would allow me to pursue my dream of working in the New York theatre. On that first trip to New York when Joe Banderia had treated me, I saw my first two Broadway shows. The first was "The Dark at the Top of the Stairs", starring Pat Hingle, Dorothy McGuire & Eileen Heckart , and I was blown away! I had never seen live acting like this in my life. The second show I saw was "Westside Story", which was a terrific show, but "The Dark at the Top of the Stairs" had completely floored me. You can imagine my joy at meeting and becoming friends with Pat Hingle decades later.

Now, back to getting that regular job in order to survive. On a Monday morning I set out on the first of many job hunts in New York City, and, boy, did I have many different jobs while trying to become an actor. Much more about that later. My first stop on my job hunt adventure was to have "breakfast" at Nedicks. A place on the corner of 72nd Street and Broadway where you got a powdered donut, a small watered down glass of something resembling orange juice and a cup of coffee, all for the amazing price of 15 cents! Absolute nutrition!

Once again I lucked out on the job front. While looking at ads and walking down Fifth Avenue, I passed a shoe store named Marilyn's. It was a bit of an upscale ladies shoe store, quite a bit different than Canons Shoe Store where I had worked in Baltimore. I don't remember if they had a sign in the window, or if I just wandered in and asked for the manager, but I presented myself very well. I had on one of my two good suits, a shirt and tie, hair cut and combed, and was well groomed. Hey! I was looking for a job. It was a different time people, late 50's, none of this lazy-ass attitude that is encountered today. The manager interviewed me. When I was younger, I was always a rather charming fellow, and well-liked by most people (a trait I've tried to maintain throughout my life and career – mostly, but not always, successfully). I managed to convince him of my sales experience, and I got the job!

I had only been in New York a few days and I had found work. I felt great!

I remember the manager's first name was Robert, and I believe his last name was Walls. He was a very nice man and always treated me and the other employees fairly.

During the time working at Marilyn's shoe store I had my first real life encounter with a "star". Ethel Merman. I remember the first time she ENTERED the store, and, believe me, it was an ENTRANCE. Miss Merman was a huge star in those days, and she was just as boisterous and as loud in person as she was on the stage or screen. When she came into the store, everyone knew she was in the store! Obviously, only the manager waited on her. I was picked as one of the "gofers" to replace the shoes she tried on but didn't buy, and to bring out other ones she wanted to try on. I believe that she bought about seven pairs the first time I saw her in the store. I know she had them delivered - it was too many pairs to carry out – which she would never do anyway. There was always a very silent sigh of relief after Miss Merman had left the store. We would all live to sell ladies shoes another day.

That December, we roommates had a small Christmas party at the apartment and invited some of the residents of the building, which included a female neighbor from a downstairs apartment. Her name was Dee DeLagarde, and she was beautiful. She was just a few years older than me, divorced, with two kids that lived with her mother in Queens. She liked what she referred to as my "boyish charm" and good Southern manners. As she left the party that evening, she invited me to come down and see her before the Holidays ended. I took her up on the offer, and in a couple of days I was spending all my nights with her in her apartment, even though I kept most of my few pieces of clothing in the upstairs apartment I shared with the guys. They liked the fact that they had a little more room and I still paid my share of the rent. Dee and I would have this arrangement for quite a while, and it was great. As I mentioned before, Dee was a very pretty lady, a good cook and we both liked to watch Jack Parr from the bed. It was a wonderful experience. When I moved out, a young actress, who later became known as Sharon Farrell, became Dee's new roommate.

 While working at Marilyn's shoe store, I still stayed in touch with my friend, Joe Banderia in Baltimore. Joe called me one evening to tell me that the annual actors awards, called "The Camille", were being given out, and I had been nominated for Best Supporting Actor. Joe was on the committee, and they wanted to know if I planned to attend the ceremony. Obviously I was very happy to discover that I had been nominated, but in my mind I thought it would be a "big deal" if I just showed up at the ceremony without letting anyone in Baltimore know I was coming. Joe advised me that this was not a "good idea", but I didn't listen. I was all caught up in the "New York Actor returns to Baltimore to attend The Camille Awards". Joe again tried to talk me out of not letting anyone know I planned to attend the awards ceremony. I still wouldn't listen, and insisted that he not tell anyone that I was going to attend. The first of many mistakes I would make as an actor, even though, looking back, it was just an award, not a job or opportunity. Regardless, at the time, on the evening when I had made such a grand entrance, receiving all the hugs and handshakes, and "how are you" – "how's New York"- "do you like it" -"are you working?" comments, I felt bigger than I should. While I was sitting at my table with two other nominees, a few friends, and, of course, my friend Joe, enjoying the meal, which was not your usual "rubber chicken fare", I noticed that a few members of the committee were meeting and had summoned Joe. After Joe had returned and we'd finished our dinner, the presentation of the awards began. Joe leaned over to me and very softly told me not to be disappointed, that I was not going to win the Best Supporting Actor award. He told me the voting was very close, and I had won by a couple of votes, but since no one expected me to attend, and the older gentlemen, Walter, still a resident of Baltimore (he had played my father in Sabrina Fair), had been nominated a few times before, and the votes were so close they decided to present him with the award. I still remember the evening, and it's been over fifty years, when they were getting ready to present the award and reading the nominees, Walter turned to me and said, "Hey kid, go on up and get your award" – then they announced his name as the winner. I have to write that he was absolutely thrilled to receive the award. After that, the rest of the evening is pretty much a blur, as I drank a bit and made my preparations to return to New York the following morning. Good lesson learned.

    Back in New York, I realized I would need to leave Marilyn's shoe store and find some type of job where I could work during the evening, and devote my days to a process known as "making the rounds", which is simply another term for seeking work.

    I quickly learned how to make the "rounds". It entailed getting up early every day, and beginning the day by walking down to that local Nedicks coffee shop at 72nd Street and Broadway that I mentioned earlier, having that nutritious breakfast of the very small watered down glass of orange juice, the powdered donut and coffee. All for that staggering price of fifteen cents. Making the rounds, you would visit every casting office that would allow you to drop off a picture and resume, plus try and cover every casting notice that was listed in the trade papers - Backstage and Variety.

    The first one of these jobs I got was in a restaurant named Lüchow's. I was a "host" - another name for a greeter. I would meet and greet the customers as they entered the restaurant, then, if we had space, or if they had a reservation, I would escort them to the proper dining room (the place had four), and turn them over to the Maitre d'. I also met another actor friend working there, Joe Jamrod, and we remained friends for years. Many of you have seen Joe in a number of films over the years as a doorman, a cop, a next door neighbor, always with a few lines and a couple of scenes. Joe did a lot of small theatre in New York, and always lived in the City, never venturing out to L.A., the West Coast.

    I had a lot of jobs in New York as a young struggling actor, trying whenever possible to work nights so I could make the rounds in the day and hope to find work as an actor. These jobs included a magazine salesman (store to store rather than door to door), parking attendant, the above-mentioned shoe salesman, driver for a delivery service, host at the original Lüchow's Restaurant on 14th Street, also mentioned above, where Mr. Jan Mitchell, the owner, offered to send me to Switzerland to learn all the art of being a first class Maitre d'. He said I would earn more money in the New York restaurant business than I would ever make as an actor (He was probably right). After Lüchow's, I became a page at the exclusive Four Seasons Restaurant, were I was absolutely awestruck when John Wayne attended one of the many celebrity events that were held at the restaurant. . Little did I know that later I would actually get to work with the Duke. I also came into contact with a real live gangster at the restaurant, ran a number of errands for him the night he attended the Four Seasons. The floor manager, Mr. Stich, pointed out his bodyguard to me. I guess the bodyguard didn't do a great job because about a week after the gangster left a picture of him showed up on the front page of the New York Post – he had been shot dead in a barbershop in Miami.

    I worked as an usher at Radio City Music Hall where I actually did a routine with Cary Grant, who was visiting his ex-wardrobe mistress that now worked at the "Hall". This was during a time when North by Northwest was playing.
I had been promoted to the Executive Elevator, which was used to take all of the visiting dignitaries up to the executive offices. When Mr. Grant entered the elevator with two of the executives of the Music Hall, I took a chance and repeated an old routine that Mr. Grant had done in one of his movies, the "You remind me of a man. What man? The man with

the power. What power? The power of voodoo. Who do? You do. Do what? Remind me of a man". Mr. Grant (dare I call him Cary?) didn't miss a beat, and joined right in with me, appearing to enjoy the encounter.

The executives obviously missed the humor because the next day I was transferred to operate the backstage elevator. This wasn't all bad because I took both the Rockettes and the Corp de Ballet up to the stage all the time, and enjoyed helping one or two of the female ballet dancers zip up a costume and help out with a "tuck" or two every now and then. I believe that's where I became enamored of dancers, because later I would date more than a few, and eventually married one.

I was a toy demonstrator for Mattel Toys at the Toy Fair, a model for romance magazines, a demonstrator and spokesperson at the boat show, a pitchman for a beauty product - the Roll-a-Curl (that didn't work) – at Macy's Department Store and Woolworth's. But my all-time favorite job as a struggling actor in New York was the summer I worked for Mary Martin and her husband, Richard Halladay, as a driver.

During this time I met Mary Martin's son, Larry Hagman, who would go on to great fame as J.R. Ewing on the hit series, "Dallas", after his first series, "I Dream of

Jeannie" with Barbara Eden. Of course I met Larry in New York with his wife, Maj, when he was struggling just like me, but with a lot more contacts. Larry was a good guy, and would give me his movie pass to The United Artist Theatres on occasion to catch a film. We stayed in touch, and I saw him again in Hollywood when he was filming "Jeannie". I even met Barbara Eden. Driving for Mary Martin and Mr. Halliday was a very enjoyable job, and I got to meet a lot of show people, like Gower and Marge Champion. They had been a famous movie dancing duo in films, and Gower went on to become a very successful director. He directed "Hello Dolly" on Broadway. He was always a very pleasant man, and extremely nice to me when I would drop him at his place, as instructed by Mr. Halliday after an evening out with them. Marge was not always pleasant. One evening as I was driving Mr. Champion home, he had been out with Mary Martin and Mr. Halliday on his own, I had my first wedding anniversary coming up on November 8th, 1964, so I went out on a limb, took a chance, and asked Mr. Champion if it was possible to get seats for "Hello Dolly", starring Carol Channing. It was the hottest ticket in town. I explained my anniversary was coming up, and I also said I would certainly pay for the tickets. He said, "Of course, you can have my house seats". He gave me the number of his secretary, told me to call her and she'd make the arrangements. His house seats were the regular price, and the night I took my wife to the show, I was offered $200 a piece for the tickets as we were going into the theatre! Like I said, the hottest ticket in town! They were fourth row center! I made a lot of points with my first wife that night! Mr. Champion was a nice man. In addition to meeting Gower and Marge Champion while driving for Mary Martin and Mr. Halliday, I also met Carol Channing and Josh Logan. I was always looking for an opportunity to talk to Mr. Logan about a movie he was preparing to do, entitled "Parish". It was based on a book that was a best seller. I thought I was perfect for the title role of Parish, a young man raised on a tobacco farm in the Carolinas – and I still believe I was perfect for that role. I could never find the time to talk to him, and a Warner Brothers heartthrob, under contract to the Studio, Troy Donahue, got the part. Another opportunity missed!

After that summer driving job was over, I went to work at the Hotel Taft as a room clerk where I had sexual encounters with a few of the women guests and took the risk of losing my job. But it was worth it! With four actor friends, and the support and help of Joe Chino, we started "coffee shop acting" at Café Chino in the Village. Joe Chino was a great guy and loved actors, so when we suggested performing in his coffee shop. He agreed. Joe told us he couldn't pay us anything but he'd feed us and let us pass the hat around after performances. We battled Actors' Equity for the right to perform in the coffee shop, but since none of us were yet in the union, Equity had no jurisdiction. Eventually, Actors' Equity approved this type theatre and later it evolved into Café LaMama Theatre.

Along the way I got involved with the folk music craze, learned to play the guitar and took my first "side trip" out of the acting profession. I became one-half of The Castaways with Michael Equine. In addition to performing in a nightclub and being the opening act for a Mime, Richmond Sheppard, a protégé of Marcel Marceau, we actually cut an album for Premiere Albums.

During this period I was introduced to, and turned on to, "pot" for the first time. Hell, it was the late 50's, early 60's and almost everyone I was meeting was doing some type of weed, pot, MaryJane, etc. Thank God, cocaine had not yet become the socially acceptable drug it would later become, and screw up so many lives as it continues to do today. Later, I did do two "acid trips", LSD and Mushroom, one year apart – which scared the hell out of me. A little more of that later in the "trip", no pun intended.

Chapter Seven

My folk-singing journey deserves a bit of space because it was such a lark and strange happening. But first I need to continue sharing with you my acting education once I had managed to leave the daytime job of selling ladies shoes and found night time work that afforded me the opportunity to concentrate on acting. After all the title of this book is A Blue Collar Actor, so let me explain how that came to be.

My roommate and friend, Ed Beres, had been accepted and was attending the New Theatre School of Theatrical Art. This is not to be confused with any New Theatre School or Organization operating today. This was the original New Theatre School that had such teachers as Karl Redcoff, Evelyn King and Dr. Ila Mottloff, who had worked with Stanislavski in The Moscow Art Theatre. One evening Ed invited me to attend class with him as his guest to observe.

Now like many young actors that knew about the Actors Studio, and not all did – many still do not know, I had already auditioned for the Actors Studio, because Brando and Dean had been touted as coming out of their ranks. More importantly to me, if you got accepted, you didn't have to pay. You could study for free. I couldn't afford to pay, and

I wanted to study. However, after auditioning, I was turned down, didn't even make it to the finals. In those days I believe you could audition every six months. Today you can only audition once a year. Regardless, I was rejected. Not once, but three times, only making the finals once. And being rejected by Strasberg himself in that final!

So, I was excited about going with Ed to observe his acting class. On that evening, Ed was in the class that Karl Redcoff taught. When I first saw Karl Redcoff I had never seen anyone that looked more like an actor. He was dressed in a cable knit turtleneck sweater, casual tan slacks that hung in and out of these three-quarter high desert boots, and a black leather trench coat opened with the belt-tie hanging loose.

He had dark hair, piercing blue eyes, a very European mustache and a little goatee, like the one Alfred Drake wore in a number of plays. If you check out a picture of Alfred Drake, you'll find one with this look. I learned later that Karl admired the talent of Drake, and was actually a protégé of Drake. So he fashioned himself after some of those stage-role looks that Drake wore. And it fit him to a T!

Karl was very charismatic, presenting both a charming and commanding presence. He was a wonderful actor and had worked with Lunt and Fontanne, Tallulah Bankhead,

Constance Cummings and of course, Alfred Drake. These were all actors that excelled in the theatre, and, for the most part, did very few films and little television. These people were stage actors, trained stage actors, not movie stars.

Karl was one of the most influential teachers in my life. He was an excellent teacher, and I don't remember him using, or quoting any particular "method" of acting. He worked on the premise that to act, you had to do. You needed to listen and react, according to the situation, and use your imagination. That acting advice has served me well throughout my career. I began to learn the process of acting from Karl Redcoff. Back in Baltimore I just got up and did it! I guess I had some natural ability and instincts, and I was doing basically what Karl was teaching – to act is to do, I just didn't know it at the time. Yet I had never learned the process of acting, and bringing certain emotional feelings to the work. That started in New York with Karl Redcoff.

That evening, the fates, or some guardian angel I never knew I had, stepped into my life, and once again smiled on me. In the class, the other actors were doing the scenes they had prepared; some good, some not so good, but they were all trying like hell. This one actress was missing her scene partner. Turns out he had to work late that night and had to miss the class, so this young lady had no scene partner. Karl asked if there were any volunteers that would like to read the scene with this actress. She was prepared, knew her lines and was obviously disappointed that she wouldn't get to do her scene and receive her notes and constructive criticism, if any. When the actors in the class all hesitated, Karl looked at me and asked me if I'd like to read the scene with this young lady. I said sure. I asked if I could have a minute to look over the scene, and Karl said we'd take a five minute break, everyone could stretch their legs. I looked over the scene. All I remember is it was a boy and girl scene, and I believe the boy was going off to sea and leaving the girl behind. Other than that, I don't have a clue. I do remember I was a little nervous, but I always got nervous when I was acting so it wasn't any surprise. We got up and did the scene. I remember the girl was quite good; honest, and lots of eye contact, so I tried to look at her as much as I could without being glued to the page of scene.

When we finished, the class broke into a little applause, as did Karl. Then Karl went off on a rant; explaining how that was good acting, complimenting the young actress on her work in the scene, how honest she was, and saying how real I was even though I was reading the text. I felt about eight feet tall! After class broke up, Ed and I were hanging around talking about the class and his scene, which I thought was good, when one of the associates at the school asked me if I would come into the office. For a minute I thought I was in trouble because I had participated in class when I was just there to observe. I didn't know that Karl had gone into the office and talked with them. I went in, was invited to sit down, then I was asked if I'd like to attend the school, because they'd like to have me as a student. I could only say yeah, sure I'd like to attend but, before I could finish my stammering about the cost, the associate said those magic words, "...on a full scholarship". Fate and the Angel had done it again. I now had a place to study and try to learn my trade, and I could afford it! Later, Ed gave me a good ribbing about how in the world could I come into class just one time and get a scholarship!

  I owed him BIG TIME! How many burgers was I going to buy him and for how long! But he was happy that we'd be attending class together. We also decided that we'd move out of the apartment on West 76th Street with the other two roommates, and get our own place. We found a good large two-room apartment up on West 82nd Street between Columbus and Amsterdam Avenues that we could both afford.

  During my time at the New Theatre School, in addition to Karl being one of my teachers, I became good friends with him and his wife, Evelyn (I've managed to be in contact with their only daughter, Nikki, over the years). I discovered that Karl's parents were from the old country. They were Russian immigrants. When Karl was a kid, the other kids would tease the hell out of him about how his parents spoke. They did it without mercy. Karl made a vow that he'd learn how to speak better than any of these assholes, and he'd show 'em! Karl became one of the best dialecticians in the business. He was so good, he'd get roles because he could do any accent needed. Needless to say, he did an excellent Russian – plus he looked the part!

    We had some great times together in New York. I'm sure at times our cutting up and clowning around drove Evelyn a little crazy. Even though Karl was fourteen years my senior, we were like a couple of kids together. I guess it was the Gemini in us. We only got into big trouble one time, when I agreed to help Karl put down a new tile floor in their kitchen. They lived in a building over by 32nd Street and 8th Avenue. Lee J. Cobb's uncle lived in the same building and Lee would come to visit often. I was always hoping to get a chance to meet him, or at least see him and say hello. Little did I know that years later I'd get to work with him on a TV show, "The Young Lawyers", when he was one of the Stars.

    Back to the kitchen. Karl and I were hard at work

putting these tiles down, when we started doing some silly comedic duo complete with accents and actions, and it reached a breaking point with Evelyn. She wanted that floor done and her kitchen put back together, and the two idiots, as she called us, were "goofing off". We couldn't break her up, so we had to settle down and complete the floor – while still laughing together. Great memories.

During this time of studying at the New Theatre School, I auditioned for every theatre acting job I could find – all with no success. I believe it was during this time that I began to truly learn, and to scratch the surface of how to use whatever talent I had and to apply it to the job of acting. I did a couple of these "Showcase Productions", where we would present scenes from different plays for an invited audience of producers, directors and of course, agents. One of these Showcase Productions was directed by Karl. It was an adaptation of "Anatomy of a Murder".

The film version starred James Stewart, Ben Gazzara and Lee Remick. In the Showcase, I did the role of the young military husband, the role Ben Gazzara played in the film. He was being tried for murder. Karl told me I did a good job, but obviously none of the producers, directors or agents were impressed – I didn't get offered any job, or get an agent. But I continued to keep knocking on those doors. Again, little did

I know that I'd meet Ben Gazzara and have dinner with him at the Cannes Film Festival years later! I also got to meet Lee Remick through her voice coach out in Hollywood.

    I don't know where or how I got the "entertainment gene" that made me pursue acting as a career. I guess I got it from ole Dad. He was a natural talent, and if the fates had treated him differently, I might have had that "in", that "connection in the business" to help you get a foothold. Who knows? My dad had a lot of musical talent as I expounded upon earlier in the book. He could play almost any string instrument - the guitar, the banjo, the fiddle, and the mandolin - all by ear. He could even figure out a tune on a piano. With a guitar, people would ask him if he knew a certain song, he'd ask them to hum the tune, and in no time at all, he'd pick it out on the guitar.

    My only entrance into the entertainment field prior to doing the Tom Sawyer Operetta at Hope Valley High, which I wrote about earlier you'll recall, was doing a puppet show on the porch at our basement house in Durham. I fashioned a stage out of large cardboard boxes, got inside and did all the hand puppets and voices for a few kids in the neighborhood. I charged a nickel a piece, and I'd put on a completely made up show each time. My imagination has always been fertile. I guess all that will explain my "entertainment gene". It'll have to do until something else comes along.

Chapter Eight

Finally, after two years of auditioning for about everything I could find, I got hired for my first summer stock job out of New York to be the leading juvenile for the season at Playhouse-on-the-Green in Worthington, Ohio. There I met two of my friends, and developed a friendship that has lasted over 59 years. One of those friends, Art Wolff, became a very noted director, directing scores of TV sitcoms, including the Seinfeld pilot, many television series, and some TV films, plus theatre and teaching. The other friend, John Quincy Adams, III, is a noted Christian Science Practitioner and lecturer. We've shared many adventures together and are still in touch.

Once I got the job at Playhouse-on-the-Green, I decided to leave New York and make a quick trip to visit my mom, who by this time was married to the nameless son-of-a-bitch I alluded to earlier. I hadn't seen my mom since I had arrived in New York, so I thought a visit was in order. I also managed to get a short trip in to see my dad's sister, my Aunt Geraldine in Portsmouth, Virginia. I discovered that my dad had been there for a short while after he sobered up from his bender. He had the car I had been making payments on in Baltimore until it was repossessed.

Now it was over three years later, and I still hadn't heard from him.

My friend and roommate, Ed, had also nailed a summer job in the Catskills in New York. It wasn't an acting gig, but he would be working all summer as some kind of camp assistant, so I wasn't leaving him stuck with the apartment rent. We just gave our notice. In New York at the time, you didn't have to sign a lease unless you wanted to. We never did because none of us ever knew when we might have to move. Ed and I decided we'd hook up after we returned from our summer jobs.

I took my first plane flight out of Virginia and headed to Ohio for my first real professional summer stock job; – Translation: you got paid every week!

I settled in and everything was good. I had been hired to play the role of Eugene in "Look Homeward Angel", a role I had lost out on to replace Anthony Perkins on Broadway, to Andrew Prine. Andrew Prine, who strangely enough wound up dating Sharon Farrell, the ex-roommate of my first live-in lady, Dee DeLagarde. Ain't life strange??

I wound up working with Andy years later in the original "Wonder Woman" pilot with Cathy Lee Crosby in the title role of Wonder Woman. I played another "side-kick" to the character Steve, the agent that worked with Wonder

Woman to capture all the "bad guys". Kas Garris played the male hero and agent, Steve.

In addition to the role of Eugene in "Look Homeward Angel", which would be one of the two main productions that summer, performing two weeks instead of the usual one, I would also perform all of the young leading man roles for that season at the Playhouse. We did an Agatha Christie mystery, some type of wild farce for the kids, a zany comedy in the Marx Brothers tradition – "How to Make a Million", and "Auntie Mame". "Auntie Mame" was the other two week main production. I played Patrick as the grown up young man. This was when I had my first crush and affair with a leading lady, Greta Markson. She was a working actress out of New York, and married to a writer at the time. She was beautiful, bright, and the "young leading man and leading lady syndrome" took place.

It was there in summer stock that I met John Quincy Adams, III. He was a local guy out of Columbus and was working as an apprentice. I mentioned him earlier. We hooked up when he came to New York and began a friendship that has lasted over 60 years. More about our adventures later in the book.

Summer stock in Ohio was a great experience. Learning and honing your acting skills, and getting paid for it. Stock companies, summer or winter, even repertory.

Stock is one of the best training grounds we have in the theatre. Once the season starts and you get the first show underway, as you perform each evening with that play, you are busy rehearsing the next week's show during the day. This continues for the entire season. You perform at night, then rehearse the next show during the day. It's hard work, but a great way to improve your concentration and continue to develop your "acting chops". I worked with a varied group of actors and actresses, some of them were very good, some okay, but they were all dedicated to their craft on different levels. I wish I could remember all their names, but memory doesn't allow it. I remember the director, Phillip Pruneau, Art Wolff, the stage manager that became one of my oldest friends, actors Art Kassal, William Whitman, IV, Greta Markson, the leading lady I fell in love with, and Lois Kibbee, the niece of character actor, Guy Kibbee. I guess I remember Lois because she never really liked me, always referred to me as "that aging Juvenile". In our stock company you had the Leading Man, the Leading Lady, the Leading Juvenile (a young leading man, that was me), the Ingénue (young leading lady), the Leading Character Man, and the Leading Character Lady.

There were a number of sexual encounters with a few

young ladies in the area, and, of course, the blockbuster of the affairs for me was with the leading lady, Greta. This was quite wonderful for a young guy, until her husband showed up toward the end of the season. Obviously, it came to a halt. She did see me once in New York after we had both returned from stock for what I would now call a "mercy visit". That was the last time I ever really "saw" her, but I've never forgotten her.

Back to New York

I returned to New York after that season of stock in an unusual way. Bill Whitman, IV (he came from a wealthy family, hence the "Fourth"), had a European sports car (I can't recall the name) and he asked me if I'd like to drive it back to New York for him. He agreed to pay me, plus money for the gas and any expense I might have on the trip.

Obviously, I agreed. I loved to drive, and had been doing so since I was about 14 years old on country roads. And, of course, I had a driver's license. So I drove his sports car back to New York City and delivered it to him at his apartment on the East Side.

I then found myself lodging at a shabby little hotel up on Broadway around 82nd Street. I was familiar with the area, and I've always been partial to the Westside. It was a one-room apartment with a bed, a dresser and a closet. The bath was in the hall. Summer stock was over and I was back to reality. I knew I needed to find a job, and a decent place to live. The only time I enjoyed my digs at the shabby little hotel was the one afternoon when Greta paid me the "mercy visit". Just like summer stock – it was a wonderful and memorable afternoon, but never to take place again.

    Back to reality. I managed to get in touch with my friend Ed Beres and asked him where he was living and if he could use a roommate. As it turned out, Ed had met a lady and they were sharing an apartment in Forest Hills, on Long Island, just a short subway ride from Manhattan. We agreed to meet up in the City and catch up on our summer adventures. I asked Ed about his girlfriend, and he was a little reluctant to give me many details. He kept beating around the bush. I asked him to tell me her name, and what did she do? Was she an actress, a dancer, a singer? Ed replied, "If I tell you, you're going to laugh." I assured him, I would not laugh. After a long pause, he said, "Her name is Marty and she plays the trumpet." I don't know if it was the WAY he said it, or if it really struck me funny for a girl to be named Marty and be a trumpet player, but I did laugh! I couldn't help myself. Ed was just so serious. But I apologized, stopped laughing, and encouraged him to tell me more about Marty, his trumpet-playing girlfriend. He told me she worked during the day at a regular job. She was the secretary and assistant to Bob Marcucci, the manager of both teenage singing idols, Frankie Avalon and Fabian. We had a good visit, and I was invited out to Ed's and Marty's apartment in Forest Hills for dinner so I could meet Marty. She was a very pretty young lady and she was good for Ed.

Ed and I continued to attend the New Theatre School for classes. The New Theatre School still honored my scholarship even though I was now considered to be a "professional actor" as I had been paid for acting work in summer stock and I'd received my Actors' Equity card. While attending the New Theatre school, I made another effort with an audition at The Actors Studio. Failed again. As I wrote previously, I was a perennial failure at The Actors Studio in New York, but I did eventually perform at The Actors Studio West in Los Angeles years later, and I was invited to join. However, at the time I was firmly entrenched at the Melrose Theatre which had quite a good list of members, including Richard Dryfuss, Tommy Lee Jones, Karen Valentine, George Murdock, Richard Bull, Jennifer Rhodes, Charles Rome Smith, Barbara Colintine, Robert Pine (father of Chris Pine), Tom Troupe, Carol Cook and Barbara Rush. So I stayed with the Melrose Theatre group.

Since Ed was sharing an apartment with his girlfriend

Marty, I found myself a one-room studio apartment up on West 85th Street, a four-flight walk-up. But, as I wrote previously, I was always partial to the Westside. I had managed to save some of my summer stock funds, but I knew I needed to find a survival job. Since I was now a member of Actors' Equity (AEA), I was now a professional actor by trade. However, that wonderful feeling and pride of becoming a member of Actors' Equity that existed in 1960 ,is no longer enjoyed by me after being a paying member for sixty years. I will provide a bit more of the reality that AEA is NOT "The Actors Union" that it professes to be, later in the book.

Regardless, at that time, I thought it was wonderful to be a member of Equity. I could go up to the Equity office and check on the job listings, visit with other Equity members, and also find out about part-time employment that was available.

One of the actors I met at Equity in those days was Percy Kilbride - "Pa" Kettle. He was a gentle man, and didn't mind being bothered by a young actor wanting to talk to him.

I tried a number of jobs as I attended audition after audition. I was a "store-to-store" magazine salesman for about two weeks. Then (as I mentioned earlier) I got a job at Lüchow's restaurant on West 14th Street downtown. It was a very well-known and "classy" restaurant. I was hired as a "Host". The Host stood inside the restaurant and greeted the patrons as they came in. I would inquire if they had a reservation, I had a little reservation list that was given to me each evening. They had two Hosts, me and Joe Jamrod, also an actor. That way when one of us was taking the patrons to "hand-off" to the Maître d' in a specific dining room (Lüchow's had three dining rooms) there was always a Host at the door. The first night I showed up for work, I had been asked to "dress up". I thought they meant really dress up, and since I had a tux, I "dressed up" and showed up in my tux. As a result, each time I would take the customers to one of the dining rooms, I was hit in the palm with a nice tip! The customers thought I was the maître d'. Well, that didn't last long – with me in the tux. Even though Mr. Mitchell, the owner, liked the look of me in the tux, he took me aside and explained that I couldn't wear the tux, as nice as I looked, because the patrons were confusing me with the maître d', (hence the tips I was getting). So I should just wear a suit in the future. He ended by saying I did add class to his restaurant, but closed by stating, I was not allowed to take tips! Well, being the enterprising young man I was (remember I'd been looking after myself since I was 14 years old), I learned that when the restaurant was really crowded, and customers had to "wait in the bar for a bit" before getting their table, it was not unusual for them to put a nice bill - $5, $10, even $20 - in my hand, to see if I "could hurry things along for them". I found two of the maître d's more than willing to work a split with me for a table in their dining rooms. The French maître d', Jean, was more than willing to work with me for his dining room, as was the American maître d', but the head maître d', Max, a European German, was not willing to do any type of split. I was warned by Jean, so I avoided Max's Dining room whenever possible. But old Max found out and reported me to Mr. Mitchell. Mr. Mitchell brought me up to his office and told me he knew what I had been doing, and it was not allowed. I was to cease doing this immediately or he'd have no choice but to fire me. Well, I don't believe I have to write that I was making a pretty good piece of change with those tips, because the job just paid the minimum hourly wage (I can't remember what it was back then, but it's only $15 an hour today, so use your imagination for the 60's), and we only worked four hours a night – so I was not about to give up those tips. The people that attended Lüchow's in those days had a few dollars and certainly were willing to part with a tip.

During the holidays I really made some money. One

Christmas, I had a guy at the bar with a party of four and without a reservation offer me $100 to get him a table. I tried like hell, but there was just nothing available. I had to let that one go! I was able to keep this up for a while, until good old Max caught me and reported me again. This time Mr. Mitchell let me go. He said he was sorry to lose me, but I left him with no choice, so I left Lüchow's with some terrific memories for a part-time job. Parties were attended by celebrities like Zsa Zsa Gabor, her sister Eva Gabor (by far the prettiest), George Saunders, Zackary Scott (the first guy I ever saw with an earring, but I was told that he "earned" it by crossing around the Horn), and even Murray Hamilton (I had to tell Mr. Mitchell who Murray was). It was a lot of fun.

I'll never forget that the first time I ever saw a man in a coat lined with mink, it was Mr. Jan Mitchell. He also owned the first Chrysler 300 I ever saw. His wife was a young European actress that gave up her career to marry him, and of course most people knew that Mr. Mitchell was also gay. I liked the guy, and we got along very well until I was caught the second time for taking tips and he had to fire me.

Fortunately, the older lady receptionist at Equity, she liked me like a son, pointed me in the direction of the Hotel Taft. I was hired as a room clerk, the young man at the check-in counter that assigned the rooms. I also met another "star" at the hotel – Rin Tin Tin. A beautiful German Sheppard dog that was really a "star". He had his own room, with a door adjoining his owners.

Once again I took some chances with my job, but I managed to stay out of trouble. Meaning I never got caught! Now, before you start to think I was into thievery or some other nefarious activity, it only involved the women guests. This was a time when a few ladies, while making either a pleasure or business trip to New York City, were looking for a little "adventure" or "tall tale" to take back home, or keep as a memory. And there I was! A fairly good looking, unattached young man that they didn't have to visit a bar to meet. Obviously it was totally against all rules of the hotel for an employee, other than a cleaning person, to visit the room of any guest. This was in the 60's well before the sexual revolution of the 70's, but also long before AIDS appeared on the scene. And even though I was certainly no Don Juan, I must have presented some southern charm, because I had several occasions to find my way up to a lady's hotel room. One young lady, whose father owned some big chain of department stores in Canada, gave me a beautiful set of cuff-links adorned with a small sapphire and diamond after a three day (or rather evening) rendezvous at the Hotel. Needless to explain, I had to carefully sneak up to her room, and I could only meet her outside away from the Hotel. She was accompanied by a little older female friend, her traveling companion and chaperone. The companion had her own room, and was certainly a bit more worldly than her young friend. She encouraged her young lady friend and traveling companion to fully enjoy herself before returning to her home in Canada. I have to admit I did my best!

Of course, we promised to stay in touch, but that never happened. As for those beautiful cuff-links, they visited a pawn shop on a couple of occasions, later when rent money was needed and acting work was scarce. I am sorry to admit that I finally had to leave them to be adopted by another customer, failing to redeem them during the allotted time.

I really enjoyed working at the Taft Hotel.

Chapter Nine

I managed to get a couple of acting jobs during this time period and wound up leaving the hotel gig. I did an off-Broadway play entitled "Lily and the Sergeant" at a small (very small) intimate little theatre that was housed in a building on West 57th Street (Another strange note: I currently reside in a building on West 57th Street that is five buildings down from that building). Richard X. Slattery starred as the Sergeant in the play. Readers may remember Richard as the tough "redneck" in the first "Walking Tall" film that starred another friend, Joe Don Baker. Richard had a very good career. He was a retired New York City Police Detective, and he went on to do a number of films and TV shows in California. He was the Captain on the "Mister Roberts" TV show that starred Roger Smith as Mister Roberts. Richard got me the role of Sparks, the radio operator on Mister Roberts, years later after I arrived in L.A. I guess he enjoyed breaking me up so much during "Lily and the Sergeant", which he managed to try to do every performance, that he wanted to work with me again. Later, we would do a few different Movies-of-the-Week and TV shows together. A little Equity note here. They have no record of "Lily and the Sergeant", and no record of another off-Broadway show that I did. It appears the only records AEA was really good at keeping for me during the 60's, was if I paid my dues on time.

    A couple of interesting turns occurred at this time. I met an actor, Bill Smith (real name), and he owned the rights to a beauty product named "Roll-a-Curl". It was a plastic device that supposedly allowed women to easily roll curls in their hair, clip it with a hair pin, spray it and set it. A demonstrator, i.e., a "pitchman", demonstrated this product, and Bill had a booth set up in Macy's Department Store. He needed a pitchman, and I needed a job. With an outgoing personality, nice presentation, shirt, coat, tie and always with a great gift of gab, I was the guy. Only real problem – the "Roll-a-Curl" didn't work! It never worked! The guy that invented this hot selling little item did all this research back in the 60's and discovered that less than five percent (5%) of women were willing to admit that they couldn't use a beauty product. Today's women would string that guy up! But I sold it. And I sold it everywhere. I was in Macy's. Later I was selling it in Woolworths five-and-dime store. I even sold it on the Boardwalk in Atlantic City. A famous pitchman that most people will remember, also worked on the Boardwalk in Atlantic City – Ed McMahon. He did well with Johnny Carson.

    While working at Macy's, I met another young guy,

Michael Equine, who was working there. He was hired to roam around the store during the holiday season, dressed in a suit as Yogi Bear. Michael and I became friends and started hanging out together. He had a friend, Chuck Morley, and they both played the guitar. Michael also lived with an older lady, only by a few years, Sykes Equine, up on West 76th Street. Can you believe it? They lived about two buildings down from where I had first lived with Ed and the roommates, plus Dee, over two years before. Michael had actually taken the last name of Sykes as his own because he had a lot of issues with his dad, a guy named Fred Herwig. Soon we were hanging out together. I had taught myself how to play the guitar, so me, Michael and a friend of his, Chuck Morley played whenever we would get together. Dreams of The Kingston Trio? My time at the New Theatre School had ended, and my scholarship had run its course. Karl Redcoff had left his teaching position to go on the road with a play. Evelyn King, his wife, had gone with Karl, and I had dropped Dr. Ila Mottloff's class after just a few weeks in the beginning. Even though he had worked with Stanislavski in the Moscow Art Theatre, I could never "get the guy".

Dr. Mottloff broke everything down into "bits" (mini-beats) and he would spend what seemed like hours doing that to each scene. I just didn't get it. So I dropped the class, even though I was on a scholarship and it was free! Hey, if it doesn't work for you, you have to walk away.

During the next year and a half I lost touch with my friend Ed Beres. Someone told me that he gave up acting and went off to become a Franciscan Brother in the Church. . I'm sorry we lost touch. I was spending a lot of time with Michael and his live-in lady friend, Sykes Equine. Sykes covered most of the cost for the apartment, food and expenses. One evening a very popular mime, Lionel Sheppard came by. Later he changed his name to Richmond Sheppard. He was an ex-husband of Sykes, and also a protégé of the world famous mime, Marcel Marceau.

Richmond was a bit older and a great deal more mature than either Michael or me, and obviously we trusted him – maybe even more than we should. He had brought over three "sugar cubes", which was referred to as a "mushroom", but in fact was the liquid LSD, a hallucinatory drug with a dose soaked in the sugar cubes. We had all been hearing about LSD (even though we never called anything, including pot, a drug) and once someone like Richmond told us it was okay to "try it", we were all game. , It was the 60's, we were young people doing a lot of crazy things, which we just thought was perfectly okay!

Richmond told us to take the "sugar cube" around

midnight, because we would want to "come up with the Sun" keeping our spirits and minds fresh and open. It was a Saturday night in early spring, 1962. All three of us followed his instructions and took the "sugar cube" around midnight. The effect hit me and Sykes first within about an hour and a half. It took a little longer for the effect to hit Michael. Now, I'll not bore the reader with all the goofy, crazy hallucinations we each experienced, like objects moving and falling in slow motion, and the difficulty in trying to perform a simple task, like combing your hair. You can read about the varying effects of LSD, and the way people have been affected, with both good and bad doses of the drug in any number of research magazines, and stories about Cary Grant's experiments with the drug, on the internet today. I'll just say it was an incredible "trip". The three of us, Michael, Sykes and me on our "adventure". We heeded the warnings of Richmond not to start staring at the rising Sun, and not to do anything truly stupid like step in front of a moving bus to see what it might feel like, or jump off any height because you "believe" you can fly!

So, as a "traveling unit", we set off to "see the sights". We walked to the subway and took the train down to South Ferry, where we boarded the Staten Island Ferry and traveled to Staten Island. I did make an attempt to buy a cup of coffee and a donut from the concession stand on the Ferry Boat. But after three tries of asking for the coffee and donut, which I thought I was stating perfectly clearly, but the lady behind the counter kept saying, "What?" – "What?" – "What is it you want?" I decided that maybe I was not speaking clearly in a language she could understand, so I retreated to the giggles of Michael and Sykes.

When we departed from the Ferry on Staten Island, the three of us, staying in our "unit", began walking around the Island. The only interesting and spooky item to share is about a tall man that was walking on the opposite side of the street where we were walking. He was dressed all in black, and was wearing one of those stovepipe hats, the type that Lincoln wore, and as we were fixated on him, the three of us agreed that the man was indeed, the Image of Death! We continued walking, and watching him as he moved down the street – then he stopped at a mortuary, unlocked the door and went in! We freaked out!

We continued to walk around Staten Island. It was now about 10 a.m. on this Sunday morning, and we had been really high for a good eight hours with no immediate feelings of "coming down". We returned to the Ferry, took it back to Manhattan, got on the Subway and returned back uptown to Sykes' and Michael's apartment after taking another walk down to the boat basin. We called Richmond to "check in" and he advised us to go to a movie until we completely "came down" off the trip. I remember the film. It was a James Cagney movie, "One, Two, Three", playing at the Astor Theatre on Broadway. Sorry, I don't have a clue what it was about.

We came home, again as our "unit", but an unusual thing had developed during this trip. I had become the "leader" of our "unit". I had taken over, took charge, became assertive, but not in any aggressive or hostile manner, I just became the leader of our "group". Neither Michael nor Sykes objected in the least. Sykes did look at me in a different light from that time on.

After the film, we all returned to the apartment. Sykes opened up a very sturdy daybed out in the living room, and we all decided it was time to call it a day. Michael and Sykes retired to the bedroom, closed the door, and we all crashed.

The next thing I remember was being gently awakened by Sykes climbing into my daybed and making love to me. It was unreal! With no dialogue, just this beautiful female person, both of us completely naked, making love to me! Then after it was over, Sykes got up and returned to the bedroom. That event was never discussed.

Later, Sykes had decided she wanted to return to a

college upstate in a place called New Paltz, to finally finish her degree, and maybe teach. Her dad had left her a small but ample trust fund, so Sykes never had to worry about money as long as she was careful and sensible. It was decided that Michael could visit her once she was settled in. We both helped move her to New Paltz. Later, she and Michael got married and had a daughter.

Sykes had led a very interesting life. She was originally from Arkansas. She had spent some time in Hollywood hanging out with a group of actors that included Dennis Hopper, who was a terrific actor, Troy Donahue (he had good looks and a good voice, but I never thought Troy was much of an actor - he was a big "heartthrob") and Tom Pittman. Tom, like many of us young actors, was absolutely enthralled by the performances and short life of James Dean. Tom was a good actor, and he copied a lot of mannerisms that Dean employed. Tom also followed some of Dean's off-screen persona. He bought and drove a Porsche Speedster and, unfortunately, his life ended in a tragic car accident like Dean's. Tom accidently drove off one of the curves on Mulholland Drive high in the hills. His car could not be seen from the road, and it was days before he was discovered pinned in the wreck. The autopsy report stated he had died from exposure and his injuries. Had he been discovered earlier he would have survived.

    Sykes was the first person to introduce me to Dennis Hopper. Dennis was appearing in a Broadway show that Sykes and I attended. After the performance, Sykes took me backstage so she could say hi to Dennis, and she introduced me. The play was entitled "Mandingo" and it had a short run. Years later I'd meet Dennis again, and I worked with him in "The Indian Runner" directed and written by Sean Penn. I would also meet up with Sykes years later in Arkansas, where she had returned in seclusion. I was working with Gregory Peck, Stacy Keach, and a slew of other name actors in "The Blue and The Gray", a blockbuster mini-series for television.

    After Sykes made the move to New Paltz in upstate New York, Michael and I were hanging out and playing the guitar together most of the time. There was a place down in Greenwich Village called The Cock and Bull, with a couple of old couches, chairs, a few small tables, and a very little stage space on about a three inch riser. They had a mic and lightweight sound system setup so anybody that wanted to get up with their instrument to play and sing was free to do so. They served coffee, sandwiches and pastries. You could buy what you wanted - obviously there were no minimums - but you were required to buy at least a cup of coffee before you could sit there all night. The early 60's were one hell of a time, especially in the Village in New York City!

    Some incredible talent would perform at The Cock and Bull on any given night. I remember Bob Dylan getting up and singing. Many of us knew him as Bob Zimmerman. This was just before his first album for RCA came out. Some of the others I saw perform there were Bob Gibson and Bob Camp. Bob Camp changed his name to Hamilton Camp and went on to sing, and later became an actor with a recurring role on a TV series. One night Erik Darling dropped in. He was performing with The Weavers folk group before organizing The Rooftop Singers. Later on he had a huge hit with "Walk Right In". He was married to Joan Darling who went on to direct TV - most notably "Mary Hartman, Mary Hartman".

    Here's where my slight detour into the folk-singing world took place. One Saturday night, Michael and I were down in the Village, broke as usual, and we started home. Michael and Sykes still lived on West 76th Street and I had the little Studio apartment on West 82nd Street, both way uptown from the Village. We were down around 3rd Street and 6th Avenue, so do the math. It was a long walk, and it was winter. We started out walking up Sixth Avenue, as bundled up as we could be, both carrying our guitar cases, and it was COLD! As we were approaching 36th Street, Michael suddenly remembered that his old man, Fred Herwig, was in town, and Fred always hung out at a bar on East 38th Street called The Centaur. It was a small bar/restaurant/club place set down off the street, but upscale.

They had a large piano sitting on a two-foot high stage, where a guy that looked like Groucho Marx, mustache and all, played the piano and sang – and they called him "Groucho". We went inside and, sure enough, Fred was there at the bar with a couple of ladies and a few friends. Fred was well-known and spent a lot of money in the joint. Michael went over to him at the bar, they greeted each other, and Michael asked him if he could borrow a couple of bucks. Michael explained we needed it to get uptown. Fred, looked at the two of us, standing there with our guitars, and hands held out – and he said, "NO." He wouldn't lend us a couple of bucks, but if we got up and played a couple of songs, he'd give us $50!

Michael asked me if I thought we should do it. I would have danced with Fred for $20 …..so yeah! We'd play and sing for a bunch of drunks for $50. I should mention here that Fred had heard the two of us play together before, so he knew we could at least make some type of music.

Fred went over to "Groucho", told him his kid and his

friend were a couple of folk singers, said we were pretty good, and asked him if it was okay for us to do a couple of songs. Groucho said, sure, he'd take a break and we could do a couple of tunes. Of course the fact that Fred dropped a ton of dough in the joint on a regular basis had absolutely NOTHING TO DO WITH IT!

Groucho, took a break. He gave us a little introduction. I couldn't remember what he said if my life depended on it. I was cold and nervous. Michael and I had never played before any type of "crowd". We had never even gotten up at The Cock and Bull. We just played for ourselves and a few select friends, that's all. Well, we got up on the little stage in front of the piano, did a little "patter" as we checked to make sure our guitars were in tune. Michael played a twelve-string guitar, and I played a Martin six-string. Michael could pick and play much better than me, but our voices really meshed together, and created a very good folk-music sound. We did a song, "Skillet Good & Greasy", up tempo, and we pulled it off! The people actually stopped some of the talking as we got into the song, and were with us when we finished! We received a little applause. We did a silly little comedy skit - I would be Chester from Gunsmoke, and Michael would be Marshall Dillion, and then we went into another song, "Nine Hundred Miles". The crowd was now really into it, and we received a much larger round of applause. And of course Fred was being congratulated on the talent of his son and his son's friend – me! We thought we'd better quit while we were ahead, so we thanked everybody and stepped down off the stage, as Groucho encouraged the customers to give us another round of applause. By the way, Groucho was not sad to see us leave his entertainment domain.

As Michael was collecting the fifty bucks from Fred, I was putting up our guitars, when this very classy looking lady came over to me, introduced herself, handed me a card that read Don Seat Enterprises. She told me this guy on the card was her husband, and he managed musical talent and that I should call him on Monday. I thanked her, put the card in my pocket, picked up the guitars, joined Michael and Fred at the bar, received a few "congratulations" and handshakes, and we left The Centaur.

Outside we got silly for about a minute and talked about grabbing a cab. Our sensibilities set in and we decided on taking a fifteen cent subway ride uptown.

It had been a good night!

Chapter Ten

On Monday morning I joined Michael at Chuck Morley's apartment in midtown and, after we discussed it for about a full minute, I decided to call Don Seat, the name and number on the business card that the lady had given me Saturday night in The Centaur. The receptionist took my call and put me through to Mr. Seat. He told me his wife had recommended that he meet with us, and asked me if we could come in on Wednesday. I didn't need to check our schedule, we were wide open, so I made the appointment. Chuck wasn't exactly thrilled that I was playing guitar with Michael most of the time (he considered himself a much superior guitar player to me - and he was correct), and he thought we were wasting our time meeting with a manager of musical talent.

On Wednesday, we both put on our good dark suits and a tie, took our guitars, and went to Don Seat's office on West 57th Street. Funny how West 57th Street keeps popping up in my life. We went up to his office and his secretary escorted us in. At that time Don Seat was managing Conway Twitty, and this was before Conway crossed over from Rock to Country, the Four Freshman and a number of other diverse musical groups, but no folk-singing groups. Don said his wife had told him she thought we had a good "folk-singing sound" after hearing us perform at The Centaur.

He then asked us if we had a demo he could listen to. Now, don't think that we were dumb – we just didn't know what a demo was. Remember, I was an actor, and Michael was just floating along with any part-time work he could find. We both knew nothing about the music business. I asked Mr. Seat, "What is a demo?" He explained it was a recording of at least two songs on a record that he could play to hear what we sounded like. He said, "You guys need a demo." I told him we would get one. We left his office, and right across the street, again on West 57th Street - At 111 West 57th Street - was Nola Recording Studio! We went in, and I asked the person at the desk how much did it cost to record a demo. He replied it was twenty-five dollars an hour. Now you have to remember, we had just received twenty-five bucks each from Michael's dad on Saturday night when we played at the Club, so I didn't see any way we could spend half of that to record a demo.

I asked the guy, "How much for a half-hour?" He looked at me like I was crazy and said, "Kid, nobody can record a song in a half-hour." I assured him we could record two songs in a half-hour. He paused for a minute – thankfully it was a slow day for Nola – and he said, "All right, twelve-fifty for a half hour....but if you go over it'll cost you the full hour."

We went into the studio, took out our guitars, made sure we were in tune, did one mic check, and cut two songs. The first song, "Skillet Good & Greasy", we did in one take. The second song, "Nine Hundred Miles", which featured me as the solo, took us three takes, but that was only because we had time left on the half-hour.

I still have the original 78 record of that demo session.

We took the demo to Don Seat. He signed us, and told us we needed to get a publicity photo taken. I explained that we were a bit short of funds. He said not to worry, he would send us to a photographer he used, and he would cover the cost.

He'd take it out of our "bookings." The folk-singing duo, "THE CASTAWAYS" was born! The next year was absolutely crazy. John Adams, the young man I had met in Ohio at Playhouse-on-the-Green arrived in town and got in touch with me through my answering service, JU-6-6300. I believe that almost every actor in town used that service. For years they were located at 1501 Broadway. I met up with John and we became friends, a friendship that has lasted over fifty-seven years. John rented an apartment down in the

Village. Michael and I booked our first gig as The Castaways as the opening act for Richmond Sheppard's mime act. Richmond called Don Seat and booked us, almost as a favor, because he discovered we now had a manager. Richmond had a guitar player named James Gavin that supplied the musical accompaniment, and sounds for the various mime routines. James was a very talented guy, he played the guitar really well and it complimented the mime routines that Richmond performed. James was also an actor and later got an opportunity in the film business in Hollywood, but he fucked it up with his eccentric behavior. He'd stay up all night smoking pot and drinking, he would show up all disheveled, unshaven, and then, when he was on the set doing his first film, he'd roll up in a blanket or rug, and take a quick nap between setups. The assistant director would have to wake him up for the next shot, then he'd forget his lines. He finally told the studio he thought this was all bullshit, so they released him from his contract and he returned to New York.

    That first job, opening for Richmond, was at some college upstate, I don't remember the name. I do remember it was the first time I had ever smoked pot before trying to perform. Michael could play just as well stoned as he could straight, and that night in our dressing room Michael broke out a joint and lit up. I was surprised and asked him what in the world was he doing? He replied, "Oh come on man, we'll be great. Have a couple of hits, that audience will never know the difference." Well, he was correct about the audience. Once we started to play and sing the first song, they were all yelling, shouting and trying to sing along. Just a few chords into the song I looked over at Michael and discovered he was playing in the key of C and I was playing in the key of G! I spent the rest of that number trying to change chords and catch up with him. The college kids loved it! They whopped and hollered the entire time we were playing, and gave us a rousing cheer and applause when we finished. We came off stage and Michael thought we were great! I had no idea how we were, and I vowed to Michael I would never get stoned before a show again! And I kept that vow until years later when I broke it just once during an actual shoot (you will read about that later).

  That period of time is hazy, and as I stated, it was a crazy time and really flew by. After just a couple of gigs, Michael's dad, Fred, told us we could move into his apartment in a luxury building on East Thirty-fourth Street while Fred was living in Jamaica, where his factory that made children's clothes was located. Fred made a lot of money because his labor cost was practically nothing. I found out much later - after they had an uprising down there - the workers were paid about six cents an hour. No wonder they had an uprising.

So, we went from me living in my small studio apartment on West 82nd Street and Michael sleeping on a couch in Chuck Morley's midtown apartment to this luxury full two bedroom apartment on the Eastside, with a number of hot-and-cold-running young ladies in and out all the time.

After just a few jobs Don Seat called us and said we had an appointment with the head guy at Premiere Records. He had sent them our demo and they were interested in talking to us about doing an album. I couldn't believe it! I had been banging my head against the acting wall for about a year and a half after my summer stock job, with absolutely no discernible success, and here, in a matter of weeks in a folk-singing duo, we were going in to meet with a record company! The meeting is worth describing. We went to the offices of Premiere Records, located on the Westside in Midtown. We were shown into this young executive's office. I remember his first name was Steven, but I have no memory of his last name. He didn't look much older than we were, maybe not even as old! He was standing next to a big desk, dressed in a medium blue velvet sports jacket, open collar shirt, dark slacks and expensive loafers, with no socks. He introduced himself to us, asked us to call him

Steve, we shook hands, and he invited us to have a seat in the two chairs opposite his desk. Then he sat down, opened up his desk drawer, took out three joints, tossed one each to me and Michael, then lit one for himself. Michael and I exchanged looks – like, is this guy a narc?? Because in the 60's in New York City, you could go to jail for marijuana! But we figured if he was smoking, it was all right, and he was not a narc! He offered us a light, and then told us he had heard "our sound", and that they were interested in doing an album with The Castaways. We sat there smoking pot with this young record executive, Steve, and listened as he explained his idea for the title of the album, and that he wanted us to record the standard folk tunes he would select (which Premiere would cover the royalties for), and were we interested? Without even asking about the contract (or anything else for that matter) we told him yes we would like to do the album. He said he would send everything over to Don Seat Enterprises, and they would give us a recording date. I remember we put out what was left of the joints (the "leftovers" were referred to as "roaches"), he gave us a little plastic vial to put them in, we shook hands and left – absolutely stoned out of our gourds! We were wasted for the rest of the day.

    Before the week was out, Don had called us and given

us the date to show up at the recording studio of Premiere Albums. We were due in at 5 p.m., which we thought was a bit late for a recording session, but we later learned that the late hours were less costly for the company than the early hours. Later hours were for the "new and unproven" talent, early hours were for the "tried and proven" talent.

    We showed up, and here's where the fun begins! First, they put us into two separate recording booths with our guitars and asked us to "lay down the music tracks." Michael and I had no frigging idea what they wanted us to do – play without singing? So, the engineer explained that this was how it was done. We would play the musical part of the song, then we would do the vocal part to a playback of the guitar music. Now today, almost every kid in the world knows about this procedure – but this was fifty years ago, and we did not! We didn't consider ourselves musicians, we just liked to sing together! Plus, neither one of us could read a note of music, we just knew how to play and sing TOGETHER!

    Well, we tried it their way. We each got into a separate booth, thankfully we could see each other through the glass, and we started to play with a "one and a two and a nod" and we started to play our guitars, and at the same time we mouthed the words to the song. We did three songs just playing the guitars – and mouthing the words. It was the only way we knew how to do it. After we finished laying down the guitar tracks, the producer and engineer told us to put down our guitars, put on some headphones so we could hear our guitars playing, and we were supposed to sing to the "music track" of our guitars. We tried, but just couldn't get the feel of the music, and when we were supposed to start singing! After a number of really frustrating tries, with no success, I spoke up and asked the music producer if we could do both the singing and playing at the same time, since this was the way we always performed. We had been in the studio about four hours since we started well after 5 p.m., and now it was around 9 p.m. The producer made a call to Steve, the young executive, who was now at his apartment getting ready to go out for the evening – probably to "discover" another singing act, and explained the "problem" to him. Steve told the producer to wrap it up for the night, and have us come in to see him the next morning.

  We showed up the next morning and briefly met with Steve – no offer of any pot this time – and he told us he had this brand new idea of how he wanted to record us. He was going to get the studio to set up a room where we could play the guitars and sing at the same time, with an invited group of people, and call the album, "At Home with The Castaways".

Written By Jordan Rhodes

The following week, Steve had invited five or six of his friends, all young, and we'd invited a few people we knew, some from the Cock and Bull crowd. So, with about twelve people sitting in this room on couches and comfy chairs, and a few mics, one each for me and Michael, and a couple around the room, we were going to cut this album in one night. The producer and engineers were all set up and ready to go. We started around 7 p.m. Steve offered joints to anyone that wanted to indulge at this "Home with The Castaways" evening of songs. I'm sure at some point I was "contact high" as almost everybody in the room was smoking. We would do a song, and the group would applaud. We'd introduce another song, play and sing it, and the group would applaud and make a few good comments. We'd do another song, etc., etc, and this continued until about 3 a.m. We finished up, everybody was happy – hell, everybody was stoned, Steve did have some good weed! There were congratulations all around. We met some of the people for the first time since we didn't know all of them before we started the evening singing/playing/entertaining. And we called it a night, even though it was early morning. Michael and I were so beat, we both declined the offer of two young ladies that volunteered to accompany us back to the apartment. Those were the days!

Three days later we went to Don Seat's office. Premiere had sent a couple of LP demos over to be heard. Don wanted us all to hear them. The three of us listened to one complete LP demo together, and it was LONG. After it finished, we sat there shell-shocked. IT WAS PURE SHIT! It sounded awful! It sounded like two guys singing and playing guitars - and not doing either very well - with a group of drunks at a party!

Don was not pleased. I was mortified, and couldn't believe it when Michael said later, "Well, I didn't think it was that bad." It was THAT BAD. After that episode, the folk-singing career began to fade just as quickly as it had started. Don lost interest in a heartbeat. But, in all fairness, his other clients like Conway Twitty, who had just crossed over to country music, and was becoming as hot as a two-dollar pistol, were taking most of his managing skills and time. Premiere Albums had a contract with us that allowed them to do whatever they wanted with "The Castaways Album" – I heard the album was a big hit in the supermarkets of Brazil, but no one was clamoring for us to do a tour.

One thing that still sticks in my mind about the weekend after the recording session, and before we heard the disaster in Don's office, was on Sunday, August 4, 1962. Me, Michael and two young ladies had just gotten up and out, about three o'clock in the afternoon after a night of fun and frolicking, when we heard the news on a radio at some newsstand – Marilyn Monroe had been found dead! It brought that day's outing to a standstill!

Chapter Eleven

After the recording disaster, I looked for and found a furnished one-room apartment on West 71st Street, where the street dead-ended into the railway yards long before the area was developed. The room had a single bed, a desk, two chairs, a table, very small refrigerator, a closet and a very large window that faced out to the street. The bathroom was shared with two other rooms in the hall. During this time I hooked back up with John Adams and would occasionally hang out with him at his apartment in the Village. One day, out of the blue, I got a call from an agent I was free-lancing with (couldn't find anyone to sign me at that time) and he told me that MGM out in L.A. was looking for some new talent to possibly sign for a new program they were starting, which was similar to the old studio system of contract players. He asked me if I could afford to go out – at my own expense of course!

    I told him I would think it over. He gave me the name of this talent scout at MGM and a phone number to call if I decided to go out to California. That night I was discussing this with John (while we were getting stoned) and we decided, what the hell! Let's go out to California.

    We began to plan our trip. We knew at that time you

could call a service which hired drivers to drive an owner's car from New York to Los Angeles. They would supply the gas money, additional funds for at least one oil change - which you were required to do - and pay you a very small – a very, very small - fee. The fee was so small I can't even remember how much it was – a pittance! The company would allow you five days to deliver the car. We decided if we could drive out there in three days, we could have the car for the additional two days (we knew you had to have a car in L.A.). Then we could sign up for another car to drive back to New York, and use it for two days in L.A., which would give us transportation for four days in Hollywood, as long as we could drive it back to New York in the remaining three days!

This way we could make a trip to Hollywood, spend four days out there, and return to New York almost for free. I'd get a chance to see the talent scout at MGM, we could look around Hollywood, and go to the beach – take a vacation! We were set.

We left some money with a friend of John's, and made arrangements for him to wire us $100 via Western Union once we arrived in Los Angeles. This way we would have some additional funds to make sure we could make the return trip. Sounded like a proper plan, didn't it?

First California Trip

On the morning we were leaving for our California trip, we met up at my room on West 71st Street. Then we took the train out to Long Island to pick up the car from the company for delivery. We each had a small suitcase, a small amount of pot, obviously packed with our clothes, and a few diet pills called "Preludin" (not Quaaludes). They were little pink pills, which worked like a pep pill, and could keep you awake.

We picked up the car without a hitch, and after signing some papers and verifying our identities, we loaded up and took off. I don't remember the name of the car we drove out to California, but it was a four door sedan, and we were delivering it to an address in Brentwood. I do remember the car we drove back, a pink Oldsmobile that belonged to Ann Miller, the dancer and actress from many MGM musicals. More about the return trip later.

We left Long Island taking turns driving and sleeping, I'd drive while John napped, until I got tired, then John would drive while I would sleep. On occasion we did take a Preludin for a little extra boost. The trip across country is almost three thousand miles, and at the halfway point we stopped for the needed and agreed-upon oil change. I asked the guy that was performing the oil change if we could stay in the vehicle while it was up on the lift. I explained that we were tired and would like to rest. He said it was fine. We smoked a little joint, then laid down, me in the front seat and John in the back. Once the oil change was finished, we were back on the road.

We arrived at Hollywood and Vine in fifty-eight hours from the time we left New York. Two days and ten hours! We were young, we were beat, but we were THERE! After getting a little something to eat, we went down to the Western Union in Hollywood to check on our money order from Gary, John's friend. We just had a short message – MONEY DELAYED. We only had a few dollars left and we desperately needed a shower and some place to sleep. I saw the Hollywood Roosevelt Hotel marquee on Hollywood Boulevard. I knew from working at the Hotel Taft in New York that you could check in without paying and were only required to pay when you checked out. Remember, this was the early 60's, and not everyone and his brother had a credit card. All that you needed was identification and a place of business to check in. I talked John into going and checking in at the Hollywood Roosevelt Hotel. I presented my identification and told them I represented Rhodes Refrigeration headquartered in Miami, Florida. They checked us in. Once we were in the room, we ordered a meal from room service, and I signed for it and charged it to the room. My education at the Hotel Taft was serving me well. We showered and got a good night's sleep. We knew we had the car for another day, so I called and made the appointment to see the talent scout at MGM, using the name of the agent in New York. This was the first time I would discover how impressed talent scouts, producers and production companies in Hollywood were with "New York talent" – regardless of whether you had any actually talent or not! The talent scout agreed to see me, so we drove out to MGM Studios and I went in to see him while John waited in the car. The meeting was over so quickly I don't even remember it. Can't remember the guy's name, or what little was discussed, only that he stated once I decided to move out to Los Angeles and relocate, I should give him a call and they'd arrange a screen test for me. Shook my hand and showed me the door! Thank you and goodbye!

    John and I decided to go to the beach. After the beach, it was getting late in the day, and we decided we'd go back to the hotel. Heading by the front desk, the manager, who had not been on duty when we checked in, called us over, and politely said there had been a little mix up, and I would need to settle up our hotel bill since they could find no record of a "Rhodes Refrigeration Company" in Miami, Florida. Of course I had to be a little indignant, and explained it was probably because I was now headquartered in New

York, as shown on my driver's license, so it was unfortunate but I'd go up to the room and make a call and have everything straightened out. The manager said that would not be possible as we were locked out of the room and would need to settle the bill in order to get the key. Of course what we didn't know at that time, was that Gary, John's friend, had sent a Western Union telegram, which was delivered to us at the hotel, stating; SORRY. NO FUNDS. SPENT IT. GARY. The manager could probably be sued for reading that telegram today, but not then. I was out of explanations. We were locked out! All of our belongings, including the pot we had in our suitcases, were now locked up!

    I did the only thing I could think of – I called my mom, collect in Hawaii where she was with the S.O.B. step-dad husband who was stationed there, and asked her if she could wire me any money. I told her I was in Hollywood, and a guy who was supposed to send us some money had really hung us out to dry. Mom asked me how much did I need. I told her $100. She said to give her the address of the Western Union office and she'd send it first thing in the morning.

    Mom always believed in me, and I'm happy that I was able to repay her for that loan many times over through the years.

    Okay, I had now arranged to get us some money.

But that was going to be tomorrow, the same day we were due to deliver the car to the owner in Brentwood. We still had to find some food and a place to sleep for the night. I knew my mom wouldn't let me down, and if she said I'd have the money tomorrow, then I knew I'd have the money tomorrow. We left the car parked on the street by a meter, but you didn't have to put any money in the meter after 6 p.m. We were walking up Hollywood Boulevard and came to a restaurant named "Johnny's Steak House". It was a nice restaurant, but not an upscale place, just very nice. I told John we were going in and I was going to talk to the manager and see if we could wash dishes for a meal. I asked the cashier if the manager was in, she told me the owner was there, and his name was actually Johnny. I went over to him and told him the whole story, obviously leaving out the part about lying and giving bogus information to the hotel. I told him we had been locked out of our hotel room, because the money we were expecting wouldn't be arriving until tomorrow and would he be willing to let us wash dishes or cleanup in exchange for a meal? He looked me over for a minute, then he called over a waiter and told him to put us in a booth and serve us a steak dinner – on the house! I couldn't believe it! We had a great meal, and I asked him to give me a check, and I told him I would return tomorrow and pay him. Johnny just smiled and said, "Okay." We left and walked back to the car, with John saying a time or two, "I don't know how you did that, Jordy." That night, after sleeping in the Hollywood Roosevelt Hotel the previous night, we slept in the car!

The next morning, we went to the Western Union office and just like my mom, bless her heart, had said, I had a $100 wire waiting for me. We paid the Hotel bill for the one night and the room service, got our belongings back – no one had searched our suitcases, and nothing was missing. I apologized to the Hotel manager about the "mix-up", and he also said he was sorry for any inconvenience.

We then called and made arrangements to pick up our "return to New York car". It was a pink Oldsmobile that belonged to Ann Miller, as mentioned before, the dancer actress of MGM fame. I drove the Oldsmobile, and John followed to deliver the four door sedan we had driven out from New York. We deliver the car to the owner in Brentwood after having it washed and cleaned, and he gave us a TIP! I believe it was either twenty or forty dollars. So now, in addition to the remaining money we had left from the one hundred dollars mom had sent me, we had the extra tip money.

That evening the first stop we made was to Johnny's

Steak House. We walked over to Johnny and I paid him for the meal he had so graciously given us the night before. When I paid him, and thanked him again, I asked him if he had ever done that for anyone before, he looked at me and replied, "A few times." I asked him if any of them had not paid him back, he smiled at me and replied, "A few." We had dinner again there that night. And years later, once I had moved to Hollywood, I went in and reintroduced myself to Johnny. I'm not sure if he remembered me or not, but I did eat quite a few meals there, and never forgot that he fed us that night when we were broke and hungry.

    Well we had two days and a pink Oldsmobile plus a few dollars, so we tried to enjoy ourselves a little. John talked me into bleaching my hair at the beach, so for a while I was a blond. We found an inexpensive motel for one night, then we drove down to Laguna Beach where I knew a single lady, her name was Sandy, I had met in New York at the Hotel Taft. I had her number, gave her a call, and John and I went down and spent an evening with her, which got a little dicey because she was entertaining a few Marines that were stationed there, and one of the Marines was almost a full-blooded Mohawk. I made the mistake of mentioning that I was part Cherokee. Obviously this Mohawk didn't like Cherokees, or the way Sandy was eyeing me and John (more

John than me), and this guy didn't care for me. His Marine friends settled him down and we were able to stay the night.

The following morning we drove back up to Hollywood. I had seen an ad in the paper where this guy was advertising for drivers with cars, to take passengers to their home in Oklahoma. We went over to meet the guy. He was working out of a parking lot on Seward Street, with a phone booth on the corner. He told us he had two guys that needed to get to their home in Oklahoma and they would pay some gas money and a few extra dollars for a ride. We had already been given our gas allowance for the trip back to New York, so we thought a few extra bucks would be okay, and where we had to take them was not very far out of the way in Oklahoma for our planned trip back to New York. We made arrangements to pick up the guys the following morning at 9 a.m. for our return trip to New York. It had been an adventure. And it wasn't over!

The next morning we arrived at the parking lot a little before 9 a.m. We met the guys. They were two young guys, both looking like a couple of Oklahoma cowboys. We didn't see anything threatening about them, so we agreed they were okay and threw their bags in the trunk. They hopped into the Olds and we pulled out of the parking lot for the drive to New York, knowing we needed to get there within three days.

Return to New York

There are only two incidents worth sharing about our return trip. John and I had traded places driving as we were traveling through the Panhandle of Texas. John was driving and I took the backseat behind him so I could catch a little shut-eye.

The two Oklahoma cowboys were napping, and John was really making some time. Translation - driving like a bat out of hell. One thing about those open highways during that time, you didn't have to necessarily follow the speed limit, just look out for the Highway Patrol. I was resting my head against the window, now just dozing a bit, about to wake up – when my eyes spotted an animal in the road way down in front of us, which we were rapidly approaching. As we got closer, I could see that the animal was slowly moving across the highway – it was a brown and white spotted cow! We flew by the cow, his nose literally inches away from my head inside the closed window – with a WHOOSH! I sat up. The cow's head was turned by the wind draft from the car. The two cowboys never woke up, as John said to me, "Damn, did you see the size of that rabbit?" I immediately told John to pull over, it was time for him to take a break. I would drive. John pulled over as the two cowboys came awake. I asked

John, did he not see the cow? John replied, "Was that a cow? I thought it was one of those big Texas jack-rabbits." I knew then that John had been driving too long. We were all wide awake by now, and I pulled back on to the highway to head into Oklahoma.

The next incident worth telling is a bit unbelievable, but completely true, and of course could never be accomplished in today's world.

As we came into Oklahoma on this beautiful four lane highway with a big grass covered divider, we had to travel north to get the two cowboys to their destination. I knew this detour was going to cost us about four hours – two hours up, and then about two hours back to get us headed east again to New York. John was once again driving, and I was riding shotgun, when two young ladies slowly passed us in a big Cadillac convertible. One of our cowboy passengers commented about the name on the dealer frame of the license plate. It was a dealer in their home town!

I asked John to speed up and pull alongside the two young ladies. I rolled down my window, stuck my head out and started talking to the ladies. I was able to shout loud enough, and I guess they thought I was cute enough, so they listened to me. I asked if they were going to that city on their dealer frame – they were! I explained that we were giving a ride to these two young men, but we were on our way to New York and I'd like to see if we might be able to get them to take these two young guys the rest of the way. I convinced them to pull off the side on the shoulder of the highway. They pulled over and stopped, we stopped behind them. I got out of the car with the two cowboys protesting that this was crazy, these girls were never going to take them the rest of the way, but John said, " You guys don't know Jordy. Let him give it a try." I went up to the ladies Caddy, and was as charming as I have ever been, explaining we'd been out to Hollywood and were now on our way back to New York. I was an actor, and we had decided to help these two guys from Oklahoma and give them a ride to their home, and you ladies could really save us some travel time, because we had to be back in New York in a short time. These guys were really nice young men, I paused for a minute, and didn't want to beg, so I just said, "Please, what do you say?" They looked at each other, then one said to me, "Let us meet the guys." I ran back to the car and asked the two cowboys to get out and meet the ladies. John stayed in the car slowly shaking his head. The ladies asked the guys where they lived. One of the young ladies knew the area, and – believe it or not - they took the two cowboys! We grabbed their bags out of the trunk, I thanked the young ladies, the two cowboys got in the back seat of the Caddy, and I went back and got into the Olds. We followed them on the highway until the next turn around which we took – and we were back on our way to New York! John's only comment was, "Jordy, I don't believe you did that. Nobody else could have pulled that off!"

Chapter Twelve

The remainder of the trip was uneventful. We took turns driving and sleeping, and had the car washed before delivering it to an address out on Long Island. It was a nice house. I have no idea if it was Ann Miller's house or not. Our instructions were to deliver it to a man at the house, that's what we did and after a brief inspection, we got a signature on the paperwork, received another tip, were given a lift to the Long Island Train Station, and we headed back to the City. Mission accomplished!

Once back in the city, I checked my answering service, and I had a message about a meeting for an off-Broadway show - a new play entitled, "The Night is Black Bottles". The play was being produced by the Showcase Theatre Production Company. It was the same production company that I did "Lily and the Sergeant" for, starring Richard X. Slattery. I mentioned that a little earlier in the book. After my meeting, which took place on West 57th Street – there's that street again! – I was told about the production schedule and that they planned to open the play in late November or early December as soon as they could lock down a theatre. I read for the play and they told me on the spot that I had the part of Louis Boy, a young drummer in a sleazy bar that catered to hookers and pimps in addition to the regular customers. Louis Boy had a big crush on one of the hookers and clashed with her pimp during the play. The play was directed by Mark Justin and had a formidable cast, including Leon B. Stevens, Lydia Bruce and Charlotte Jones. That certainly took a little of the sting off the recording disaster. I was now back to my acting career. Michael moved up to New Paltz to be with Sykes. A few years later Michael would play drums with "Cat Mother and her All Night Newsboys". They appeared on a few TV shows, most notably the David Susskind interview show. Michael and I would get together years later in Los Angeles when I hired him as a grip for a commercial shoot I was directing.

During this time back in New York, and after the Hollywood trip with John Quincy, we continued developing our friendship. My friend, John, even though now he is a very successful Christian Practitioner and lecturer, had ventured to New York to try his hand at an acting career. He had a very talented aunt, Dodie Goodman, whom I knew about and had seen on the Jack Parr Show long before I met him at the Playhouse-on-the-Green. John was a character. He did have a real talent for publicity ideas, and he did two things I don't believe were ever done before, or have ever been done since. The first was that he figured out a way to make the New York Times honor a loophole in their classified ads wording, which enabled him to put a classified ad on the front page of the paper! He had a classified ad at the very bottom of the front page of the New York Times, advertising, "John Quincy Adams III is a new actor in town seeking work. Call JU-6-6300". The answering service went nuts! John received a number of calls – unfortunately none of them were about the type of work he was seeking!

This next story of what he did is unbelievable – BUT ABSOLUTELY TRUE! At that time in New York, the most successful producer on Broadway was David Merrick. He had more hits on Broadway than anyone at the time. John devised a plan and a way to get in to see Mr. Merrick. He decided to ship himself to Mr. Merrick in a box! He took great care in making sure Mr. Merrick would be in his office, which was in a building above Sardi's restaurant on West 44th Street. He had called a week before representing himself as The Long Island Express Company and needed to deliver a package to Mr. Merrick, but Merrick would have to sign for it himself. No one else could sign for the package. John was given a day and time when Mr. Merrick would be in the office and able to sign for the package.

On that specific day, John had a large cardboard box and sealing tape, plus an authentic delivery book which needed to be signed. I can't remember if I was supposed to meet John outside the office building, seal him in the box, take him up to Mr. Merrick's office, drop off the box and get Merrick to sign (which I thought was insane) – and I couldn't make it because of an audition or rehearsal, or maybe I was never the designated delivery guy, but, for whatever reason, another friend of John's, Gary Flanders, was assigned the duty. You'll remember Gary - he's the "friend" that left us high and dry in Hollywood, the guy that DIDN'T send us our money!

  John, dressed in a seersucker suit and tie, got into the box. Gary was wearing a delivery hat and jacket, with the delivery book, and had a dolly push cart, all the items John had gotten for him, plus the sealing tape. Gary taped up the box with John in it, wheeled him up to Merrick's office, delivered the box into Merrick's office, had it signed for and left. John said he stayed in the box for a bit – then he POPPED OUT! David Merrick was stunned! According to John, and he'd have no reason to lie since he was not thrown out the window, Merrick sat behind his desk looking at John in stunned silence. John stepped out of the box with a picture and a resume in his hand. He introduced himself to Mr. Merrick as he walked over, took Merrick's hand, explained he was an actor looking for a job and said he had a picture and a resume he'd like to leave. After a pause, Mr. Merrick looked at John and replied, "Young man, you have made an impression on me that will live with me for the rest of my life, so I don't need a picture and a resume. Now get the hell out of my office!"

As I said, John was a character! I don't know anyone else that would have the guts to do anything like that! John had many unusual, ironic and even funny things that happened to him while he was pursuing an acting career, but this book isn't intended to be about my friend John, so I'll only share two of the outrageous stories that occurred during my Blue Collar career with my friend, John Quincy Adams, III. I did manage to get John a small part in the play I was set to do, "The Night is Black Bottles".

Another note about Equity here, and the reasons I don't consider AEA the "actors" union it professes to be. After being a dues paying member since 1960, and continuing to work as a professional actor in both film, television and the theatre, I went to check on my pension eligibility in about 2004 as I was approaching the age of sixty-five, only to discover that since I had less than seven earned pension credits, and due to not signing an Equity contract in a seven year period of time, Equity had invoked the "break-in-service" rule, a rule that penalizes an actor for NOT working, and the Equity pension plan had taken my seven earned pension credits! That's worth writing again, Equity took my seven EARNED pension credits, and I had none! I went in to discuss this with the Pension Department. A gentleman retrieved my "records", the ones they had on file. He told me that Equity had no record of me working prior to 1964. As I looked through this file he handed me, I discovered a New York Times review and a photo from the play, "The Night is Black Bottles". The photo clearly showed me as Louis Boy, and three of the other actors from a scene in the play, and listed our names. The date on the picture and review was December 5th, 1962. I slid the picture and review over to him, pointing out the date – 1962. I asked him why did Equity claim to not have any record of me working prior to 1964, with this clear proof that I was appearing in an Equity production dated 1962. He had no answer. I've been fighting with Equity over this penalty rule for about sixteen years, as I write this, and they still will not return my seven EARNED pension credits they stole with some penalty rule. This is not the actions of an "actors union".

Well I had a few weeks before we were to begin rehearsals for "The Night is Black Bottles", and I was going to start looking for another part-time job. Fortunately, my rent on the room on West 71st Street was only nine dollars a week, so I didn't need much to get by. I had listed with a number of print agencies and, out of the blue, I received a call from one about doing some print work for these Romance magazines. I hot-footed it down to the agency and got booked. These print jobs were of the low-level entry type. They paid about twenty-five to fifty bucks a job, no union was involved, and, basically, if the photographer liked you, the agency would book you again. They liked me. I was your all-American looking clean-cut guy that would be photographed as the young husband of the unfaithful wife, or the unfaithful husband of the young wife. I must have done about fifteen or twenty of those jobs. The photographer liked to "direct" a scene, give you an action before he started clicking off pictures. I'd be an angry husband, lover, or boyfriend – shouting or pretending to hit the girl. – Whatever girl I'd be working with, we'd have to keep up this kind of silliness for hours until the photographer believed he had the shot he would need to accompany the story in the magazine.

    These stories were all made up, of course, none of them were true, even though one of the magazines was called, "True Romance". I did manage to get four decent paying photo shoots during that time. One was for M&M Candies – me and a girl making silly faces while eating M&M's in a fake movie set on a date. Another was a picture story of "Father was a Schoolboy". We were photographed in Central Park. I was in a cap and gown, having just graduated and holding my baby daughter in my arms, with a small beagle dog on a lead wrapped around my leg, with my wife running to the rescue in the background. It was a funny picture.

Another of these "better paying" print jobs involved me as a young father pretending to be Santa Claus that got hung up in a tree while trying to parachute down to see the kids. It was all shot in a studio with me hanging from an overhead setup, fully dressed as Santa, and with the magic of stills, the tree above me and the sky, plus snow, was all put in after I was photographed yelling for help!

The highest-paying photo shoot I ever got was with one of the highest-paid female face models at the time. I remember two things; her name was Bonnie – and she would have absolutely nothing to do with me! It was an ad for a classy magazine, and the ad was called "The Sandwich Game". You saw our faces looking around a tall huge sandwich, smiling at each other, which really looks like we were a couple. We were not! It turned out this model was dating the guy with a hit record called, "I Saw Mommy Kissing Santa Claus". Bonnie was gorgeous – he was not! I thought I was being paid really great. I was paid two hundred dollars and this was 1962! I had been getting twenty-five, sometimes fifty dollars for the print work, and made seventy-five bucks for those other "better paying" photo gigs. , So making, two hundred dollars for this day's shoot, which took four to five hours, a lot of it with wardrobe and Bonnie's make-up - I was a happy camper. Later, after the shoot, when I was talking about the job, and how great I thought the pay was – one of the company people asked me if I knew what Bonnie made. Of course I had no idea, and would never discuss anyone's pay on a job, a rule I followed for my entire career. This person told me that Bonnie was one of the highest paid in this print field – she received five hundred dollars an hour with a five hour guarantee, plus a hundred dollar "travel fee" (she lived all the way on the Eastside!). I'm guessing that was for any cabs she wanted to take from the Eastside down to midtown on the Westside. I later learned that she used a car service – no cabs! Regardless of all this unsolicited and not needed information regarding Bonnie and her boyfriend, I was happy with my two hundred dollars.

  During the time I spent doing these print jobs I did meet a few models. They were completely different than any of the actresses I had met, and would continue to meet during my career.

None of the models I met were interested in being an actress. They all made good money doing print work mostly, but some would occasionally work in some show, where they would just walk around at an invited designers party wearing the clothes of that designer. These were not Runway models. Another interesting thing I discovered with all the ones I dated – they all had two things in common (apart from all being beautiful); They all lived on the upper Eastside between the sixties and the seventies, and they all had hardly any furniture! I never saw more than a few large throw pillows on the living room floor serving as a sofa, and the lamps set on the floor. All the apartments had a breakfast counter/bar with a couple of stools, and the bedrooms had a large mattress, some with a box spring, all on the floor, and a large closet. That was it. I learned later that a lot of these models traveled for work, both in the States and to Europe, so they never wanted to have to get rid of a lot of furniture. Made sense to me – but what did I know? I lived in a one-room furnished apartment with a shared bath, on the Westside! Another thing I learned was that these ladies didn't care for phony guys. They enjoyed the company of a regular down-to-earth type guy, with a good sense of humor, that could make them laugh, and NOT try to impress them. I guess I fit all the qualifications. Being from the South, I was down-to-earth. I've always had a good sense of humor, and I could make them laugh, and there sure as hell was no chance that a struggling actor with very little money was going to impress anybody! I found the ladies in the modeling profession that I had the pleasure of dating were all just regular girls that had been blessed with incredible looks, but were never the "image" that they portrayed in the profession.

As for the "impress you" bit, I have one interesting anecdote. One evening, the young lady, a model I was dating, had plans to attend a New York Rangers Hockey game with a friend of hers, who was dating a very well-to-do young fellow. Her friend insisted that she bring her date, being me, for a double date to see the hockey game. My lady explained her date, me again, wouldn't be able to afford the tickets, and her friend immediately said, it was their treat – "their" being her date.

We agreed to go on this double date. Two interesting experiences happened that evening – I took my first ride in an expensive Mercedes, belonging to her friend's boyfriend, and saw my first professional hockey game in Madison Square Garden. I met Kathy, my date, at her apartment, on the Eastside, of course – remember I told you that all the models I knew and dated lived on the Eastside. Her friend and boyfriend picked us up in his Mercedes. His name was Chuck and the girl's name was Trish. Chuck was really a nice guy. In fact, he was the kind of guy I would have hung out with if we traveled in the same crowd. When we pulled up to Madison Square Garden, Chuck had a guy take his car. The girls stood on the side as Chuck and I walked toward the box office. I grabbed Chuck's arm and said let me help with the tickets. Chuck said, forget it, I've got this. I insisted, and said let me at least split the tickets, he said forget it, he had it. He got the tickets which were in his name. As we were walking into the Garden, I made another effort to pay something toward the tickets, when Chuck took me aside and said, "Hey man, I know you don't have much money, this is my treat so forget about it." When I suggested that I could pay something toward the tickets, he said, "Okay, you got two hundred dollars? That's the price of your ticket." The shocked look on my face said it all. He laughed and said, "Hey man, don't worry about it. It's on me, just enjoy the game." The seats where right down where you sat behind the glass behind the players. It was an incredible game. It was an incredible evening. We all went someplace and had a bite to eat, Chuck making it clear it was his treat. They drove us to Kathy's apartment, we bid them a goodnight and thanked them for the evening. Kathy and I went upstairs for a romantic ending. The next morning I walked home through Central Park, to my little one-room on the Westside.

I had enjoyed an incredible evening.

Chapter Thirteen

In late October/early November, 1962, we started rehearsals for "The Night is Black Bottles". We rehearsed for a couple of weeks at a rehearsal hall, then we went into The Cricket Theatre on Second Avenue. We rehearsed for two weeks in the theatre, had our dress rehearsal and opened. It was a small off-Broadway Equity house with seating for about 150 to 160 audience members. We didn't have any previews. We opened on December 4th, 1962 and we received awful reviews! Very little was liked by the critics. One important critic opened his review by writing, "Last night I attended a new play at The Cricket Theatre, it was entitled, "The Night is Black Bottles" – and it was!" We performed for three nights, then had our "dark night", the night you're off before returning to the show. When we showed up on December 7th, the theatre was closed and there was a sign on the door that read: The Night is Black Bottles has closed.

They listed a contact number to call for any refunds. After those reviews, I doubt if there were many refunds to be made.

Out of work again and Christmas was just eighteen days away. I applied for another "pitch job", selling this little toy called a Gyroscope. It was an actual small gyroscope, and, unlike the Roll-a-Curl, it actually worked – until the kid broke it. I was set up in a big department store in a mall on Long Island, which I could reach by subway and a short walk. I'd pull the string on the gyroscope and get at least two of them going at the same time. I placed one of them on this string I had rigged up, like a tight rope in the circus between two small poles on my table. Then I'd put the other one on the end of a pencil and demonstrate how it would balance and rotate on the pencil while the first one "walked" across the little string. It was a great stocking-stuffer - the kids loved it - and I sold them like hot cakes. As most pitchmen, I worked strictly on commission, thirty percent of what I sold. . I broke some kind of a record at this store, according to the guy I worked for. I sold 537 Gyroscopes in one day. As I said, the Gyroscope was a great stocking-stuffer, and at ninety-nine cents, it was a last-minute grab.

Christmas was over. I don't remember doing a lot that holiday season, but it had been a very eventful year for this Blue Collar Actor. The trip to Hollywood with John Quincy, getting the print jobs, doing another off-Broadway show, even though it flopped, and finding a last minute job selling the Gyroscopes to put a few bucks in my pocket. I remember attending some party on New Year's Day way up on the Eastside with a lot of people I didn't really know, and having a short encounter with a young lady dressed all in black. I believe we got snowed in up at that apartment and people wound up sleeping (really?) all over the place.

In January, my former singing partner left me a message that he was back in New York for a while and wanted to see if we could get together. Before I could call him back, I got a call from an agent about a Gillette Foam shaving commercial audition. He had seen a picture of me and Michael as the Castaways (I don't have a clue where he found that picture) and read my resume that listed under "special talents" that I was a guitar player. The advertising agency wanted to see "folk singers". I called Michael and asked him if he wanted to go on this audition. I knew he always had his guitar. But I had misunderstood the casting agent that called me. I thought they were looking for folk singers - plural, but when I told the agent that my singing partner and I would go on the audition, he said he didn't know if they were looking for a duo or not, but if we let him represent both of us – meaning collect the commission if either of us got the job – then he would send us both in together. We went in together, did a number for the agency together – and they liked us but couldn't decide which one of us to use, so they hired us both. They asked us both not to shave for week starting that day, then to come back. They called the agent that sent us, and booked both of us for the commercial. We didn't shave for a week, as instructed, and returned to the agency for a "look-over." They decided we both looked fine with our one-week stubble, and gave us a shoot day, including a wardrobe call. They filmed the commercial with both of us on the same day. As I remember, I went first. The storyline was this guy is playing the guitar and singing (which the audience never heard – ah, the commercial business) but he has this "stubble" of beard so the girl doesn't like him. Then he uses Gillette Shaving Foam, comes back into her life clean-shaven – and she likes him! After I was done, they shot the exact same commercial with Michael. We both got paid for the spot, it was SAG (Screen Actor's Guild) minimum, BUT you could get your SAG card because you had signed a SAG contract if you could pay the initiation fee and wanted to join. I had the fee and wanted to join. Michael wasn't interested in joining, so he didn't. The agency wound up going with my spot instead of Michael's, so I got residuals which over time more than covered my fee to join SAG. I also was now a member of SAG and AEA. I had been in New York for five years, and I was in two of the actor's unions. I could now call myself a professional actor. Hell, I was in two acting unions and now the world would just open up for me, right? Wrong!

But at least I could go to the Equity office, and check out their job board, then I could go to the SAG office and check out their job listings, if any. I started applying and showing up for almost every Equity or SAG call. I had a couple of agents that I could freelance with, but I still couldn't find one agent to sign me. So, I needed to find a job. I got back in touch with Bill Smith, the Roll-a-Curl entrepreneur, and asked him if he could use me. He could. I went back to work pitching the Roll-a-Curl at Macy's Department Store.

Around this time, a friend of mine was working in an office and I went up to meet him for lunch. A young lady, Jan Wilson, was working as a receptionist. She had long dark hair, dark eyes, and was built like a work of art - tall, shapely and curved. When she walked down the hall to let my friend know I was there, she immediately brought to mind Jack Lemmon's line about Marilyn Monroe's walk in "Some Like It Hot,", when he said, "She moves like Jello on wheels." Jan moved like firm Jello on skates. I was smitten. When she came back with my friend, and, isn't it funny - I can't remember the name of my friend that was working there! –I asked her if I could have her number. Surprisingly, she gave it to me! I will eliminate some of the suspense that you'll discover later in the book by injecting this information here. This lady became my first wife. Later she changed her name and has enjoyed a very successful acting career. She is one hell of an actress, and you have most likely seen her in both films and in television series for more years than she'd like for me to include. She has also done a good number of theatrical plays, appearing off-Broadway, and she loves performing in the theatre.

      Obviously I called her. We went on a number of dates. I stopped seeing other girlfriends, and, eventually, we were going "steady." We had one of our early dates at Jones Beach – she was a knockout in a bikini! When she went off to stock in the Catskills that first summer we knew each other, I made a trip up to see her, and spent one night with her on the Q.T. Neither of us wanted to stir up any questions or do harm to her reputation. Remember, it was 1963. Jan lived in an apartment building on West 67th Street, right off Central Park, and she had two other roommates. I still had my one room on West 71st Street. I don't remember the name of one of her roommates, but the other one was a gal named Nancy. Nancy was just a couple of years older than Jan, but acted like a "mother hen" towards her. Translation: Nancy didn't really care for me! After Jan returned from the season of summer stock in the Catskills, we started spending most of our time together. She got another job, this time as an assistant to Warner LeRoy, Mervyn LeRoy's son. Warner projected himself as a big-time producer, but for my money he was just a rich kid with a famous father. Warner treated Jan fine, but he always had a bit of an edge with me. Warner and his wife invited us to their apartment in the Dakotas Building a couple of times - very pricey real estate in New York City on West 72nd Street right off Central Park - and world famous as being the place where John Lennon was shot by a crazy guy whose name I refuse to give space to. Warner was always asking me, a struggling actor living in a one-room furnished apartment, dumb questions, like what was my favorite dream car? When I told him at the time, it was a certain model of a Ferrari, he replied, "Well you better get busy acting, because they cost a lot of money." He was always doing shit like that to me, so he was not a favorite person of mine. Once, when Jan and I had gone up to his apartment for her to deliver some papers, we were asked to wait in the living room while he and his guest finished dinner. There was a nice chess set on the coffee table, so we started a game. Warner came out from the dining room, saw us playing chess, did a "panic take," came over immediately and asked us not to "mess" with the set – he said it was very expensive. He treated us like a couple of five-year-old kids. It was easy to see why I thought he was a jerk!

I continued selling Roll-a-Curl at Macy's and occasionally slipping out for an audition or applying for any SAG jobs I would hear about.

In those days when I was making the rounds and attending any audition or "open call" that I found out about. I banged around and bumped into a number of actors. Some, like myself, would later go on to have decent careers, with a couple becoming stars and enjoying tremendous careers, well above the "Blue Collar Actor" status of yours truly. I made the rounds and auditions with: Tom Signorelli (friend, passed away), Joe Don Baker (of Walking Tall fame - we've kept in touch - I always thought Joe Don was more than a notch or two above the rest of us, because he had done two Broadway shows!); Dustin Hoffman (star - doesn't remember me); Alan Sklar (lost touch); and, of course, friends mentioned earlier in the book, Richard X. Slattery, John Quincy Adams, III, and Ed Beres, plus many other actors that I will apologize to for omitting them from my New York years.

It was late in the year 1963, and, after going with Jan for just a few months, I knew I was in love with her, and I asked her to marry me. She said yes, and we were married on November 8th, 1963, in an Episcopal Church on West 69th Street right across the street from where we had found a little furnished one-bedroom basement apartment. The Episcopal Priest that married us was later defrocked by the Church, leading to a comment by Jan saying, "It must have been an omen". Art Wolff, one of the friends I had met at Playhouse-on-the-Green (his career as a very successful director was mentioned earlier), served as my Best Man. Nancy, the "mother hen" roommate of Jan's, was Maid of Honor (much to her chagrin - not at being in the wedding party, just at the choice of husbands – me!). Art and his wife threw us a wonderful wedding party at their apartment in Queens, and Bill Smith, my Roll-a-Curl man, gave me a few days off so Jan and I could go to Atlantic City on our honeymoon. We spent a glorious four days, including a weekend in Atlantic City. Then we moved into our little apartment.

Ten days after we returned from our honeymoon, November 22nd, John F. Kennedy was assassinated in Dallas, Texas. Everyone that I knew was devastated! I heard about the news while pitching Roll-a-Curl at Macy's. JFK was the first President I voted for. I was surprised when my boss wanted me to keep working – my heart just wasn't in it. The rest of that year was very "blue". I don't remember that Christmas. I believe we attended a party with Jan's former roommates at her old apartment. Of course, Nancy was there along with a few people I didn't know very well. The year was coming to a close, and 1964 in New York City would start a new chapter in my acting profession and alter my life.

Chapter Fourteen

In the New Year, with my SAG card firmly in hand, I started to get some small roles on TV. A couple were just "Featured Extra", which today they refer to as "Background", but I would get a few lines in some of the shows. The first one of these I did was "The Defenders" with E.G. Marshall and Robert Reed. On the heels of that, I got a small shot on "The Reporter" that starred Harry Guardino, and the guest star was Dyan Cannon, she was dating Cary Grant at the time, and later they were married. Casting directors were beginning to hire me. Next was "Mr. Broadway" starring Craig Stevens, and one of the guest stars was Jill St. John, who is married to a good friend of mine, Robert Wagner, and I still stay in touch with them. Then I did "For the People" that starred William Shatner, well before his "Star Trek" journey. On one show, an episode of "The Doctors & The Nurses", which had Zina Bethune as one of the young stars, I learned the value of listening and paying attention on a set, rather than doing a lot of bullshitting between setups. I was on the show as an extra, and I'd always try to hang around the cameraman (making sure I didn't get in anybody's way), because I was interested in directing and learning. On my first day, I overheard the director tell the assistant director that they were going to need an actor that played the guitar and could sing for the scene around the fireplace in this ski resort. I walked over and said, "Excuse me, but I play the guitar and sing." The director looked at me, making sure I didn't have two heads, and asked me if I was on the shoot. I nodded yes, and he told me to bring my guitar in the next day. I brought my guitar the next day and did a quick little ditty for him. He asked me if I knew a public domain folk song that wouldn't require them to have to get a clearance, I said that I did. He told the assistant director to give this kid the job. I signed a principal contract. I played the guitar and sang the song, and had lines! Viola! – from extra to actor just by paying attention.

During that time in New York I had bought a Vespa Motor Scooter. It was a 150 model, in a light blue color, and I rode it everywhere. I had registered it in New Jersey because that was cheaper, and you could have the minimum insurance required; different times, different years - different rules. I hope the statute of limitations has expired because this tidbit of information about my Vespa is unique, and I'm not proud of it, because it was obviously illegal. The New Jersey Department of Motor Vehicles had issued me a registration with a number for my Vespa as SP-209, (not sure if those numbers are correct, but the situation is the same) but my plate number read SP-210. I discovered this when I received a parking ticket one afternoon because I was delayed on an audition, and spent more than the allotted time allowed on the street. Later, when I was preparing to pay my ticket – and I was not a happy camper because it was a stout ticket - I noticed the ticket was written up for a Vespa with the plate number of SP-210. My registered number was for a Vespa with plate number SP-209. The ticket was not written for my Vespa, because my Vespa had a plate with the number of SP-210. . I put the ticket into one of the little compartments on the bubble side of the Vespa, and I started parking any place that was convenient. I filled up both of the bubble compartments with tickets. I never worried about getting a ticket - on paper my Vespa was SP-209 and it never got a ticket!

    A few actors I knew had Vespa's in New York in those days, it was a great way to get around. Michael J. Pollard had one, and Dustin Hoffman had one, even though there is some confusion about that. I will attempt to explain. As I wrote earlier, I made the rounds and auditioned with Dustin. As everyone knows today, Dustin is a very talented actor. I also thought he did an excellent job directing a fine film, "The Quartet", with an incredible group of international actors. It's one of my favorite films. The first time I attended an audition with Dustin, it was for an Equity Library Theatre production of "Dead End". Before we went in to audition together, he popped into a little grocery store and bought a loaf of bread, which he had in a paper bag as we went up to the studio space where they held the auditions.

"Dead End" is the play that featured The Dead End Kids, and the film version starred Humphrey Bogart as the gangster returning to the old neighborhood. The director of this ELT production would pick out a group of the young actors auditioning, and let them read together. I was in the group with Dustin. I don't remember which of the "Dead End Kids" I was reading for, but Dustin was reading for a character nicknamed T.B., because, obviously, the character had T.B., and coughed on occasion. During this reading and auditioning, Dustin made an actor's choice to reach into the paper bag and rip out a center piece of the loaf of bread, and start eating it as he delivered his lines. An interesting actor's choice – he got the role!

I didn't get cast in that production, but later I would do my first children's play with the Equity Library Theatre, "Niccolo and Nicolette," in which I played the title role of Niccolo, The Puppet Prince. We toured the city and performed with Joseph Papp's Shakespeare in the Park productions, performing in Central Park for the public, doing matinee performances for children and families, before the evening productions of the Shakespearean plays. I kept one of my most cherished "fan letters" for years from those appearances in Central Park. After a performance of "Niccolo and Nicolette" one afternoon, a lady was waiting as we actors exited the stage, which was built up high, with dressing facilities underneath. She was waiting there with her son, a youngster about five or six years old. She told me that today was the second time that they had seen the show, because her little boy insisted, and he had a note for me. I bent down and took this card he had put in a small envelope and opened it. It was a card he had made with two characters glued on it, and very nicely I might add, one of my character, Niccolo, and the other one of the young girl, Nicolette, that saves me, The Puppet Prince, in the play. Written inside was this, "To my most favorite actor in the whole world". I can't even write this without it bringing tears to my eyes. I hugged him, thanked him very much, and signed a program for him and his mother. And people ask me, "Why are you an actor?" ARE YOU KIDDING? Sadly, and regrettably after keeping that "fan letter" for more than thirty years, it was misplaced and lost in one of my many moves.

    Quickly back to Dustin, and the Vespa, as promised. When I wrote about the different actors I made the rounds and auditioned with, I mentioned after Dustin's name, "doesn't remember me." We both were tested for The Graduate, but so were about twenty other young actors, so there is no call to remember that. Here's where there is a bit of confusion as written earlier. One evening while Jan and I were still dating, we were walking up Riverside Drive just past 72nd Street. We were coming from my one-room apartment on West 71st Street, and we bumped into Dustin, who was out looking for his Vespa which had been stolen – a common occurrence for us Vespa owners in those days. They were quite easy to steal, you just had to twist the front bars very hard, which broke the lock, know how to turn on the gas switch, snap down on the pedal to start the engine and drive away. I offered to lend my Vespa to Dustin so he could ride around town looking to find his, but he thanked me and declined. Now, years later at some party in Hollywood, I was retelling this story along with the Graduate story, when Jan overheard part of it, and interjected, "Who are you talking about? Dustin Hoffman? I never met Dustin Hoffman". I then started explaining the night this all took place on Riverside Drive – she insisted that was NOT Dustin Hoffman, it was just some little guy, but she never met Dustin Hoffman! So, my recollection and Jan's does differ, but the same can be said for the other side of the coin – Dustin may not remember me, but Jan doesn't remember him. I guess it all comes out in the wash!

For Christmas, 1964, we made a trip to Illinois to finally meet Jan's family, they all knew her as Janice. I met her dad, Ben Wilson, her brother and family, plus her aunt who had been her mother since Jan's mom had passed away. I flew my mom up from North Carolina, where she had returned to live after the horrible marriage with the nameless SOB, to meet Jan's family, and we all spent the holiday together. I really liked Jan's dad, Ben. We got along great and he was one of the few old remaining honorable gentlemen I had the pleasure of knowing. My mom and Ben got along very well. In fact, we thought for a short time a spark or two might develop into a major flame, but it wasn't to be. I enjoyed meeting Jan's family. We flew back to New York, and mom flew back to North Carolina after a really fun and memorable holiday.

Back in New York, the year 1965 brought a few events and changes. I got lucky and got my first film role in a low-budget film, filmed on Long Island and in New York. It was called "Who Killed Teddy Bear" and starred Sal Mineo, Juliet Prowse (she was dating Frank Sinatra at the time), Elaine Stritch, and Rex Everhart who had a small role. Rex would go on to replace the role of Ben Franklin in the Broadway production of the musical "1776". I did the film version of "1776" in the role of William Hopper out in Los Angeles much later. In "Teddy Bear", I played a waiter who was a friend of Sal Mineo's character. Sal was a nice guy and we got along great. I avoided asking him any dumb questions about James Dean, as many people did, and he appreciated that I didn't. Years later I was visiting friends in Hollywood after a performance of a play I was doing, and just two days after my visit, Sal was stabbed and killed in the carport right under their apartment.

    In February, right after getting the role in "Who Killed Teddy Bear", a new series was being developed by David Susskind. It was called, "Esso Repertory Theatre". A production company would visit different Repertory Companies across the country, and would tape a live performance of some classical play the Repertory Company was doing. The plays would be "flushed out" a bit, add a few characters, etc., to give them a little more of a "filmed" production, which was actually not filmed, but taped. I auditioned and was cast in a production of "Saint Patrick's", being performed by a Boston Repertory Company. Since this was a taped production, I was signed to an AFTRA contract, which in those days, before the SAG-AFTRA merger, was a separate union that covered all the taped shows, like your

Written By Jordan Rhodes

daytime drama, i.e., "soap operas". We rehearsed in New York for a few days, then flew up to Boston to rehearse the additional scenes and characters with the Repertory Company, before performing it live for taping. Now, I was really a full-fledged professional actor that belonged to all three actor's unions: SAG, AEA and AFTRA. This guy from a tobacco farm in North Carolina, without a single connection in the world, was a professional working actor!

Shortly. in 1965, most of the New York film productions began to disappear. Jan had discovered a wonderful acting teacher, Wendell K. Phillips, who had worked with Lee Strasberg, Cheryl Crawford and others in the original Group Theatre. Wendell also had a good acting career and went on to direct some of the most innovative theatre pieces in San Francisco and Los Angeles. Both his son and his daughter were actors, with Wendy, his daughter, enjoying success, most notably as the wife of Bugsy Segal, portrayed by Warren Beatty in the film of the same name. Jan and I both studied with Wendell, and maintained a friendship with him for the rest of his life.

Unfortunately, with the film work drying up in New York, and it becoming all but impossible to book a Broadway show, even though much earlier I had been cast in my first Broadway show. It was a play entitled, "Beautiful Dreamer" to be directed by Eddie Bracken. I attended an open call, was singled out for a call-back, returned, auditioned, and was told on the spot that I had the young lead role of the Beautiful Dreamer. The story was about a traveling carnival that comes into a small town. A young man goes to the carnival and falls madly in love with a young carnival dancer, a little older and much wiser in the "ways of the world" than the young man, the Beautiful Dreamer. Of course, after a brief encounter with the young lady, his first ever, he is head-over-heels in love and intends to marry her, which she does not discourage but she has no intention of marrying this "dreamer." After making all kinds of plans, you can imagine his absolute devastation when he comes to the Carnival at the appointed time and discovers that both the young dancer, the love of his life, and the Carnival have left town! Curtain down!

    I remember rushing out of the rehearsal hall the day I was told that I had the role. I went right to Times Square, climbed upon the George M. Cohan statue and yelled "I'm gonna be on Broadway!" Days later, when I went to Equity to check out how I would go about all this, and did I need an agent, etc., I was informed that the money – the funds – the finances for the play did not materialize, and Mr. Bracken would not be directing "Beautiful Dreamer". This beautiful dreamer was crushed!

By June of 1965, we had decided to make the move to California and see what the film business and theatre, if it had any, would offer us. I made arrangements for us to acquire another "drive this car to California" with an agency. We loaded up our few belongings, including our black cat, named Mnemosyne, one of the nine muses out of a play I had done. The cat was nicknamed Moss. Then we started to California. The same trip John Quincy and I had made three years earlier, but this time with a wife, and a cat called Moss, who didn't enjoy the trip at all! We had six days to make the trip. I had no idea what I would face or accomplish in California.

Chapter Fifteen
Moving to California

We left New York for our car trip to California in late July 1965. It was a fairly uneventful trip for us, but our cat, Moss, she didn't care for the trip at all. Moss didn't like being confined to the cat carrying case, which we set on the floor of the car in the backseat area. It was cooler down there, but she hated having to go to the bathroom outside with anybody watching. We also had to keep her on a collar and leash, while she did her "business" in whatever dirt or sandy spot we could find. Moss was not a happy camper!

We tried to average about 600 miles a day, which allowed us a full day once we arrived in Hollywood to find a motel and arrange our own transportation.

We found a little drive-in motel on Sunset Boulevard where we checked-in without making any mention that we had a cat. We immediately grabbed a couple of papers and starting looking for an apartment. I also checked out one of the "Rent-a-Wreck" car agencies to make arrangements for a car, once we turned in our Drive-to-Los Angeles wheels. We picked up our Rent-A-Wreck, appropriately named, I believe. It was a 1958 Olds, whose better days were long since gone, and I was instructed to put in a quart of oil at least every five or six days if we planned on doing a lot driving. We didn't plan on doing a lot of driving with this car. We had better luck with the Apartment. We found a furnished one-bedroom apartment two blocks above Hollywood Boulevard, literally within walking distance of the infamous Hollywood Roosevelt Hotel where John Quincy and I had been locked out of during our trip to California a few years before. The apartment building allowed cats, so we were able to have Moss without having to sneak her in. Of course, we had to pay an increased deposit in the event of any damage she might do to the furniture, etc. Moss developed a new way to pee over the litter box onto the floor, which made me have to install a plastic "shield" around three sides of the litter box. I'm convinced Moss developed this habit to punish us for the trip across country.

We had managed to arrive in Los Angeles, in Hollywood, just before the Watts Riots erupted in August of that year. .

As soon as we settled in at the apartment, which was only a few blocks from the hotel where Janis Joplin would overdose five years later in 1970, and just up the street where Sylvester Stallone lived while he was shopping his "Rocky" script. The apartment was quite nice, much larger than our New York City one-bedroom basement apartment. It was on the second floor with large windows overlooking the circular drive. It also had a pool in the back, laundry room in the garage and a parking space for one car. We started looking for a car and work almost at the same time. I didn't want to drive around Hollywood in the Rent-a-Wreck any longer than absolutely necessary. We found a used car dealer close to the airport that would take a down payment, and allow us to make monthly payments, using their own finance company, which charged an enormous rate of interest – but a beggar can never be a chooser. So, we bought a Triumph sports car, red with a black convertible top. Jan drove our new (well it was new to us) car with the temporary tags and followed me to return the Rent-a-Wreck. Then it was on to the job hunt. Jan nailed a job almost immediately, and why not? She was smart, had excellent office skills, and was very pretty. She got a job at 20th Century Fox Studios, working for Paul Monash, the producer of Peyton Place. At that time, Peyton Place was the first nighttime, prime time soap opera, and it was shown three times a week in the beginning.

  By that December, Jan had made a number of friends and the people in the office knew her husband was an actor from New York. She kept her own acting desires to herself, not wanting to jeopardize her job. For some unknown reason, someone connected to the show made the suggestion of, "Why not give Jan a Christmas present and hire her husband for a small part on the show?" I was hired to do this small part of a guy recovering from an accident, receiving therapy from the same doctor that was treating Allison, the character that Mia Farrow portrayed. The doctor was played by David Canary. My scene was a physical one where my character is attempting to walk, using this apparatus with two wooden bars, where you support your weight with your arms extended as you try to walk while being encouraged by the doctor. During the rehearsals, I worked up quite a sweat, giving the impression to some of the crew and the director that this New York actor had been trained through "the method." In those days, Hollywood "loved" New York trained actors, and mistakenly mistook any physical exertion or intense concentration as an actor using "the method". Obviously none of them knew of my failed attempts at The Actors Studio. As we were getting ready to "make one" (do a real take of the scene), a make-up person rushed over to mop the sweat off my brow, but the director, Jeffrey Hayden, the husband of Eva Marie Saint, shouted, "No, no, leave that alone, that guy worked hard for that sweat. Let's see it." It was a good scene. The director gave me a nice compliment, as did David, the actor I worked with in the scene. We did some coverage of the scene, and I was dismissed with,

"Thanks, good job." I left feeling pretty damn good. I had been in Hollywood for four months and I had been given an acting job. Much thanks to my wife, obviously!

A month later, after the holidays, they had decided to add a few regular characters to Peyton Place. They wanted to create a little "small town" feeling, and thought an intern from the hospital, showing up in the bookstore, and the local bar and restaurant would be a nice addition, as well as being seen in the hospital. Jeffrey Hayden, the director I had worked for back in December on the "gift job", suggested me with a glowing recommendation. Mr. Monash, the producer, had viewed the scene, and he okayed me for the job. I didn't have an agent, so they contacted me directly. Obviously, there was no discussion about money. I received SAG minimum, and was perfectly happy to get it! I worked with three directors on Peyton Place. Ted Post, always a good natured guy and treated me fairly. Jeffrey Hayden, he was great to me. After all, I was his suggestion, and I had my best scenes working for him. The most memorable scene I had was with Lee Grant, which Jeffrey directed. Her character, for which she won an Emmy, was stealing drugs from the hospital for her boyfriend, played by Don Gordon. My character came upon her stealing the drugs, but was so busy "hitting" on her for a date, that he didn't notice she was stealing the drugs. I remember prior to shooting the scene, during the rehearsals when I was introduced to Lee, I mentioned to her that I had a big "crush" on her like all New York actors. Lee smiled at me and said, "Use it baby, use it." The scene went well, and we got it in one take. My intern had scored well! The third director I worked for was Walter Doniger. I didn't care for him, and the feeling was mutual. I was Walter's "whipping boy". He obviously didn't like the fact that I had been hired for this "recurring role". I was too new in the business to object to the crap he would throw at me. Example: When I was in a scene at the bar talking with the bartender, as Walter would have the camera move in (dolly is the term), to feature the leads, and I would need to move, Walter would instruct me to take (strike is the term) the barstool I was sitting on and move it out of the shot with me. Even the prop guys would come up to me and say, "Hey kid, you don't have to take that shit. You're not required to move any props." I didn't want to make waves, too insecure, so I put up with Walter's direction and crap each time I would work for him. Later in my career I didn't put up with that nonsense from any director, and more importantly, none of them ever tried such antics. Of course, that's not to imply if something was needed for a scene, if it was discussed with me and the other actors, and if it was a reasonable request,

I was more than happy to comply. But I was never another director's "whipping boy".

After a few weeks on Peyton Place, as my character became more and more relegated to doing these "introduction scenes" for the various featured leads on the series, I was beginning to become a little disenchanted. During this time the interesting episode with Mia Farrow and her infamous "haircut" took place. Mia was engaged to Frank Sinatra at the time, and they had planned a weekend get-away on his boat. Obviously I don't know any of the details other than what was reported about the trip, but the gist of the reports was that Mia had expected to enjoy the trip with just her and Frank. She was not aware that Frank traveled with his entourage of friends, and I'm guessing that's why she got so upset – but that is a guess. What I know is that on Tuesday after they returned, I showed up on the set about 9 a.m. I had a late call, I believe it was for 10 a.m. – but I have always had a habit of showing up early. It was one of the good things I learned from dear old dad. He said if you just showed up on time you were a half-hour late. Anyway, as I was arriving at the make-up department, an A.D. (assistant director) flew by me in a major hurry and shouted, "You're on hold, you don't work today." I looked around the set and it was like a beehive. Everybody was scurrying about. I found an assistant and asked him, "What was going on?" He replied that Mia had gone into her dressing room and chopped off her hair! Interesting turn of events, because her character, Allison, was in the hospital with her long flowing locks, and she was bedridden, so some rewriting had to be performed to explain how Allison managed to get a haircut!

I really enjoyed reading all the press stories about this new "Jean Seberg" look, that Mia had received from some major hair stylist! The media was just as dishonest with cover-ups in those days as it is today. That year we were invited to the Peyton Place Christmas Party at the Studio, and one of the funniest outtakes they showed was Mia lying in the hospital bed, with her long locks cascading over the pillow - then a blackout followed by a blood curdling scream, and cut back to Mia still in the hospital bed with her "Jean Seberg" short hair! Long locks gone! It was a funny outtake!

I do remember the day I resigned from Peyton Place, after becoming disenchanted as I wrote. I was in my little dressing room, and I had received the next two scripts for my character. I looked over the scripts and again I was really doing nothing. One scene had me in the book store buying a book, while the young actor playing one of the major roles of a guy recently blinded, accidentally knocked over some books. I reached down to help him pick up the books and he shouted at me, "I can do it myself!" to which my character mumbles, "Sorry," and exits the store as the main scene continues. I don't remember the second script, but it was about the same. I really had nothing of importance to do.

I just decided I didn't want to do this anymore. I didn't feel like I was acting. I was an actor. I wanted to act! So I walked across the lot to Mr. Monash's office, ,went inside and asked his secretary if I could see Mr. Monash. She buzzed him on the intercom and said, "Jordan is here, he'd like to see you." I was shown in and greeted by Mr. Monash. Boy, do I remember that conversation. After the greeting and, " what can I do for you,?" – Here is the conversation: ME- "Mr. Monash, I just received the next two shows I'll be doing". PAUL MONASH- "Yeah." ME- "Is this all I'm going to be doing on the show?" PAUL MONASH- "Yeah, pretty much." ME- "Well, I don't think I want to do this anymore." PAUL MONASH- "Okay. Do you want to finish these two shows?" ME- "Yeah, I'll finish these two." PAUL MONASH- (Rising to shake my hand) "It's been a pleasure having you on the show." ME- (shaking his hand) "Thanks." I turned and walked out of the office. As I was walking across the lot, my mind began to talk to me – "Let's see, I'm an actor, came out here to act, and I just quit an acting job!" I completed those two shows and left Peyton Place with a few memories and actor friends.

During the weeks I was on Peyton Place, I had managed to get my first agent, not really a problem when you're working. I only remember that her first name was Maxine. She was an older lady, and she had me accompany her to drop off gift baskets of fruit to various casting agents. Not anything I enjoyed but I kept up a "good face", and was always polite. Even though I thought it was silly, it did pay off for me. After being out of work for a few weeks having quit Peyton Place, in March I was booked on "12 O'Clock High". I went four months before the next television job which showed up in October, when I was "tested" for the lead role of a new series, "Love on a Rooftop". I didn't get the lead, it went to Peter Duel, who later became a friend of mine. Yet I got cast in a good supporting role in one of the series episodes. Pete did a lot of good work, but developed a drinking problem, and tragically a few years later, he shot himself.

Shortly after the Peyton Place journey, I had a dry spell. With the exceptions of the previous named shows, I wasn't being sent out very much by Maxine, so I had to find a "regular job". I took a job working for this guy that had the parking lot concession at a restaurant called "The

Gallery Room". It was a nice little place right in the heart of Hollywood on Santa Monica Boulevard. This guy had arranged a deal with the owner of the restaurant for the parking concession, and I parked cars for the customers. Quite a few names frequented the place. This was one of the first times I met Paul Lynde. He used to come in often for dinner. I had been working there for a few weeks, and one night when I was off, I received a call from the owner of the restaurant. The guy that owned the concession, the guy I worked for, hadn't shown up and the lot was getting full, with no one to park the cars. He asked me if I could come down and help him out. I was only hesitant because I had taken a couple of "hits" - "tokes" off a joint, and had a little "buzz".

  My hesitation prompted the owner of the restaurant to offer me the parking concession for free provided I'd come down and help him out. I straightened out as quickly as I could. Stuck my head under the cold water in the shower, jumped around a bit trying to take the "edge" off, so I could go park cars! Jan was very understanding, especially since she wasn't fond of smoking pot anyway. I jumped into the Triumph and drove down to The Gallery Room to organize the cars in the parking lot. It took a bit of doing, but I was able to round up the keys to the cars from the customers inside, and put everything in order on the lot. One of the owners (The Gallery Room was owned by two guys) was so impressed with the way I handled the situation, he not only gave me the parking concession for free but allowed me to have a meal there each night before I started work. The guy that had operated the parking concession previously only came back once, during the day to tell the owner he was sorry but he had a personal problem and wouldn't be able to operate the parking lot for the restaurant anymore. There was never any problem between me and that guy.

The only problem for me in the beginning, was I had to work six nights a week, including every weekend because the restaurant was closed only on Monday. I resolved the problem by hiring a guy to work for me, part time! I would work Thursday through Sunday, and my hired dude would park the cars on Tuesday and Wednesday. I also knew he was stealing from me, but it was okay – he didn't steal from the customers or cause any problems, so all was well. I had most days free for any auditions and I still brought in a decent amount of money.

During this acting drought I thought it would be an ideal time to seek out a new agent. Because I was so new in Hollywood, and had been tested for a sitcom, "Love on a Rooftop", I managed an appointment with The Louis Shurr Agency.

Louis Shurr was still a huge agent with a lot of clout. Among his previous clients were Bob Hope, Dorothy Lamour (her son still worked at the agency) and Ginger Rogers. I went in for a meeting with Mr. Shurr himself, and I got the full treatment, i.e., I was going to be the next Dick Van Dyke, they were going to get me meetings, and have me doing so many shows I'd need a secretary! Sounded great for this young actor, who by night was parking cars for the people that the Shurr Agency was going to contact, and have them transform me into the next great comedy star! The most fun meeting I ever had while being represented by the Louis Shurr Agency was the day I went over to Columbia Studios to meet two big comedy show writers, Bill Persky and Sam Denoff. They were a writing team, wrote for the Dick Van Dyke Show, and they were developing a new series. When I came into the office, Sam was on the phone. Bill Persky greeted me and had me sit down. Sam was talking on the phone and told whoever he was talking to that I had just come into the office. Sam said they were seeing me for a new series. Then he said, "Okay" on the phone, and told me Carl Reiner wanted to talk to me, and he handed me the phone. I took the phone and said "Hello." The guy on the phone was Carl Reiner. He said, "Hi, Jordan, I like your hair, now give the phone back to Sam." I handed the phone back to Sam. After a few words, Sam hung up the phone, turned to me and Bill Persky and said, "Carl says we should hire this guy, he likes his hair." Being familiar with Mel Brooks and Carl Reiner, I thought the whole "meeting/interview/phone call" was funny as hell! He liked my hair over the phone? Come on – that's funny! Especially coming from Carl Reiner!

However, I didn't get the job. In fact I never got a single job from The Louis Shurr Agency. But I kept parking cars at The Gallery Room.

During this hiatus, as I prefer to call it, one evening Les Roberts, a writer friend I knew from New York, came into the restaurant. We greeted each other outside and spent a little time catching up. Les wanted to know if I was still acting. I told him I had been on Peyton Place for a bit, then did a couple of shows, but had hit a snag and was continuing to look for work. Les asked me if I ever watched "The Hollywood Squares". I told him I had not. He said, "Watch it one afternoon and write me ten test questions. Maybe I'll hire you for the show." Les was not only the head writer for the game show, but also one of the producers that assisted Merrill Heatter & Bob Quigley, the two creators and executive producers of the show, plus many other game shows over the years.

I watched "The Hollywood Squares" twice, wrote

fifteen questions, and drove them out to the Valley to the production offices. I met Les, exchanged a few pleasantries, and gave him the test questions. Two days later he called me up and asked me if I wanted to write for the show? He said they'd start me at one hundred and twenty five dollars a week and I had to deliver a hundred and twenty five questions each week. I didn't want to drive out to the Valley every day and work out of an office, so I asked Les if I could work from home. Les said he didn't care where I worked, as long as I delivered him a hundred and twenty five questions every Friday by 3 pm. Wow! I was now a writer!

    I watched the show a few more times to get the hang of the type of questions that the audience responded to. My first week I drove to the main library in downtown L.A., left a little late to avoid the traffic and got there about ten o'clock. I would use all the research tools available to me, newspapers, magazines, periodicals, anything with current information or items of interest. In the beginning I would finish my hundred and twenty five questions by one or two in the afternoon. I'd go home and type them up, then on Tuesdays and Wednesdays I would try to make a couple of appointments. I was seeking a new agent because The Shurr Agency was doing nothing for me. Thursday through Sunday I would park cars at The Gallery Room, and on Fridays I would deliver my hundred and twenty five questions to Les out at The Hollywood Squares office. The way a writer kept his job writing quiz questions for The Hollywood Squares was based on the percentage of "buys" the Show took from you. In other words, the amount of questions they took from your hundred twenty-five, which they might use on the Show. Anything ten percent or above, you were golden. That amounted to about twelve to fourteen questions taken out of your hundred and twenty five. In the first two weeks, they took twenty of my questions each week! Les then decided to assign me to concentrate on questions for Paul Lynde, Cliff Arquette (Charley Weaver character) and Wally Cox. I wound up writing for Hollywood Squares for sixteen weeks! Les once told me I had lasted longer than most of the "career writers" he'd hired for the show.

    I made arrangements and got permission from the owners of The Gallery Room to turn the parking concession over to one of the guys I had working for me. He paid me a small percentage of the parking fees for a couple of months, as per our agreement for the concession, and I was no longer parking cars.

    During this stretch of time, Jan and I both joined The Melrose Theatre Workshop which had a very interesting group of actors, coming in and out over the years we attended. There were a number of classes held at The Melrose, with the "professional" group attending a workshop every Saturday at 10 a.m. A few of the more notable alumni included Tommy Lee Jones, Richard Dreyfus, Karen Valentine, Paul Mantee, Tom Troupe, Charles Rome Smith, Cindy Williams, George Murdock (one of my best friends), Robert Pine and Gwynne Gillford (father & mother of Chris Pine), Paul Kent (teacher and advocate of Sandy Meisner), Richard Bull, Jennifer Rhodes, Lawrence Haddon, Frank Christi, and a number of other fine actors that I apologize for missing.

Written By Jordan Rhodes

Chapter Sixteen

    I did a few plays at The Melrose Theatre where some fine theatrical productions were mounted. More than one went on to have a successful run in a larger theatre, such as the production of "Father's Day" by Oliver Hailey. "Father's Day" opened at The Melrose and was so successful that we received an offer to do a two-week engagement at a theatre in San Diego, at the time called The Off-Broadway. We opened with a cast that included Paul Kent, Carole Cook, Gwynne Gillford, Paul Mantee, Barbara Rush (she had replaced Jacquelyn Hyde), Tom Troupe, and yours truly, Jordan Rhodes. The production was directed by Tom Troupe and was so successful, we wound up having a run that extended over two years and included bookings in The Parker Playhouse in Ft. Lauderdale, Florida, The Arlington Theatre outside Chicago, The Huntington Hartford in L.A. for two separate runs of four weeks each, and at The Marines Memorial Theatre in San Francisco in conjunction with The American Repertory Theatre, where we performed for sixteen weeks. There was talk of a revival on Broadway, where the play, when originally opened, had closed after two performances, but our revival never materialized. One of the highlights for me, besides working steady in a hit play for an extended period of time, was after one matinee at The Parker Playhouse in Florida, Karl Redcoff paid me a surprise visit backstage! Karl had attended the show as he was now living in Florida. I was absolutely thrilled to see him! He was very complimentary to me, and I received a sense of pride from him, that one of his "students", and in our case also a friend, had achieved success and was surviving as a working actor. It was a wonderful and heartwarming experience for me. Unfortunately, it would be the last time I ever saw Karl, as he passed away a few years later – enjoying his favorite pastime, playing golf! He had a heart attack on the course.

Those were exciting times at The Melrose Theatre. I did a few plays, including "Room Service" and "Home", which we also performed at The Actors Studio West, plus a reading of "Death of a Salesman" at the Studio. However, we actors believed we were getting a raw deal from Equity. The union would only allow us to perform in a theatre with no more than 49 seats and would only allow us to do three performances. The Melrose Theatre was an approved Equity Workshop Theatre. As an actor, you received no credit with Equity for your years working with an Equity approved workshop. – It didn't stop the unions "break-in-service" penalty rule from being applied. A group of actors rebelled. Along with a very fine dedicated group of actors, we broke away from Equity and organized P.A.L., the Professional Actors League. We demanded an increase in the theatre size from forty-nine seats to ninety-nine seats, and an increase in allowed performances from three performances to an open-end run.

Working in the workshop theatre in L.A., there was no pay, so the only opportunity for work was being allowed to perform long enough for casting directors, directors and producers to have an opportunity to see your work! This could not be accomplished with just three performances! Not enough time to be seen, even if the reviews were blockbuster!

We had so many actors join and support our new Professional Actors League that it brought the West Coast President of Equity, Eddie Weston, to the negotiating table.

We prevailed! We got our ninety-nine seat limit, and our open-end run! I also had a brief "outing" with a new agent. Another big agency – William Morris. I was with them for about twenty minutes! I attended one of their big soirees, held in their offices in Beverly Hills. William Morris was so large, it was housed in two buildings. At this event, I was wandering around and, while getting a drink at the open bar, I had the occasion to meet one of the agents. He asked me if I was an actor (I guess I looked like an actor). I replied yes. He asked me if I was with the agency. I told him yes. He asked me who my agent was. I told him my agents name, which was Bob. That's all I can remember, can't remember his last name, but that's only fair because he probably didn't even "know" my name. This agent paused for a minute, then said, "No, I don't know him". He turned and walked away. Shortly after, I left the party. As I was walking to get my car, which was now a Volkswagen Bug, I thought to myself, "What am I doing with an agency that is so large, one agent doesn't even know my agent!" I was seeking a new agent the following day.

    And I lucked out! I found an independent agent, Ted Wilk, of his own agency, The Ted Wilk Agency. Ted had seen me in a play, "Telemachus Clay," where most of the actors (and it was a large cast) played multiple roles. I had received very good reviews, so he agreed to meet with me. We met and he agreed to represent me, and, boy, did he represent me! Right out of the box he got me an interview with the director, John Sturges. Mr. Sturges was directing a film with Charles Bronson and Lee Remick over at MGM Studios and Ted convinced him to see me on the set. I shot over to MGM, and on a break from filming, Mr. Sturges interviewed me. He asked me a few questions about any work I had done, and, after a bit, he said he wanted to use me in the film. He told me to get back in touch with him once he started casting for a space movie, "Marooned." I thanked him and left, kind of walking on a small cloud.

Just a few weeks later, I was on an audition, when Ted called me and told me he heard that Columbia Studios was finishing up the casting for "Marooned." I told Ted that John Sturges, the director had said he wanted to use me in the film. Ted said he hadn't received any word from the casting office. This all took place on a Friday. I went down to the Western Union office and sent a telegram to Mr. Sturges over at MGM. I remember the telegram, which you could still send in those days, and not have it "phoned in." It read: Mr. Sturges, I'm Jordan Rhodes. We met at MGM-You said you wanted me for a role in Mission Control in Marooned-My agent said the casting office hasn't called, and production is starting. I'd still like to be in your film-Thanks. And I sent it off. On Monday afternoon, Ted called me and said, "Get over to the casting office at Columbia, they want you for a part in Marooned, requested by the director." I got the role of Glenn the E-con engineer in Mission Control.

In addition to a lot of weeks work on "Marooned," there were a number of highlights worth sharing with you. I got to work with Gregory Peck (years later I'd work with Mr. Peck again in a huge mini-series, "The Blue and the Gray").

I also worked with David Janssen. I met and became friends with Scott Brady (Lawrence Tierney was Scott's brother and got him into the movies). And I also met and became friends with Frank Capra, Jr. He was an associate producer who later was the head of the Screen Gems Studio in Wilmington, North Carolina where I did the "Matlock" series. Just a Blue Collar Actor, folks!

Scott and I became good friends on "Marooned." He had a lot of lines, and his reputation was a little "shaky" at that time, so he really wanted to come off well.

I would run lines with him in his dressing trailer all the time. I was fine with my lines, since they were literally "one-liners." I do remember being very nervous the first time I had to answer a question from Gregory Peck. It was a very involved and long setup shot. The camera was panning over the room on a huge crane, coming to rest and featuring Mr. Peck as he asks Glenn (me) about the radiators (technical term). I respond with, "All radiators are normal". I could only think about screwing up my line, which came at the end of this long sequence, which would have caused the director to have to reshoot the entire scene. So much for any thought of "technique or method" acting – just say the damn line and don't screw it up! I didn't screw it up!

Scott and I would go out after the day's work, usually

landing at one of his favorite watering holes, have a few drinks, and then head home. We'd also go out to lunch each day. I got to know Scott and his wife, and they met Jan when we were invited to their house up in the Hollywood Hills for dinner. Scott used to quietly show me his picture album with him and Dorothy Malone, while his wife and Jan were in the kitchen. He would always tell me that Dorothy was the love of his life. He got a kick out of me telling him that I had worked with her on "Peyton Place." After we finished "Marooned," we continued to keep in touch.

    Then another one of those "unexplained" events that seemed to take place in my life, took place again. I was continuing to work, you'll read about that next, but now "Marooned" was finished, and Columbia was planning a real old-fashioned "Hollywood Premiere." Huge searchlights, red carpet, stars, lots of press, a big premiere party on the sound stages at Columbia, a real premiere for "Marooned." There were a lot of "name stars" in the cast, so you can imagine my complete surprise when I received an invitation to the premiere! To this day, I'm still convinced that my name had to have been listed just below one of the stars, and the young secretary assigned to type up the Invitations thought it "sounded" like "somebody important." This was 1969, almost no one was named, "Jordan", combined with

"Jordan Rhodes" and probably following Gregory Peck, I'm convinced it was a mistake. Had it been Mike, Bill or Tim, etc., - no reflection on any of those names, they are fine names, but I believe she thought it was the name of an important actor, and sent out the Invitation.

Regardless, I received the Invitation and I was determined to go. For years I had always told anyone that asked me if I was ever going to attend a premiere, that I would attend a premiere, "When I was in the movie." Well now I was in the movie! I called Scott and asked him if he was going to go. Scott said he had been to so many of those things he didn't care to attend. I told him I had been invited and convinced (begged) him and his wife to go with me and Jan. I told him I'd get the limo, have them picked up and we'd all go together. He finally agreed. The rest only gets better – for me! When we arrived at The Egyptian Theatre, Scott told me to stay close to him so I'd get in all the publicity shots. There were huge searchlights scanning the sky, and the red carpet was right where we stepped out of the limo. People were being held back behind red velvet ropes. Mounted up above the theatre was a twelve-foot high production picture of the Mission Control Room with only three faces large and recognizable in the photograph – Gregory Peck, standing, Gene Hackman's face on a screen from inside the Space Craft, and Jordan Rhodes, yours truly, looking up at Mr. Peck! As Scott and I started walking on the red carpet, a lady in the crowd looked up at the huge picture, pointed at me and shouted, "That's him, that's him!" Scott threw his arm around my shoulder and we continued into the theatre. I don't remember seeing the film, just saying hello to so many of the stars in the film. But the best is yet to come!

After we left the screening, we all got back into the limo and drove over to the Columbia lot for the party. As we were walking toward the sound stages where all the tables, the bars, the food and the servers were waiting, we passed a black Chrysler Imperial being driven and parked by Robert Mitchum. He was there with his wife, and as we walked by Scott and Bob said hello. Robert Mitchum had always been one of my favorites, so I asked Scott if he knew him. Scott said, "Sure, I've known him for years."

Once inside the sound stages, it was incredible! Just imagine everything you've ever thought that a Hollywood Premiere Party would have – it had it all! Lights, tables beautifully set, huge long bars, servers all over the place, ice sculptures, huge tables full of fruit, every kind you can imagine, all of the men in tuxedos, ladies in gowns, everything was absolutely beautiful! Imagine me, a guy that as a kid, used to drive a tobacco sled in the fields in North Carolina, being in a place like this. Wow-Wow!

After we were seated, and had taken a few pictures for the press, Scott leaned over to me and said, "Now, listen, there are a lot of producers, directors, and some casting people here, so you tell me who you want to meet, and I'll take you to meet 'em." I asked Scott if he really meant "anybody?" He said, absolutely, anybody you want to meet. I told Scott I wanted to meet Robert Mitchum. Scott said, "Well what do you want to meet him for?" I just said, "I wanted to meet Bob Mitchum". Scott said all right, we got up and started walking over to where Robert Mitchum was standing at the bar. As we got closer, Scott said, "Now, look, Bob can be a funny guy sometimes, if he doesn't feel like talking or being friendly, don't be offended, it's just the way Bob is sometimes." Scott introduced me to Bob Mitchum, told him I was in the film with him, that I was a friend of his, and I was new in town. We shook hands, and Bob started talking, and telling stories about some of the moguls in Hollywood, and how Harry Cohen use to cuss out Shelley Winters, call her the "C" name all the time, accuse her of doing nothing but bitching about everything, and the stories went on all night! Mitchum would impersonate the moguls, Jack Warner, Harry Cohen, anyone he'd tell a story about, he'd impersonate them. Scott and Bob exchanged stories about people coming up to them in a bar and trying to borrow money, when they didn't even know the people. How everybody thought all actors were filthy rich. Bob said his wife would kick his ass if he gave money to any of these strangers. Other actors came by the bar and said hello to Mitchum, Scott and me! It was one of the most memorable nights of my life! Obviously I'll never forget my first film Premiere! December 12th, 1969.

Chapter Seventeen

After "Marooned," I started working and did a succession of TV shows. "Then Came Bronson," "Green Acres" (I was supposed to be a recurring character, as the young veterinarian, but Eddie Albert, the star, didn't "cotton" to me as we'd say in my neck of the woods), "Daniel Boone," "Young Country," "Mod Squad," "Brackens World" (where I'd get to see my friend Joe Don Baker from the New York days - he was visiting the studio where we were filming) ,"The Bill Cosby Show" and "The Young Lawyers" (I met and worked with Lee J. Cobb, after all those times in New York when I had hopes of just meeting him - now I was working with him!). He paid me a wonderful compliment after I finished a long courtroom scene, by saying, "You're a fine actor, young man."

I got a commercial agent through a young lady that lived at our apartment building. Her name was Lynn Marta and she was with the Bill Cunningham Agency.

They were strictly a commercial agent for TV commercials, voice-overs, and modeling. Lynn did commercials for them. I met her one day out by the pool, and she asked me if I had a commercial agent. I told her no, and she asked me if I wanted to do commercials? I said sure.

Another Blue Collar Actor decision. She arranged a meeting with me and the Agency. They signed me for commercials, and The Cunningham Agency is the only commercial agent I've ever had. The name has changed a couple times over the years, as new partners joined the Agency. I signed with them on the West Coast - Hollywood - but when I returned to New York, I continued to be represented by the Agency, now called CESD. I got so lucky doing commercials. It gave me the financial freedom to hold out for better roles in television which also came with the "Guest Star" billing, and a little higher pay scale.

  The 70's would have been even better for me, on a personal level, but I screwed the personal part up. I really started to work. But going on location with a film, "Angel Unchained," was going to change the personal part. The year before, when I was doing the play "Telemachus Clay", there was an actress in the play that I had met earlier, her name was Jean Marie. She was one of the female leads. Later she developed into a very talented artist and writer. She had been married to Marty Ingels, an entertainer of some note, who went on to manage celebrities for various shows and functions, and later he married Shirley Jones. For a while I believe Jean worked using her married name of Jean Ingels. We had become friends and, since I did photography as a hobby, I took some pictures of her. Just your usual headshots, nothing scandalous, or suggestive, just some nice pictures of her. She was an exceptionally fine-looking young lady. Shortly after we had finished "Telemachus Clay," another actor friend, Don Chastain, and his girlfriend, Karen Arthur, threw a combination party for the cast of "Telemachus Clay" and some other group, which I don't remember – but hey! It was an excuse for a Hollywood Party! Don had a good run as an actor before using his writing skills to write for a number of soap operas. He starred opposite Debbie Reynolds in her short-lived television series, among a number of other television and film credits. In addition, Don was an excellent singer and did a number of musicals in the theatre world. Karen Arthur would go on to become a very talented director, and was the first female director to win an Emmy.

    The party was a typical Hollywood Party of the late 60's that the civilians read about in magazines. A swimming pool with some nude swimmers taking part, a few people smoking a little pot, and people drinking and eating, having a good time. For whatever reason, my wife Jan didn't want to attend, and Jean Marie's boyfriend at the time also didn't come. So, Jean and I wound up spending time together at the party. When she said she should leave, I walked her out to her car, opened the door for her, and we talked for a short while. Without a doubt there was some strong sexual tension going on between us. I leaned in and kissed her. She grabbed me and said, "Get in the car." I got in and we continued our kiss, finally breaking apart and both agreeing this was not a good idea! We separated, I got out, we said our goodnights, she drove off and I went back inside to the party for about ten minutes, then told Don and Karen goodnight, and I went home. Yes, I did feel guilty, but I kept telling myself, it was okay. I didn't let my "little head" get the best of my "big head" – the one that sits on my shoulders supported by my neck.

In a few weeks Jan got a role in a Burt Lancaster film. I believe it was called "Lawman." It was shooting in Mexico with a few other names. While she was waiting to see when she would head out to Mexico, Ted got me an audition for an American International Pictures film entitled "Angel Unchained." As it turned out, a rather ominous title for me. Lee Madden was the director, and I did get the part. Oddly enough, this was the first film where I came in contact with Ken Vose, who became my writing partner years later on a very successful play. We just didn't know each other at the time. It was one of those American International Pictures motorcycle flicks, but with a little twist. In this one, the motorcycle gang members were the "good guys," and the "bad guys" were a bunch of redneck cowboys, me being one of the leaders! Don Stroud was the lead motorcycle guy, Angel, and Luke Askew led a group of flower children that just wanted to live peaceably in their commune. But the redneck cowboys didn't want no damn hippies cluttering up the countryside. So, Angel to the rescue! Other members of the cast in addition to Don and Luke, were Tyne Daly (she's said me she would have me killed if I ever told anyone we did that film), Larry Bishop (Joey Bishop's son), Aldo Ray, and Bill McKinney. Bill went on to have a fine career. You'll remember him from "Deliverance" as the disgusting hillbilly that raped Ned Beatty's character. And, of course, yours truly was in the film, on location in Apache Junction, Arizona. You'll notice throughout the Book I always seemed to get the "exotic" locations, places like Apache Junction, Arizona, Kingsville, Texas, Springer, Oklahoma, and Canon City, La Junta, Mazanola and Montrose, Colorado. No France, Switzerland, Italy, London or Mexico for me! No sir!

The cast and crew had been on location for about a week, when the two lead actors playing the redneck cowboys, me and Peter Lawrence arrived. No sooner had we checked into our hotel/motel in Apache Junction, than the assistant director knocked on my door and said, you're needed on the set. Now there is a rule in SAG, that you are not supposed to travel and work on the same day without receiving extra pay, but, for whatever reason, it didn't apply for this A.I.P. film.

So, I dropped my luggage in the room, got in the car and was driven to the set.

Imagine my surprise when I walked onto the set, and a very pretty motorcycle gang "mama" came over to me and gave me a welcoming hug, - it was Jean Marie!

She whispered in my ear, "I'm so glad you're here. You've got to save me from this co-star actor, he's driving me crazy". Well, of course, I went along! It was now just a matter of time before the "little head" was going to rule the "big head" – just a matter of time. And we had both tried to be so good at that Hollywood party!

That first day, the director, Lee Madden, had decided to film one of the fight scenes between the redneck cowboys in their dune buggies , attacking the hippies in their commune. In this scene, Peter is driving the dune buggy. I'm the passenger, and as we speed around trying to run down the hippies. I'm swinging a short rope and trying to hit them, when one of hippies stabs me in the shoulder with a pitchfork. Peter slams on the breaks, and stands up to shout at, and dress down the hippies, telling them we'll be coming back with another large group and we intended to run them into the ground. That was the scene. Imagine everyone's surprise when Peter's shouted dialogue was absolutely BRITISH! An Arizona cowboy with a very distinct English/British accent! Lee Madden was more surprised than anyone! After trying a number of takes to see if Peter could "soften" his English accent, we wrapped for the day.

Back in my hotel/motel room, after dinner, there was a knock at my door. It was the director, Lee, standing there in his Safari hat, jacket, slacks, and his Jodhpur boots, holding his ridding crop. This was Lee's "signature" directors outfit.

He came in, crossed around me, and sat down on the bed. He said, "Jordan, I need a favor. You heard Peter today. The guy has a heavy fucking English accent! I was sold a bill of goods, and a sob story by his agent [Lee always did have a soft spot for an actor's plight], plus he didn't have that damn accent when we met!" He then explained the "favor" he was asking. He wanted to know if I would take most of Peter's dialogue and combine it with my own. Peter would just stand there and look "menacing" as I basically adjusted the dialogue. Example: Instead of Peter answering a question about, "How do you feel?" my character would say, "He feels fine, what's it to you?" I agreed to take Peter's dialogue. Lee thanked me for, quote: "Saving my ass, I won't forget it". Thankfully I was a quick study, and was able to adjust to the

Written By Jordan Rhodes

Jordan With His Mom & Dad

School Days 1949-50

Class Picture

Early School Headshot

The Life of a Blue Collar Actor

Jordan With His Dad In His Navy Uniform

Three Generations - Jordan, His Dad And Daughter Cheyenne

Jordan In "Sabrina Fair" For The Players Company- Baltimore, Md.

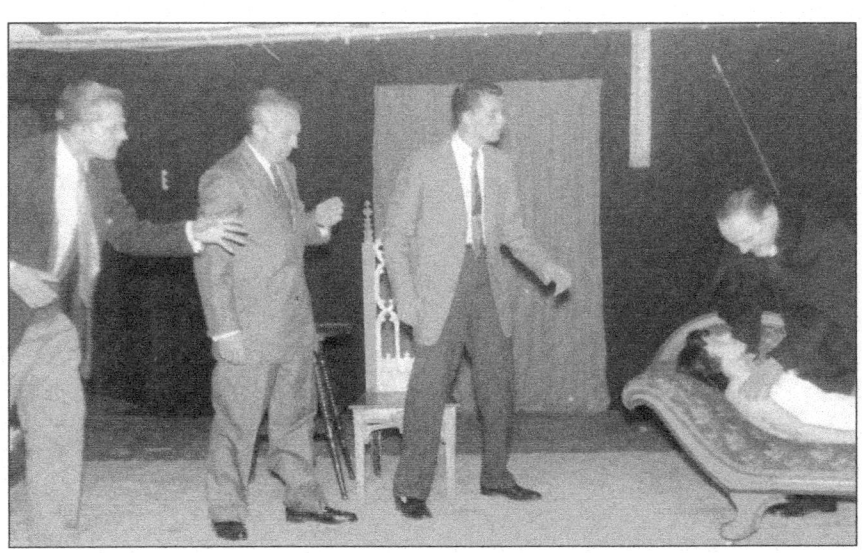

Jordan (Center) In His First Play, "Dracula" At The Hilltop Theatre-Harpers Ferry, W.VA. Payment Was Room & Board Plus Stipend

Jordan (Center With Gun) In "Desperate Hours" -Vagabond Players-Last Play In Baltimore Before Move To New York.

Jordan (Black Vest) With Joe Banderia - "Sabrina Fair"

Written By Jordan Rhodes

Jordan (Far Right) Lead In "Look Homeward Angel"-Summer Stock-Ohio

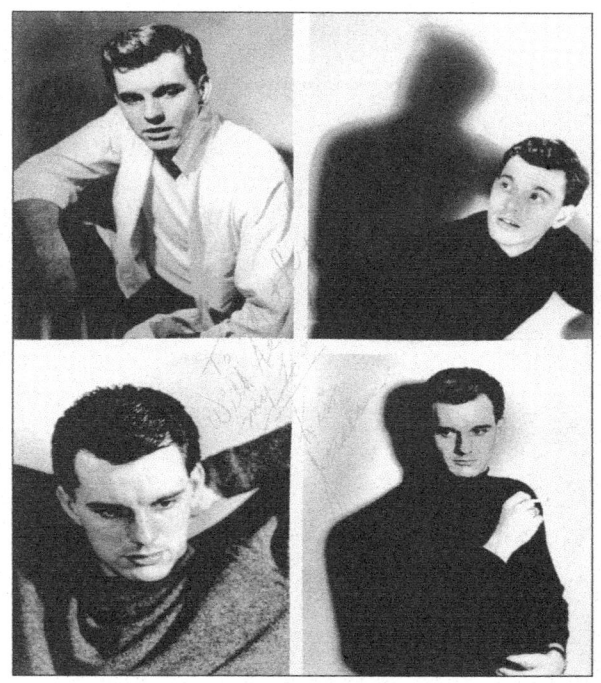

First Group of NY Dramatic Photos

Jordan (Center On Ledge) "Make A Million" - Summer Stock-Ohio

Jordan (Far Right) Doing Slap Stick Comedy In Stock

Jordan Backstage With
Leading Lady Greta Markson

Spending As Much Time
With Leading Lady As
Possible.

Jordan (Center With Art Kassal) In Agatha Christie Murder Mystery.

Jordan (In Tux Gazing Across The Stage At His Summer Love, The Leading Lady) The Play Is "Auntie Mame".

The Beginning Of The Folk Singing Adventure As "The Castaways". Jordan Is On The Left.

Here, He's On The Right.

Back In New York - Appearing In Off-Broadway Production Of "The Night Is Black Bottles". Jordan Is In The Back With A White Tie & Playing Drums As Louie Boy

Written By Jordan Rhodes

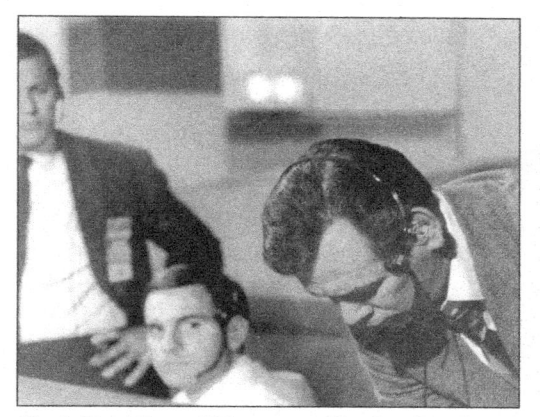

First Big Film - "Marooned" - Jordan In Center With David Janssen

Jordan With Scott Brady At "Marooned" Premier.

First Big Musical "1776" -Jordan In Back Row, Fourth From Right-With White Periwig.

"Marooned" Premier Party With First Wife Jan, Scott Brady & His Wife

The Life of a Blue Collar Actor

Publicity Shot Of Jordan In "S.A.M."

Jodie Foster, Catherine Ferrar, Paul Sand & Jordan In "S.A.M."

Jordan Being Restrained By Kent Mccord On "Adam-12".

Jordan With Paul Sand And Director James Komack Filming "S.A.M."

Written By Jordan Rhodes

With Friend, Chuck Connors Of "The Rifleman" Fame.

On Set Of "Marcus Welby, M.D." - Show That Jumpstarted My Career.

Guest Star On "Bonanza".

The Life of a Blue Collar Actor

With My Daughter Cheyenne On Location Filming "The American Cowboy".

Jordan As Randal "The Indian Runner"

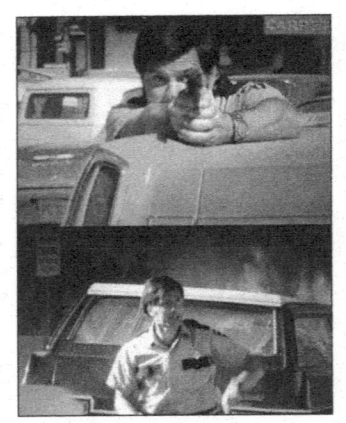

Jordan As Hal Ritchie, "Mr. Majestyk"

Jordan As Brace On "Battlestar Gallactica".

Written By Jordan Rhodes

On Set With Dennis Hopper

On Set Of "The Indian Runner" With Sean Penn

With Al Lettieri On "Mr. Majestyk".

With Linda Cristal On "Mr. Majestyk".

The Life of a Blue Collar Actor

Filming "Hart To Hart" With Robert Wagner, Wife Laura Wallace & Jordan.

With Cast Of Play, "Father's Day". Two Year Tour With Barbara Rush, Paul Kent, Tom Troupe, Carole Cook, Gwynne Guilford & Jordan.

Marriage To My 2nd Wife, Actress Laura Wallace - Mother Of Cheyenne.

With My Daughter, Cheyenne, At Our First Apartment In Queens, NY.

Written By Jordan Rhodes

With Friend & Director Leo Penn Filming "Matlock" - 3 Seasons As Lt. Harmon Andrews.

Publicity Shot From "The Jordan Rhodes Show" On WMFD - A Three Year Radio Adventure

Lynn Early In Her Career With Tom Selleck In TV Pilot, "Concrete Cowboy".

Marriage To My Third Wife, Actress/Singer Lynn Moore In New Orleans

One Of Many Posters Of The Play During The Five Year Run.

Lynn Next To Johnny Cash After Doing A Grand Ole Opera Show.

Lynn & Jordan With Friend Gary Busey At A Celebrity Event.

Starting Our Five Year Tour Of PAPA "The Man, The Myth, The Legend".

Lynn with Arthur Miller

Another Break From "PAPA" To Attend My Daughter, Cheyenne's Wedding

Jordan & Lynn With Friend & Co-Writer Ken Vose On Tour With "PAPA".

Lynn With Mr. Chips

Taking A Break From "PAPA" At Home With Mr. Chips, Our Wonderful Rottie

Jordan With His Two Grandsons, Chayton & Declyn.

Jordan & Lynn With Jill St. John & Robert Wagner At A Celebrity Event.

During "PAPA"- Here's My First Meeting With My Brother, Mark. A Brother I Never Knew I Had.

Backstage With Friends, Jill St. John & Robert Wagner After Their Performance Of "Love Letters".

Filming "House Of Good & Evil". Notice The Ax Blade In My Back.

On The Set, Filming "A Long Way Off".

combined dialogue.

    This was the film where I made friends with a number of stunt guys, including Bud Ekins, the stunt coordinator. Bud did the famous motorcycle barbed wire jump for Steve McQueen in "The Great Escape." Also, Jerry Randall, Alan Gibbs, J.N. Roberts, and Bill Burton. Billy would go on to double for me a number of times, and a couple of years later I was happy to request him to double for me in a pilot film, S.A.M. for director/producer James Komack. I loved hanging out with these guys on a location. I even got to do a couple of my own close-up stunts with Bud and Billy. My character was jerked out of a moving dune buggy by Bud Ekins. Prior to filming the scene, I asked Bud if he thought I could do the stunt with him instead of using a double. If I did it, the director could get a closer shot. Bud said, "Yeah, you can do it. Just do what I tell you". Bud told me what to do. I had to push off with my legs on his cue after he had jumped onto the moving dune buggy, grabbed me and pulled me off. Bud jumped on the moving dune buggy, grabbed me by my collar, leaned down and said into my ear, "Now!" I pushed off with my legs as he pulled me so we'd clear the rear moving wheels of the buggy, and we hit and rolled on the ground. Lee yelled, "Cut – Print. We got it!"

    I did one other close stunt in a fight scene, when Billy

Burton had me throw a punch at him and he flipped me onto the hood of a pick-up truck. As an actor, I loved it!

As I wrote earlier, it was just a matter of time before I got together with Jean. After a few days of filming, we went out to dinner one evening, and after dinner she drove us up to this little lake view. I believe it was a lake view, but we were in Arizona so I'm not quite sure. I do remember it was very secluded, and had a nice view, which we only enjoyed for about five minutes before we were locked in a passionate embrace. Jean drove us in her sports car back to the hotel/motel where we all were staying, I went into Jean's room and we did exactly what we knew we were going to do – and we did it most of the night. We were together every night for the rest of the film. I finished my scenes a couple of days before she was wrapped with hers, so I checked out of my room and moved into hers. I cashed in my return plane ticket, and as soon as Jean was finished, the picture wrapped and she drove us back to L.A. together, stopping over two nights and exhausting ourselves in bed.

Unfortunately I could not control my heart, and I fell in love with Jean. By the way, she never believed that. She always said if we had stayed together, we would have wound up killing each other.

Regardless, I had screwed up my marriage royally. I

was a dickhead. Jan had never done anything to drive me away. She didn't nag me, she didn't cut me off from sex or deny me affection. I can't remember having more than two real arguments during our seven years of marriage. We had always agreed that having kids was not in our plans, we were both career-oriented, so not having any kids was a plus at that time. In addition to destroying my marriage, I also lost one of my best friends, George Murdock. George tried desperately to talk me out of leaving Jan. He suggested that I just have this fling with Jean, get it out of my system, keep it quiet, and not let anybody else know, but that I should come to my senses and not lose Jan. But the heart, and I now admit, being greatly influenced by the "little head," wouldn't allow the "big head" to get his act together.

    Jan and I were now living in a one-bedroom apartment on the ground floor of a building in North Hollywood. I moved out only taking my personal belongings. We had two Volkswagen Bugs, so I took one and left Jan the other one. It was a very emotional time, and the scene was caused entirely by me. Leaving was very hard, but it felt (there goes that "feeling" shit again) like the right thing to do. I'm thankful, that, fifty years later, Jan and I have stayed on friendly terms. I don't know if she's ever forgiven me, and I'm not sure she should, but at least she knows that none of it was her fault.

My friend Don Chastain had a little apartment in Hollywood, which he sometimes used as an office, and he let me rent it for a while. I spent most of my nights with Jean in her apartment on Doheny Drive for the time we were together. The building was just on the outskirts of Beverly Hills and it had some interesting tenants. The dancer/actress Joey Heatherton, who was married to Lance Rentzel, a wide receiver for the Dallas Cowboys, and Jessie White, a veteran actor of many films who had become the Maytag Repairman.

I can still remember the last time Jean and I were together. It was at my little apartment, the one I was renting from Don Chastain. She came over and we had one of our sexual rendezvous. Our sexual relationship was always intense, so I don't know if we made love that afternoon, or if we just banged our brains out again. She decided to return to her apartment that evening, and the next time we spoke on the phone, she broke up with me - over the phone! She said some nice things about me being a young, good-looking actor, that was single, working, and that I wouldn't have any trouble finding ladies. She said I was sure to have an exciting time in front of me. It did hit me hard, but I avoided making a fool out of myself – well, at least I avoided making a bigger fool out of myself than I had already managed to do. I had no way of knowing that over ten years later a tragedy would cause our paths to cross again.

In a few days I vacated Don's place and found a one-bedroom apartment just a few blocks away, but still in Hollywood. Thanks to my agent Ted Wilk, I continued working, almost doing one show right after another. I don't intend to bore the reader with the names of all those television series. You can find those shows on the internet, and the information is available on IMDb, the International Motion Picture Data Bank on-line. I will just highlight the ones that contain a good or interesting - maybe even entertaining - story. One of these stories involves the way I was introduced to Leo Penn. Leo was one of the premiere directors in Hollywood, and my agent, Ted, had been chasing him for months trying to get me in to see him. Finally, it happened. Ted called me and told me to get over to Universal Studios for a meeting with Leo Penn. I drove over, and went into this office where Mr. Penn was preparing his next television show. After a quick hello, he asked me to read for a part in this "Marcus Welby" show. He read with me. After the reading, Mr. Penn looked at me for a bit, then he said, "Jordan, this part has already been cast. I agreed to see you because your agent has been driving me crazy! He's been following me everywhere and telling me that I have to see you! Yesterday, he followed me into the men's room, and continued insisting that I see you – so I just said, Okay! I'll see your client! But I'm glad I did. You're good, and I will have you back for another part, the next time I'm doing a show I believe you're right for." I thanked him for his time and left the office. I had heard the "next time" line a number of times, and usually it didn't amount to a hill of beans. But this time it did! Mr. Penn called me back for a lead role on a "Marcus Welby, M.D." episode, which was the first time the series had ever decided to do a show based on a real story, about a true event. It was an episode entitled, "We'll Walk Out of Here Together". Monique James, who was the head of the Universal talent department and the contract players, had two young actors, contract players, that she wanted to do the role of Bobby Hershey. Mr. Penn fought for me, and after a nerve-racking second audition, with more executives in the room than I can remember, I got the role!

My character, Bobby Hershey, was a young truck driver that was paralyzed in a bad wreck, and was sent to the rehabilitation wing of a hospital to try and adjust to his new life and to learn how to cope with a wheelchair that he'd need for the rest of his life. At the hospital, he meets this young female writer that has been stricken with spinal meningitis. A young actress named Sian Barbara Allen was playing the young writer. Sian was dating Richard Thomas at that time, so I met Richard when he came over to the set. Richard enjoyed tremendous success with "The Waltons" TV series.

    As for that Marcus Welby episode, I believe you can see it on YouTube these days. It was a terrific role for me and it really gave my career a big boost. I even made the first ballot on the Emmy's list that year for Best Supporting Actor. Of course, anybody could make a First Ballot in those days, you just had to have someone in the business connected with the show submit your name. In my case it was one of the producers. But, hey - it was a big deal for me at the time!

Chapter Eighteen

When I found out where we were going to be filming, I went to Mr. Penn and asked him if there was any chance I could go down to the rehabilitation hospital, spend some time in a wheelchair, and meet some of the patients? He told me to call him Leo, and he said if I wanted to go down to the hospital to research this role, he would damn sure make it happen! Leo was from New York City and was a very well-known New York actor prior to coming out to California, then getting caught up in the blacklisting shit going on during the McCarthy Senate Hearings, which destroyed many lives. He appreciated the effort I wanted to put into the role. I worked for Leo many times after that show. We became great friends. To this day, I credit Leo with putting my acting career on the map. I became friends with his entire family. His three sons, Michael Penn, a very talented music writer and composer, composing many themes for films, Sean Penn, what do I need to say about Sean? And Chris Penn, the youngest brother, an actor that unfortunately passed away too young.

Leo's wife, and the mother of those men, Eileen Ryan Penn, is my daughter's Godmother. So, yes, I'm a friend of that family.

After that "Marcus Welby, M.D." episode, I was really busy. My love life wasn't suffering either. A lot of very nice and attractive young ladies were happy to go out with an actor, especially one that was working. I moved into a good-sized apartment in North Hollywood and I bought a big Buick. I could afford the gas - the "crunch" hadn't hit yet, so I moved out of the Volkswagen family. I had started doing some of the "Adam-12" episodes a year before my "Welby", and the producer, Herm Saunders, liked my work, and suggested me to Jack Webb for a pilot. Jack Webb had his own production company, you may remember the MARK VII signature stamped on the beginning of his series dating all the way back to "Dragnet". The series pilot was, "O'Hara Treasury Agent," and starred David Janssen. I was auditioning for the role of a young Lt. Colonel, a pilot that flew jets all over the country to drop off and sometimes pickup Janssen's character after he had solved a case.

What follows will depict one of the "missteps" I made during my career, which I can now discuss in retrospect. Mr. Webb had me come up to his office in the Tower, a tall building on the Universal Studios lot, where I was to read for him and a couple of other executives, including David Janssen, plus an assistant that read with me. It was a very pleasant meeting, and though I was nervous as usual,

I settled in fairly quickly. Having looked the script over beforehand, I did a good audition. Mr. Webb gave me some of his notes after my first read through - he always liked a very staccato delivery of lines in his shows. "Dragnet" was a typical example of this. Mr. Webb would not have liked working with James Stewart. After the second reading, Mr. Webb seemed happy with my performance, so the other executives agreed, of course. Jack Webb was the boss. I left feeling like I had done a good job, which is all I believe anyone can ever do after any meeting or audition. If you believed you did your best, or did a good job, then that's all you can ask.

    Two days later my agent, Ted, called me and told me I had the job! Jack Webb had personally picked me for the role of the young Lt Colonel. I gave Herm Saunders a quick phone call and thanked him for getting me the audition. Herm told me that Jack liked me, and thought I'd do a good job. Needless to say, I was a happy camper. The following day Ted called me for another audition for a pilot series out at MGM, for director/producer James Komack. It was entitled "S.A.M. - Stories About Man," and was starring this new hot talent from the New York Stage, a young guy named Paul Sand. The female lead was also set, it was Catherine Ferrar, and everyone was comparing her to Elizabeth Taylor.

Catherine and I had both done "Mod Squad". She was a stunning looking young lady and a good actress to boot, and she continued to have a very good career. Little Jodie Foster was also in the pilot. I believe she was about six or seven at the time, and the most precocious kid you'd ever want to meet. I was auditioning for the second male lead opposite Paul in the show, the third lead overall. The cast was very good, it included Bruce Kirby (his son Bruno went on to fame in one of the Godfather films), and Bruce had a fine career, and William Christopher, who would have an entire career playing the Priest on the hit series, "Mash." I got the role! Wow, two series pilots in one week! Sounds great – right? Well, here was the problem....both "O'Hara Treasury Agent," where I had been "handpicked" by Jack Webb, and "S.A.M.," where I had been "handpicked" by James Komack, the producer and director, were both scheduled to film at the same time! I had a major decision to make, but unfortunately I had already committed to do the "O'Hara" show. Obviously, the role on "S.A.M." was much larger, it was a lead, than the supporting role on "O'Hara." I discussed it with my agent, Ted, and the only solution we could come up with was for me to explain the situation to Herm Saunders and ask him if he would intervene on my behalf, and ask Mr. Webb if he would let me out of the commitment of

"O'Hara" so I could do the role in "S.A.M." I asked Herm. He completely understood and went to Mr. Webb on my behalf, and Mr. Webb agreed to let me out of the commitment. I did "S.A.M." It didn't sell, so therefore it didn't go to series. "O'Hara Treasury Agent" did sell, and went to series – even though it was short-lived, but it was still a series!

    When I was auditioning for S.A.M., and James Komack was making up his mind, they asked me if I could ride a motorcycle. The character in the pilot was a motorcycle cop that lived at the boarding house where Paul's and Catherine's characters also resided. Of course I said I could ride a motorcycle. I even lied and said I had owned a Norton in New York City. My "Norton" motorcycle was in reality the Vespa 150 motor scooter I rode around the City! As written, I got the job. I asked if I could have some time to "familiarize" myself with the motorcycle I would be riding in the show. The true meaning of my word "familiarize" was to get to see the "size" of this motorcycle I would be riding. They told me I could have two weeks to ride the motorcycle, and get comfortable with it. On a Monday morning I met with one of the assistant directors, Mike, who was also the "tech advisor" for the show, because he was an excellent rider of motorcycles and even raced Dirt Bikes in various Desert Racing events. When I showed up on that Monday morning on the back lot of MGM Studios, and saw the size of this Harley model 74 Police Motorcycle, I guess my face must have given it all away, because Mike took one look at me and said, "You've never ridden a motorcycle in your life, have you?" It was a BIG Harley motorcycle. I came clean and told Mike I had only ridden a Vespa motor scooter, which I owned in New York. Mike said, "This ain't a scooter kid." I told Mike, I could do it. He was a cool guy, so he spent that entire morning explaining the controls, and how I would need to balance the motorcycle. By noon of that day, I was riding the big Harley around the back lot of MGM Studios. I came over every morning, including Saturday and Sunday, for two weeks and rode the big Harley Police Motorcycle all around the MGM back lot passing the movie sets of "Gone With The Wind," and "Wizard of Oz," plus others I don't remember – but I got it down. I learned how to ride and handle that big Harley so I looked like a real Cop! That I actually knew what I was doing! I only put the motorcycle down once during the entire shoot!

Since I had one of the leads in the series pilot film, I had a little "juice," and was able to request that Billy Burton be hired as my double. In the police outfit, helmet and all, Billy looked so much like me that one day, while watching the "dailies" (that's the film we shot the previous day), I saw him accelerate out of a gravel driveway onto the highway and do a little "fishtail" down the highway. Everyone watching, made a little comment about the "fishtail" on the motorcycle to Billy, about almost "losing it" – Billy replied, "That wasn't me, that was Jordan." Later, Billy told me I was lucky I didn't "lose it," and that you had to be careful when you were coming off a gravel surface on to pavement. I enjoyed riding the motorcycle so much, that I got a group of the guys, including Mike, the assistant, Billy Burton and Jerry Randall, stunt guys, to help me set up a dirt bike. They helped me "tweak" out a Yamaha 250 dirt bike with the proper handlebar and pegs, so I could go Desert Racing. The Bike was one of the first "toys" I treated myself to. I had a blast entering different Desert Races – I never won, but I always got my Finishing Pin! The proof that you had completed the race! I bought a 1964 Ford pickup so I could haul the bike to different events. Of course I also kept my Datsun 240 Z. We used to go way out in the Valley where they had a Motocross Track and ride many weekends. Steve McQueen used to ride out there, and man, could that guy ride! My stunt friend, Bud Ekins, who did the barbed wired fence jump for McQueen in "The Great Escape," I mentioned that earlier, told me that McQueen was so good on a motorcycle that he wanted to do the jump in the film, but the production company wouldn't let him. Bud said Steve could have done it, too. In fact, Steve was so good riding in the film that he put on the German's uniform and did the riding as the German that was chasing him! He was that much better than any of the stunt riders on the film! Whenever I tried to ride behind him at the Motocross track – that's where I always was! Behind him! I couldn't get within 200 yards of McQueen! Obviously, Motocross was not an event I was equipped to compete in, as I learned one day when I was lapped on the track by a guy with a ponytail flapping out behind his helmet. I pulled off the course and rode over to where we all had our trucks and refreshments set up. I got off my bike and made some comment about the "guy" lapping me with the ponytail. Jerry Randall, one of the stunt guys, laughing, said, "That wasn't a guy, Jordan, that was one of the Desert Rats. It's a girl's group of riders!" Needless to say I never tried to ride Motocross again!

    A couple of months after the dust had settled for the pilots, and some were going to series, "O'Hara Treasury Agent" was set to go into production. I was having dinner at Don Cuco's Mexican Restaurant in Burbank, not far from Warner Brothers Studios, when Herm Saunders and Jack Webb came in and took a booth. I called the waiter over and sent a couple of drinks over to them. They both looked over and acknowledged the drinks. When I finished and had paid my check, I walked over to their booth, they hadn't received their dinner order yet so I felt comfortable in saying hello. I greeted both of them, and Herm asked me how was everything? I told him okay and said I was back on the audition trail. Mr. Webb commented that he heard my pilot S.A.M. wasn't picked up. I agreed he was correct and congratulated him on "O'Hara" being picked up, and I added with a wry smile, "I didn't make the right choice there". Mr. Webb looked me right in the eye and replied, "Yeah, sometimes we make the right choices, and sometimes we make the wrong ones". They thanked me for the drinks again, and I bid them a good night and left. As I was leaving the restaurant I knew right then I was never going to work for a Jack Webb Production again. And I was correct. Much later when I spoke to Herm about the situation, Herm told me the problem was that Jack had handpicked me for that part in the show, and he never appreciated me asking for an out after I had made the commitment. As I stated, it was a "misstep," and, in retrospect, it was a mistake. One of a few I would make along my way.

  Over the next year and a half, my commercial bookings took off like gangbusters. I did twenty-one commercial spots, the majority being local and regional commercials, but I booked four nationals – Toyota, Swift's Turkey, Magic-Grow plant food, featuring a world-winning Sunflower grown by an autistic young lady that was featured in the commercial with me, and a Folgers Coffee commercial, where I would meet my second wife. But before that commercial and meeting, I would work almost non-stop. I had a good run and was doing shows that wound up being the highest-rated shows in their time slots, and some held the record for a long time. One of these was "The Night Stalker," a highly rated movie-of-the-week that became a hit series starring Darren McGavin. Many others followed including the original "Wonder Woman" movie-of-the-week starring Kathy Lee Crosby, and I did a guest star turn on "Bonanza" with Pamela Franklin, the young lady nominated for an Oscar for her role in "The Prime of Miss Jean Brody." A little rib-tickler here from my role opposite Pamela. We were playing a husband and a wife in this episode entitled "First Love," being directed by my now friend, Leo Penn. We had a bedroom scene at the Ponderosa where Ben Cartwright had invited us to stay for the night. As we were preparing to shoot the scene which required both Pamela and me to be in bed, I was starting to remove my jeans, when Pamela, in her beautiful English accent, snapped quickly, "What are you doing?"

I replied, "Removing my jeans to get into bed." "No you're not," she protested, "You will keep your pants on, Mister." I looked over at Leo, who was certainly enjoying this, and he shrugged, "You heard the lady, Jordan – keep your pants on."

I climbed into bed, wearing my jeans. After all, she was an Oscar nominee! I learned later that she was married to an English actor that enjoyed limited success in Hollywood, and he was insanely jealous! Perhaps she didn't want to have to explain that I didn't have my pants on in the scene.

During this "run" of work, I was enjoying myself immensely. I had acquired a business manager, Lee Winkler, who took me on as a client with "potential," more than my actual standing at the time. His clients included the director John Ford, Woody Stroud and Burt Reynolds. I actually had some fun conversations with Burt over the phone in Lee's office. It was great having a "business" manager. I would get a monthly allowance based on my earnings, but I'd have to clear any large purchases with Lee before I could spend the money. Lee's wife was named Peri, and a good friend of mine, Frank Christi, always kidded Peri, who was beautiful by the way, of marrying Lee just so she could be known as "Peri Winkler." Frank Christi, another Italian, became my best friend, which almost no one could understand. Frank was born and raised in New York, his father was a big shot in the Teamsters and obviously connected. Frank was a street-wise tough guy (in attitude) from New York, and I was a "shitkicker" (his favorite nickname for me) from the country in North Carolina. What could we possibly have in common? He played a number of movie "tough guys," more or less typecast. Frank used to tell me that every time he got cast in a western, and held the gun on a "good guy," he always had this urge to say, "Get off the horse, and get in the cab." Frank was my best man when I got married for the second time. He also knew Jean Marie before I did, and he became my daughter's Godfather – a title and role that he LOVED! Frank met with a tragedy he never deserved. He was shot down in his carport in the Hollywood Hills by two low life second-rate burglars that were hired by another low-life, for twenty-seven hundred dollars, because he was dating the guy's ex-girlfriend. It took the L.A. police department over ten years to solve his murder. He's buried in St. John Cemetery, Middle Village, Queens, under the family name Crifasi. He was one of my great and good friends. I still miss the guy.

 Many of the years I spent in Hollywood were filled with extreme violence. Much of it touching the film community.

Just three years after Jan and I arrived, the Sharon Tate murders took place at the hands of the crazy followers of Charlie Manson. It was brutal, and shocked the entire film community. Celebrities started installing security devices at an unbelievable rate. Doors and locks that used to be open became a thing of the past. Years later the Laurel Canyon area was thrust into the headlines with the Wonderland Murders, involving porn star John Holmes.

Chapter Nineteen

My success in the commercial field gave me the financial freedom to turn down certain roles, thereby allowing me the opportunity to hold out for better roles, better billing (which could never be overlooked in Hollywood), and a higher pay scale. With the approval of Lee, my business manager, I got my first new sports car. It was a Datsun 240 Z, metallic brown with a tan interior. Boy, did I love that car. I got it shortly after doing a Toyota commercial, which was probably the most dangerous filming I ever allowed myself to do. I was standing on top of a new high end Toyota, that was being held up by heavy chains supporting a platform to give the illusion of the car being taken off a ship. The car was locked on the platform. In order to achieve this "look" for the camera without going to the harbor and using an actual ship, we were shooting up in Mulholland Canyon. They had a large crane set up by a house, owned by Barry Sullivan, a very well-known actor from films, and later television. I was standing on top of the car holding onto those chains that supported the platform, the car and me. As I spoke the dialogue (sales pitch) directly into the camera, the crane swung the car, with me standing on top, and platform out over the canyon to give the illusion that the car was being delivered off the ship, and it was then lowered to the pavement. The production company had rigged up what they called a "safety harness," which was attached to my arm running down the sleeve of the sports coat I was wearing. I had no idea how dangerous this "stunt" was. There were no stuntmen on the shoot and after a couple of "filming takes", I was lowered back to the pavement for a short break. Then a couple of the crew guys came over to "check out" my "rigging". They asked me if I was receiving "stunt pay" since this was such a dangerous filming! I then had them unhook me from my "safety harness", and I approached the director and producer to discuss this filming with them. Once I expressed my concerns about possibly falling off the top of the car as it was being swung around by the crane and plunging down about 500 feet into the canyon, they agreed that they had enough footage of that shot and would only now need to lower me with the car down onto the pavement! We finished filming the commercial without me being swung out over the canyon anymore. As we were wrapping the commercial, Barry Sullivan approached me and said, "You've got more guts than me kid. I'd never have done that." Well, that's the life of a Blue Collar Actor. They would never ask George Clooney to do something like that! The happy ending for that commercial – I made about twenty thousand dollars in residuals, and that was a lot of money for this Blue Collar actor in the 70's!

As I continued my television and film work, I was hired for my first and only musical film. It was the film version of the Broadway hit, "1776". It starred most of the Broadway cast, including William Daniels, Howard Da Silva, Ken Howard, John Cullum, and Blythe Danner. It was one of those "good" jobs for a working actor, meaning it was about sixteen weeks! We had a few weeks of rehearsal for the roles that were being added to the film, roles that they couldn't have on Broadway, because it would have been too costly. Then we had costume and wig fittings, then both the studio and location filming. It was grand! I met a number of the actors from the New York production, and during setups (downtime) even played chess with a couple - William Daniels and Howard Da Silva. Bill wouldn't play with me after beating me a few times, as I just wasn't a challenge for him, but Howard would play with me even after beating me a number of times! He enjoyed winning. I promised to only write about the various funny or entertaining events involved with the films, rather than trying to tell or bore the reader about each television show or film I've done in a six decade career. So, here's one story that points out the things that one should never do while performing, but I was guilty of once during my short-lived folk-singing career, and only once during my entire film career. During all the rehearsals for "1776" and the filming, a small group of us became friends and talked a lot about our personal likes and dislikes. In doing so, we discovered that a few of us did enjoy smoking a joint once in a while, and, on this particular day, we discovered that our work after lunch just involved sitting around in the Continental Congress. I happened to mention that I had some "killer weed" at my apartment, which was about a ten-minute drive from the Columbia lot. One of the guys, Barry, a beautiful tenor, said that he and his girlfriend had always wanted to try some pot. So, me and two other actors, (whose names I will omit because they may not appreciate me pointing out that we got stoned while filming on that day) made a deal with Barry. If he would drive us out to my apartment, the three of us would smoke a joint, and I'd give him a joint for him and his girlfriend, but he'd need to stay straight so he could drive us back. He agreed. On the lunch break, all four of us piled into Barry's VW Bug (remember now, we were all still in complete costumes for the time period of "1776", with full periwigs, outfitted in pinks and lavender clothes of the period). We drove out on the freeway and arrived at my apartment. The three of us smoked a joint, keeping Barry away from us because we didn't want him to get a "contact high". It was killer weed, referred to in those days as "Acapulco Gold". I gave Barry the joint for him and his girlfriend for later, and we all jumped back into the car and zipped down the freeway back to the Studio, laughing and attracting attention from many motorists, looking at this group of men dressed like they were headed to a very classy Halloween party, but Halloween was not due for many months, so we just looked silly with our periwigs.

And period clothes – also, as is usual, we couldn't stop laughing! We arrived back at the Studio, Barry parked the car (thankfully, we were smart enough to ask him NOT to get high until later, when he was home!). We all agreed that we had to avoid each other on the set, because each time we looked at each other - we would start laughing. Just one of the "perks" of smoking good pot in those days, but not recommended anytime you're working!!

Back on the set, making a quick stop at hair and make-up, and being careful to avoid each other, we stayed in our respective dressing rooms waiting to be called to the set. One problem - they had changed the shooting schedule for after lunch!

We were no longer going to be just sitting at our desk and tables, listening to a debate, they had decided to do a large scene where we all had to be involved, listen for certain cues, and react! I have no idea how the other two actors felt, but I was in an absolute panic! I don't believe I have ever had to work so hard to concentrate in my life! It is now forty-eight years later as I'm writing this, and I'm relieved to say I have never even considered smoking a joint while engaged in any work situation since that day. As a matter of fact, I haven't had a buzz from anything stronger than a glass of wine, or a couple of margaritas, in the last thirty-five years.

 Unfortunately, I was aware of many people in my profession ruining their lives and careers by getting involved with "the white lady", cocaine, and other equally as damaging drugs. There was a time when so many people were doing "coke" it became a way to get a job. If you could supply certain directors or producers with some coke, you could not only get a job, you could wind up in a series. So, for a group of actors, myself included, that didn't participate in that nefarious activity, some jobs became hard to get. Then, later, when many people became involved with the recovery from an addiction, there were so many people in power who were now recovering addicts, that they only wanted to hire actors that were recovering! So, if you had managed to stay clean, and not become involved through the "supply some coke" for a job era, and missed out – now you missed out again because you were not a "recovering addict!" It was a strange, but thankfully a short-lived time in the entertainment business.

    I managed to weather that period of the business I just described, and the 70's and 80's were good to me. I continued to do Movies-of-the-Week, Co-starring roles and Guest spots in TV series, and was actively involved with The Melrose Theatre, attending the Workshop and doing a few plays. Once after I had taken a trip to New York, where I saw a play entitled "Home", starring Sir John Gielgud and Sir Ralph Richardson, when I returned to Los Angeles, a director from The Actors Studio West, Charles Rome Smith, was preparing to mount a production of that play in Los Angeles. There was a small, but effective, role of Alfred, a young man that had a frontal lobotomy performed on him, and he was one of the residents of this Home. It was just a five-character play. Two older men, two older women, and Alfred. Charles Smith (anyone who knew him called him Chuck), had cast Richard Bull (he was a regular as Mr. Olson on "Little House on the Prairie"), and Larry Haddon, another fine actor as the two older men. I was intrigued with the role of Alfred when I saw the play on Broadway, so I approached Chuck and asked him if he would consider me for the role of Alfred. Chuck couldn't believe I wanted to do this small role, and asked me if I was sure. I said absolutely I was sure, and Chuck said if I wanted to do that role, I had it! Oh, for those good old "heydays", when I was working so much that a director couldn't believe I would be interested in a smaller part!

We did the play "Home", and it was so successful at The Melrose Theatre we were invited to perform it at The Actors Studio West. It was very well-received, and later I was involved with a group of actors from The Melrose Theatre and a group of Actors Studio members to perform a staged reading of "Death of a Salesman." One of the perks of doing a lot of television, including two-hour TV movies and films, was the opportunity to go out as a Guest Artist to various universities and perform with their theatre arts department. I did one of these Guest Artist performances with Texas A&I in Kingsville, Texas. Actors would use the "hiatus period", the time in the summer when TV series would take a break before gearing up for the new season. If I couldn't get cast in a pilot for a series, I would seek a guest artist job. I did "Summer and Smoke", a fine Tennessee Williams play, at Texas A&I, where I did the male lead of Dr. Johnny. They had a wonderful group of talented young people, and a couple of the actors were quite outstanding.

These guest artist jobs were a wonderful challenge, and you would get an opportunity to work with the young people studying to become actors, or just serious about learning the craft. The guest artist would arrive to rehearse for two weeks with the students that had already been rehearsing for four weeks or longer, depending upon the difficulty of the play. Then after "polishing" the play and adjusting to the guest artist for the two weeks, the play would open and would be performed for another two weeks. Opening nights were like any opening nights at most theatres. Friends, parents and other students would show up for opening night, and I never let my young lady co-stars down, and continued the age old custom of presenting them with flowers during the curtain call. For "Summer and Smoke", I gave each one of the two young ladies performing with me long stem red roses. I also got to meet the parents of both the young ladies on opening night. Of course, because of the "excitement" of performing with a professional actor, and one that they had seen on television, and, in my case, in films, I had to adjust to the wary glances and looks from current boyfriends. Especially since there are a couple of embraces between Dr. Johnny and the two ladies. You don't just fake a kiss on stage. When a kiss is called for, you must be as real as possible! Use any method training you have!

    I enjoyed my time at Texas A&I, and while I was

there I was invited to visit The King Ranch. I couldn't believe the size of that place! They really treated me royally. I was even invited to ride one of their prized cutting horses. But after watching a demonstration from this champion cutting horse, I decided it would be better if I politely declined. That beautiful animal would have dumped me right on my keister, and Dr. Johnny wouldn't be attractive in the play with a broken arm!

Once back in Los Angeles, Cunningham, my commercial agent, sent me out for a Folgers Coffee commercial audition. Not only did I get the commercial, but the young lady, an actress named Laura Wallace, that was cast as my wife, actually became my second wife! Maybe you remember those Folgers commercials – the young wife was always trying to make coffee that her young husband would like. I need to relate the meeting between Laura and myself, as she liked to tell it. My daughter has heard it a few times. Laura always said that when I came into the casting office, she thought I had a real "full of myself" attitude, and she wasn't happy when we were paired up together for the audition. Well, the advertising agency liked us, because we both got the job. Laura was a house guest of Elizabeth Allen in Studio City. They met when Laura was cast as Elizabeth's daughter in a play entitled "Cactus Flower". Elizabeth had done the play on Broadway, but they replaced the role of the daughter for the road tour, and that's how Laura Wallace wound up in Studio City as a houseguest of Elizabeth. Laura told Elizabeth she was going to be working with this really "actor-type guy" that was full of himself, but she was happy she got the job.

During the filming of the commercial, Laura, who was new to the work in TV and film, was having a little trouble delivering the line, "Oh, Mrs. Olson, how can I make coffee he likes?" It was not that unusual in the commercial world at the time, because most of the ad executives didn't know what the hell they really wanted anyway, so they have little meetings to "discuss" how an actor should say the line. Nothing much to do with reality – but you had to deliver the line the way they envisioned it or you'd be there all day – and night. Well, I stepped in to help Laura, and give her some little tips, and a "line-reading" to show her where the ad executive wanted the emphasis placed on the "he likes" line. After a couple of tries during a little break, she got it and finally delivered the line the way the ad executive "heard it". To be completely honest, there wasn't a damn bit of difference between the way Laura started out delivering the line, and the way the ad executive wanted the line to be read.

Afterward, we wrapped the commercial and started on our separate ways. I asked her for her number, and I said that maybe we could meet for lunch one afternoon. I was dating a very tall redheaded lady at the time, named Holly, but we weren't what you'd call "serious". Just dating and having some fun. Holly was six feet tall in her stocking feet and she liked to wear the highest heels she could find, plus the shortest skirts. She was one of the editors at the new "Playgirl" magazine, the female answer to "Playboy". I actually did a photo shoot with Holly for a layout in the first issue of "Playgirl", with me in my pajama bottoms and Holly wearing only the pajama tops. I had an uncirculated copy of that first addition for years, but it got thrown out. I wonder if one of those would be worth much to a collector today?

Holly took me to a boat show in L.A., and I fell in love ... with a beautiful Ranger 26-Foot sailboat. A gorgeous Red Hull racing special. This was the second "toy" I treated myself to, after listening to Lee Winkler, my business manager, tell me about the two happiest days of a boat owner's life – the day he buys it and the day he sells it!

Since Holly introduced me to the boat show, I named the boat the "Miss Holly".

Once it was in the water, I docked it in a slip at Marina Del Rey. I started sailing in the Wednesday evening "Beer

Can" races. These were short races around a few buoy markers just beyond the breakwater, and a lot of fun. After the races, a group of us half-ass sailors would wind up at the local Mexican restaurant for dinner and a few margaritas. It was a fun time.

Chapter Twenty

Now, back to Laura. After I asked her for her number and a possible lunch date, as I wrote before, she surprised me and gave me her number. She was as pretty as she could be, and had a real cute little attitude. She had started her career as a dancer, but tore up her knee during a routine, so she concentrated on acting. And they tell you only athletes suffer career-ending knee injuries. Not true! Many dancers suffer the same career-ending injuries. After she gave me her number, she told me she was staying with a friend in Studio City. Later, when Elizabeth asked her why did she give her number to this "full of himself" jerk, Laura said I wasn't really a jerk at all, and I had been really sweet and kind, and had helped her a lot during the shoot.

Laura had a very good seasonal job for an actress. She worked the Auto Show conventions whenever and wherever they were held on the West Coast. She was known as The Opel Girl. She would stand on a revolving platform with the car, obviously an Opel, a Buick product, and demonstrate all the features of the car. Naturally since she got a tremendous discount from the company, she owned and drove an Opel.

We started dating and since I've already referred to her as my second wife, you know we got married. We stayed married for almost twenty years with a lot going on, some incredible, some very good, some great highs, and some bad lows, but the early years were truly great. I continued to work pretty steady all through the 70's doing shows that ranged from "Temperatures Rising", a comedy, playing my first "hit man" on the "New Perry Mason" series, and the first original TV Movie of "Wonder Woman" starring Cathy Lee Crosby. I again crossed paths with Andy Prine – remember, he was the actor that knocked me out of the Tony Perkins replacement on the Broadway production of "Look Homeward Angel". In "Wonder Woman", he was one of the henchmen for Ricardo Montalban.

During my relationship with Laura, I became good friends with her friend, Elizabeth Allen, with whom Laura was firmly entrenched as a houseguest. Elizabeth was quite a star. She starred on Broadway in a number of musicals, and had the female lead opposite John Wayne and Lee Marvin in "Donavan's Reef" (directed by John Ford, no less). She played the wife of Paul Lynde on both of his TV series, and toured with Paul on the Summer Henley Tour Circuit, which Paul always sold out. (Remember, I wrote questions for Paul on "Hollywood Squares). On a couple of these tours where Elizabeth portrayed Paul Lynde's wife, Laura performed the role of his daughter in the play "My Daughter's Rated X". I met Paul socially at the parties Elizabeth had all the time at her lovely home in Studio City, along with many other names, including Cesar Romero. I'm also guilty of playing a number of practical jokes on Elizabeth, one of which no one has ever corrected with the truth. She was planning one of her lavish Thanksgiving dinners. Friends would cook and bring various dishes like special potatoes, cranberry dishes and so on. On this particular Thanksgiving, I spoke right up and stated that I'd make the pies! Elizabeth was a little surprised, and said that was a lot of work, was I sure I wanted to make the pies? I insisted that I'd make the pies! I asked if she thought three pies would be enough? She agreed, and I said I'd make a pumpkin pie, an apple pie and a cherry pie. I had told Laura to go along with this, and as soon as I left, Elizabeth asked Laura in a panic tone, "Does Jordan know how to make a pie"? Laura simply said, "Yes, I'm sure he does". As the day of the lavish, celebrity and friend attended annual Thanksgiving dinner approached, Elizabeth was still questioning Laura about the pies and did "Jordan know what he was doing?" Okay, here's the setup. In the Studio City area where I lived, there was a wonderful pie bakery and restaurant named Marie-Calendar Pies. They made incredible pies. I bought three, a pumpkin pie, an apple pie and a cherry pie. Then I went to the grocery store and purchased three homemade pie plates, the type of tinfoil plates people use for homemade pies. I carefully put all three pies into the store-bought plates and proceeded to bring them to Elizabeth's for the dinner. She was blown away! She relaxed! Jordan had shown up with the pies, and once everyone was having them for dessert, Elizabeth never stopped raving about how good the pies were and she announced to everyone that I had made the pies! No one ever told Elizabeth the truth about the pies. No one ever had the heart to expose "Jordan's Pie Folly."

I had been with my agent, Ted Wilk, for about five years, and Ted had literally worked his ass off for me, and I believe I made another "misstep" in the agent arena.

A number of producers and directors were telling me that I needed to think about changing my agent. I was "advised" that I needed to step-up and go with a more "high-end" agent - that Ted had a habit of annoying casting people, directors and producers by his constant "badgering", and "they" believed it was costing me jobs.

Looking back, I don't know if that was really true or not, but I did leave Ted, and I signed with Alex Brewis, who also had his own agency and wanted to take me on. Saying this was a misstep is not meant to slight Alex. He did very well with Ed Harris, Leonard Nimoy and a friend of mine,

Peter Jason. But I should have stayed with Ted.

I was moving up in the Guest Star ranks, thanks to directors like Leo Penn, Kenneth Gilbert, Harry Falk, Jud Taylor and E.W. Swackhammer, even though I had accomplished that with Ted on Bonanza before going with Alex.

1973 and 1974 were better years than any of the seven before, and it was about to get even better for this Blue Collar Actor. I bought my first house! It was a little two-bedroom ranch and cottage-style house on a large piece of property in a section of Studio City which actually had the post office address of Valley Village – but nobody used it. It was in a neat little neighborhood. No through streets, so no commuters were ever tempted to "fly through" the neighborhood. My next-door neighbors were Hap, an old grip that had worked for years at Universal Studios, and his wife, Bunny. She was Judy Garland's stand-in for all those MGM musicals.

Two blocks down, just around the corner, was where Mickey Rooney lived. I'd see the "Mick" all the time with his station wagon full of kids. Right across the street from Mick lived Don "Red" Barry. Don had been a cowboy movie star in a bunch of "B" westerns in the 50's, and later he did a lot of character work in some big films. I'd see Don all the time, too. It was a great neighborhood. I put a pool in the backyard and bought my first Mercedes Benz. I felt like Janice Joplin from her song! Now before you start thinking - Boy! This guy has gone material-crazy, a house, a sailboat and MBZ - just remember where I came from, my background. I never owned a TV until I was twenty-one! Even then it was a black and white, not color! My family never owned a home, and every car we ever had always came with payments! I was just enjoying my life, which I was earning and paying for, no entitlement sought or expected!

Now with a house, I decided I wanted to get a dog. I liked German Shepherds, and I found a breeder, Eric Reiner, who also ran the International Guiding Eyes, which was a terrific organization. They raised and trained dogs to be guide dogs for the blind. The dogs were given to the blind, no fees or charges. If you were blind, and wanted to have the freedom a guide dog could give you, then you made an application. When your name came up, they'd call you. You would go to their place where they had the rooming facilities, you would meet your dog, then you would spend the next two weeks training with the dog, always having the dog with you, even at night the dog would sleep on the floor right next to your bed. Each day you would have a routine. You would get up, take a shower, have breakfast and then go out with your dog. To watch these dogs work with their new owners was really something to see. I met and became friends with Eric when I went to see him about purchasing a puppy. When Eric found out I was an actor, he asked if I might be able to help him get some "names", some TV personalities to be the host or hostess at the Graduation Ceremonies when the people had finished their training and were taking their dog's home. I volunteered, and I hosted a graduation, and I promised to find them celebrities for future ceremonies – which I did. I also had picked out a little male puppy, which Eric said I couldn't have until he was twelve weeks old and also had his hips checked. He told me not to get too attached to the little guy until he had a clean bill of health. The puppy was certified as healthy, and Eric told me that he had a small defect, only one testicle had "dropped", so I wouldn't be able to breed him. I had no intention of breeding him anyway, I just wanted the little guy. Eric said that normally he wouldn't sell a puppy with what was considered a defect, but if I still wanted him, he was going to let me have him. I wanted him and I got him. I named him "Rayne", and he was with me for twelve years – a great dog! Laura was a bit intimidated by big dogs, so she told her friends that as soon as Rayne grew up to full-size, she expected our relationship to be over because she didn't think she could live with a large dog, and she knew I wouldn't give him up. Funny about that! She came to love the dog, and Rayne became her complete protector! He would go everywhere with her, and she loved it! One thing I'll add about the guide dog training, Eric asked me one day if I'd like to experience what a blind person experiences using a guide dog. Of course I wanted to do it! I've always believed that as an actor (maybe even just a civilian) you should take every opportunity to learn something, even if it's something you might fear. So, off to downtown Los Angeles we went one afternoon with a group of blind people all in training. A fitted blindfold was placed over my eyes which allowed my eyes to be open, but I could not see anything! No bleeding light at all, absolute total darkness, with my eyes opened! It was certainly disconcerting. Eric gave me my guide dog, and instructions about where I was to go. It was just around the block. I never had to cross a street, but I had to pay attention to my guide dog, who would stop me before I got to each corner. It was both an incredible and terrifying experience. Hearing all the traffic noise and people walking by you, and having to trust the guide dog, my eyes wide open and not be able to see a thing! Eric and his helpers were watching me, which I didn't know - as far as I knew I was on my own for four blocks! When I had completed the task, which the guide dog performed beautifully, bringing me safely around the entire block, I was soaking wet! I had perspired completely through my undershirt and casual shirt! And it was not a hot day! An unbelievable experience!

As I previously said, these years were good years. My work luck continued and I got cast in two films, a small role in "The Terminal Man", which starred George Segal, and, on the heels of "The Terminal Man", I was cast in a film with Charlie Bronson in a supporting role. Nineteen years later I would do another film with Charlie. This first one was entitled "Mr. Majestyk", and it also starred Al Lettieri, Linda Cristal and Lee Purcell. It was being filmed on location in Colorado for twelve weeks. Laura agreed to move into my house in Studio City and take care of my dog, Rayne. By this time she had fallen madly in love with the dog, despite his size. A good friend of mine, Pat Anthony, a musician that played bass with Phil Everly, and Anne Murray, volunteered to cut the grass while I was gone. "Mr. Majestyk" was directed by Richard Fleisher and produced by Walter Mirisch, a real gentleman. As for Richard, I wouldn't put him at the top of my "directors I'd like to work with" list. I enjoyed working on the film with people like Frank Maxwell, whom I had known in Hollywood, Paul Koslo, Linda Cristal, Lee Purcell and Al

Lettieri. I became friends with Al and we stayed in touch until his untimely death just two years after we finished the film. Two of my best stories from "Mr. Majestyk" concern Al, who I thought was a great guy, and one hell of an actor as displayed with his work in films like "The Getaway" and "Godfather". While we were filming "Majestyk" in this small town in Colorado, Al was called back to L.A. to complete some voice work on "The Don is Dead", another film he had finished filming prior to starting "Majestyk". Al left this little town of Manzanola, Colorado, on a Friday, and was flown on a private plane back to L.A. to do the voice dubbing needed for the "Don is Dead". He returned very late on Sunday night back to Manzanola. Now Al had already been with us on location for a couple of weeks before having to make that return trip to L.A., and he knew that there was very little, if any, type of entertainment or evening enjoyment of any kind for the crew and supporting actors. Al, being a big-hearted guy, brought two young ladies of the evening - hookers - back with him to introduce to the crew guys. In addition, Al also brought back a small pillow case half-full of marijuana – again to be shared with any cast and crew member seeking to partake in the evenings or weekends. From the private airport, Al loaded into a waiting car arranged by the production company, accompanied by the two ladies of the evening and his small pillow case, and told the driver to take them to his motel. Unfortunately, Al gave the driver the address of the wrong motel. At the motel Al, with the ladies and the small pillow case, plus one suitcase, went up the outside staircase to what he assumed was his room. Obviously his key wouldn't open the door – it was the wrong motel. Al, being tired, and it being quite late in this little town, got frustrated that the door wouldn't open, so he just kicked it in! You can imagine the surprise this gave the older couple that were fast asleep in the room! Seeing this gangster looking large man standing in the doorway after kicking in the door! The police were called. Al was completely confused, because he thought he had come to the correct motel where he had been staying prior to flying back to L.A. So Al was arrested and taken to the local police station, where he made a call to one of the production assistants, who came to the station and explained the situation. Everyone in the town knew that actors, and especially Charles Bronson, were making a film in their little city. Now, you're wondering what happened to the two young ladies of the evening, and the small pillow case of marijuana? When the police arrived and arrested Al, they left the two ladies with the small pillow case and Al's suitcase at the motel! When Al was released, he went back to the motel, apologized to the people, and picked up the two ladies with the "baggage" that were still waiting at the Motel – where could they possibly go? And then he went to the correct motel and finally crashed for the evening! By the following morning the story had spread like wildfire through the entire company. I will add that many of the single crew guys welcomed Al back with open arms. The ladies and the small pillow case were a big hit!

Al had been working back-to-back on three big films before coming to Colorado to do "Majestyk". He had finished "The Getaway", "The Godfather" and "The Don is Dead", so he was trying to relax at every opportunity. He liked his Blackberry Brandy, and he was not opposed to partying when possible. He had a tendency to find out-of-the-way places, and convince them to open for breakfast while traveling to a location. Sometimes this would delay him just a bit before arriving at the filming site. Due to this happening on just a couple of occasions, the director decided that when the company made the move to a very remote, large log cabin-type resort way up in the mountains, where the final shootout scene would take place, we actors would be sequestered for the number of days needed to finish the sequence. That meant Al couldn't have his Blackberry Brandy, or any other way to relax, after a hard day's work.

So Al was getting a bit cranky, and with all the action taking place, requiring a larger number of "takes" more than normal, it made for some long tense days. On our final day, which started early in the morning (it was cold on the mountain top at this resort location), the director wanted to film this shootout scene that required Al's character to be on top of the roof with a shotgun. He was to shoot the various characters as they ran out of the resort.

    As they were preparing to film the scene, Al shouted down to the director and asked, "Who do I shoot, Richard?" The director looked up at Al and replied in a very prissy manner, "Well, if you had read the script Al, you'd know who to shoot." I don't need to add that this was the last straw that broke the camel's back completely in two. Al had been a bit like a caged animal, and he was not in the mood. Al shouted back at Richard, the director, in a growl that resonated throughout the mountains, "Dick, if I had read this fucking script – I wouldn't even be here!! So tell me who to shoot, and I'll shoot 'em!" We did finally finish the filming at the resort, and we were returned to civilization that evening. I loved Al Lettieri!

    I enjoyed working on the film, and, with the approval of the stunt coordinator and the director, I was able to do all of my own driving in the film, and I learned how to do a roll out of a car right before the trunk was blown off and come out firing my pistol at the bad guys. All great fun!

When the film was finished, I headed back to Los Angeles with a flight scheduled out of Denver. Of course with me there was always a little drama! I arrived at the airport in plenty of time, in fact way too much time, to make the last remaining flight to L.A. For some unknown reason, after checking in at the gate (which was a hell of a lot simpler in those days), I wandered around the airport and lost track of time. While meandering back toward the departing Gate, I spied a very frantic airline hostess (we called them stewardesses in those days) calling my name. Due to SAG rules I was flying first class of course, and I was the one first class passenger that was checked in - but missing! I ran out to the departing gate and was stopped by an airline employee who had just closed the gate – No Passengers Allowed Beyond This Point. I went around him and ran out onto the tarmac where they had just removed the rolling stairway from the plane. Obviously my luggage was already checked on the plane, so here I was, alone, standing in front this large jet plane that had just started to move. I begin jumping up and down, waving my arms frantically, finally falling to my knees with my hands placed in a prayer-like manner, and literally pleading with a "please-please" let me on the plane look, as an airline employee was rapidly approaching, and just as he grabbed my arm, I saw him look up at the Pilot. Being part of the ground crew, he had on headphones. I heard him say, "Okay, I'll tell them." Then I saw the rolling staircase being guided back to the plane, the plane had stopped, the staircase was rolled up to the door of the plane, the door was opened and I was instructed that I could board the plane! The passengers on the plane must have thought that this was some incredibly important person that the plane had stopped for. As I got into the plane, and thanked the pilot profusely, he was still laughing and remarked he couldn't have continued moving anyway – I was in his way! As I took my seat in first class, most of the people in coach (where I usually sit) were straining their necks for a look at this obvious V.I.P. None of them know to this day that the plane was stopped by the kindness of an airline pilot, just for this Blue Collar Actor! Of course if I did that today at the airport , I would simply be shot! (And rightly so.)

    Once I arrived back at my house in California, and was properly greeted by my girlfriend Laura, and received a wonderful face licking by Rayne, "the wonder dog", I was informed that my agent, Alex, wanted me to call him as soon as possible. I was wanted for a new TV Movie-of-the-

Week, "The Vince Lombardi Story", starring Ernest Borgnine. I had literally been cast while I was in the air returning from Denver, Colorado! I had one day for a wardrobe fitting, and then the following day I was to report to the downtown L.A. location where my scenes would be filmed. This was the first time I met Ernest Borgnine, when he invited me to share his limo so we could run our lines on the way to the location. I got to know him, and less than ten years later, Ernie and I would be guests at a Buckingham Palace cocktail party hosted by Prince Phillip!

After "The Vince Lombardi Story", I was cast in my first "hit man" role for the "New Perry Mason" series starring Monte Markham, thanks to my director friend, Leo Penn. The end of the year was approaching and there was talk of doing a road tour with a play we had performed with great success at The Melrose Theatre. It was Oliver Hailey's "Father's Day". Barbara Rush had seen the play at The Melrose, plus she was great friends with Tom Troupe, the director, and Carole Cook, one of the female leads in the play. Barbara had been approached about touring in a play of her choice for a legitimate theatrical production company and she liked "Father's Day". While this was taking place, all the discussions and possibly dates, the New Year arrived and I was hired to do an episode of "Owen Marshall". I also asked Laura to marry me. She agreed, and the next thing I knew we were planning an August wedding at St. Charles Borromeo Catholic Church in North Hollywood. Of course, there was a slight hurdle to overcome – my first marriage! However, since my first marriage was not performed in a Catholic Church, it was not recognized by the Catholic Faith. So if we were willing to attend the proper classes, since we were both members of the Catholic Faith, we could have a sanctioned marriage performed by a Catholic Priest. Laura, being Irish-Italian, and her family were all Catholics and expected us to have a Catholic marriage ceremony. While we were busy dealing with all the instructions for the upcoming nuptials, I was hired to do the original "Wonder Woman" Movie-of-the-Week starring Cathy Lee Crosby as Wonder Woman. Another young actor, Kaz Garis, did the leading male role of Steve, the Interpol Agent. I played his sidekick, the guy always trying to date Cathy while not knowing that Cathy was really Wonder Woman. I also ran into a couple of the actors I had some history with from New York. Richard X. Slattery, still up to his old tricks of trying to break me up at every opportunity, and Andrew Prine – remember he bumped me out of the replacement role for Tony Perkins on Broadway in "Look Homeward, Angel". . Once again I learned a valuable lesson in the film business. In a scene with Richard, my character has to carry and load a bag filled with three million dollars onto the back of a donkey, money to be paid to the bad guys so they don't blow up a factory. I'm standing outside the door where Richard's character, a science professor, has fitted a tracking device on the donkey. On a light cue, I enter the room with the bag full of loot, take it over and throw it across the donkeys back. During the rehearsal I noticed that the bag, supposedly full of three million dollars, was very light. So in my "true-to-life actors training," I made a comment to the prop guy about the bag being too "light." It wasn't believable that it contained three million dollars, so I "requested" that they give the bag some weight. Big mistake! Young actor should never tell old prop man how to do his job! Young actor should "fake or act" the weight, not say, "it needs some weight." The prop guy shouted out to his department, "Hey, this guy says the bag needs some weight, so give it some weight." The bag was brought over and set down by my feet. The director called "action" for the scene – I stood by waiting for my light cue, then reached down to pick up the bag. It now weighed about sixty pounds! My cue light came on, I entered the room struggling with the sixty pound bag, walked over to the donkey and somehow managed to get the bag over the donkeys back! The director called "Cut!" we had the shot, now only needed to film the close-ups. As I was waiting to do the close-up, the prop guy walked past me and said, "Was there enough weight in the bag?" I saw Slattery chuckling, and my guess is he had something to do with the "weight" the prop guy added to the bag! Lesson learned!

After the "Wonder Woman" job, we were all hoping it would go to series. While waiting, I was told that the play "Father's Day," was booked to open at The Huntington Hartford Theatre in Hollywood in August, the same month my wedding was planned. I had done "Father's Day" both at The Melrose Theatre in Hollywood and The Off Broadway Theatre in San Diego with Barbara Rush joining the cast in San Diego. Prior to the start of rehearsals to get the play back on its feet, I was hired for a "Doc Elliott" episode. The series starred James Franciscus. I had worked with James on the feature, "Marooned", and three years later I would be doing another series with him. Laura and I were making our wedding plans, trying to figure out how to make it all work. We had made plans to bring her family out for the wedding - her mother, father and two brothers. Plus I had arranged to bring out my mom and new step-dad (this one was a good guy, never to be confused with the S.O.B. that mistreated my mom). In the meantime, while we were rehearsing "Father's Day" to get ready for our Huntington Hartford opening scheduled to run from July 10th to August 4th, we were told that we had a booking with the tour of the play in Arlington Park, Illinois, just outside of Chicago, after we closed at the Hartford.

The actress playing my ex-wife in the play didn't want to continue the tour after the Arlington Park/Chicago outing, so Laura had been asked to replace her. This meant understudying the role and rehearsing in Arlington Park. The "Father's Day" company had to be in Arlington Park by Friday the 9th, so we could set up and rehearse for an opening on Monday the 12th. So, we closed "Father's Day" on Sunday the 4th at the Huntington Hartford to make way for "Hughie" starring Ben Gazzara. Laura and I were scheduled to be married on Monday August 5th, with all the family and friends, then we were due in Arlington Park by Friday the 9th. For a brief honeymoon, we decided to take all the family to Las Vegas for two days. They all had a grand time and I even won a little money, which helped with the cost of this family honeymoon trip. After the two days, we all went our separate ways, Laura's family back to New York, my mom and step-dad back to North Carolina, and we would go to Arlington Park via Chicago. I told Laura that we would go to Europe on our "real" honeymoon later after the tour with the play was over and no other work was pending, which we were able to do in a little over two years. I was about to enter into my second marriage, and I promised myself that I intended to "behave" and not screw this one up!

Chapter Twenty-One
Wedding-Europe-Daughter

I made arrangements to bring my mom and Herman, my step-dad, out to Hollywood a few days before the wedding so they could catch a performance of "Father's Day." Mom always loved to see me perform. She saw a couple of my films at a drive-in in North Carolina when drive-ins were still operating. Plus, I wanted her to get a chance to meet Laura before the wedding. I knew she was going to love Laura, just like she loved Jan. My mom was saddened when I messed that marriage up, but never dogged me about it. My mom was a pretty terrific lady who went through her own hell with a couple of men, my dad being one.

We managed to get all of the families out to Hollywood for the wedding, and the ceremony went off without a hitch. The wedding party, in addition to the bride and groom, included Frank Christi, my best man, Eileen Penn, Laura's maid of honor, Laura's two brothers and our friends Pat Anthony and Billy Kidd as our ushers, and of course, the rest of the family members. Elizabeth Allen graciously arranged the wedding reception at her lovely Studio City home and it was star-studded for a Blue Collar Actor's wedding. Our guests included Paul Lynde, Barbara Rush, Cesar Romero

(Elizabeth's date), Frank Maxwell and his wife, Robert Pine and his wife Gwynne Gilford (parents of superstar Chris Pine), Carole Cook and Tom Troupe, Paul Kent and his wife, Eileen Penn's two sons, Sean and Christopher (both enjoyed the pool immensely) and Todd Martin (a dear friend and Actors Studio alumni). I apologize to the many friends that attended and I have left off this list. It was a grand wedding reception with a fountain of margaritas continuously flowing (I believe this was the only time I ever saw Robert Pine "tipsy"), great Mexican food and a few people partaking of a little pot. All in all, it was truly a fine affair which ended in time to allow our respective families a little leeway to prepare for their departure to Las Vegas. They all joined the bride and groom on their brief honeymoon, and then everyone finally went their separate ways.

    Laura and I joined the cast of "Father's Day" in Arlington Park, Illinois, for the two week engagement, which was met with a more lukewarm reception than our previous performances. The audience in Arlington Park didn't "cotton" to the profane language being spoken by our leading lady. On our off day, Barbara always had an invitation from some VIP's to join them for a lunch outing, always held at some upscale establishment. Barbara, a truly classy lady, always insisted that the entire cast be invited to these events, so our off days were always very enjoyable. Regardless of the reception from some of the people that attended the play, it was still considered a success, and we were to continue onto The Parker Playhouse in Fort Lauderdale, Florida, after first returning to L.A. We were losing two of our cast members. Gwynne Gilford, who played my ex-wife, didn't want to continue the tour. And Paul Mantee, the actor playing the ex-husband of Carole Cook, had another commitment. Laura stepped in for Gwynne, and Tom Troupe, our director and also the husband of Carole, took over the role vacated by Paul Mantee. This cast would stay together for the remaining run of the tour, which was substantial.

    We had four weeks at The Parker Playhouse, then we returned to The Huntington Hartford in Hollywood for another three week engagement, where we had enjoyed such success in our previous run. Being back in Hollywood, Laura and I were finally able to start setting up our house and rejoining our dog, Rayne. Erich Renner had been kind enough to watch over Rayne back at Rayne's original home while we were on the road.

    While putting the house together, I had my eye on a large four-poster reproduction of an early American circa-1800 bed. It was a bit costly, so that entailed a trip to my business manager, Lee Winkler, to make sure that I could afford it, or, more accurately, to find out if he was going to advise me that I could afford it. Arriving at Lee's office, I enjoyed my first encounter with Burt Reynolds, one of Lee's big clients. Lee was on the phone, but motioned for me to come on in. As I came into the office, he greeted me, which prompted the guy on the phone to ask him, "Who is it?" Lee was talking to Burt, and they were discussing a number of things, most notably Burt's centerfold for Cosmopolitan Magazine, which he regretted doing. Lee answered his question by replying, "It's Jordan Rhodes, he wants to know if he can afford an expensive large four-poster bed." Burt said to Lee, "Tell Jordan, I have one of those beds, and it's great." I called over the phone and asked Burt if his four-poster had the two steps to get up into the bed. Burt replied back, "Tell Jordan my ladies don't need steps to get into my bed." I answered back and told Lee to tell Burt, "The steps were not there to help my ladies get into bed, the steps were there to help them get out of the bed!" I could hear Burt's great infectious cackling laugh over the phone as we all broke up. It was a terrific introduction to Burt Reynolds. I admired Burt through his entire life and career. Lee approved the purchase of the bed.

As we were winding down our second engagement of "Father's Day" at The Huntington Hartford theatre in

Hollywood, we found out that a branch of The American Conservatory Theatre, namely, The Marine Memorials Theatre in San Francisco, had offered us an engagement to bring "Father's Day" for an unlimited run starting March of 1975. Obviously, we were all thrilled as we were continuing to work.

After we closed at the Hartford, Laura and I continued to improve the house. We brought in Billy Kidd, a very good friend and extremely talented designer, who did wonderful improvements adding wallpaper. I put in a second bathroom in the master bedroom, which turned the house into a two-bedroom, two-bath living space. We did some more wallpapering and flooring in the large kitchen, and we had the exterior of the house painted white with red trim which gave it the appearance of a little cottage. Laura picked most of the colors and wallpaper, consulting with Billy "The" Kidd, as we called him.

During this break from the play, I continued to audition for parts whenever my agent would call. But mostly we were enjoying the time. One Sunday, as it was getting close to Christmas, we were driving out to a favorite Mexican restaurant in the Valley and we drove past the Gabriel & Olsen Porsche-Audi Dealership. Roman Gabriel and Merlin Olsen were two outstanding players for the Los Angeles

Rams and they were partners in the dealership. I was a big Rams fan. Much later I would become very good friends with Roman Gabriel, the quarterback of the Rams, and I played in a number of his celebrity golf tournaments for various charities. I would also work with Merlin in his TV series, "Father Murphy". But this day, a beautiful Porsche 911, metallic brown with a tan leather interior, caught my eye. I whipped my car into the dealership lot, got out, went in and enjoyed the beautiful lines of this incredible machine. A salesman approached me and asked if I'd like to take one for a test drive. I took one for a test drive. Within two weeks I was asking Lee, my business manager, if I could afford one. Lee had already set me up with my first ever lease of a Mercedes, but I wanted to purchase the Porsche. After all, Laura's little Opel didn't have air-conditioning, so we could sell that, and she could drive the Mercedes. That sealed the deal with her - she wanted me to get the Porsche. I would take the Porsche as my car, because it was a stick-shift and Laura couldn't drive a gear shift car, so she would drive the Mercedes and I would drive the Porsche. To help me with my plea to Lee and soften the blow to my finances to purchase the Porsche, I was cast in a "Barnaby Jones" episode starring Buddy Ebsen. Then I got called for another "Marcus Welby, M.D." Laura had also been cast in a daytime series,

"The Doctors," as Nurse Penny Peters. "The Doctors" was syndicated and not on a major network. But one advantage of that meant they didn't work all the time like a regular daytime series, such as a network soap opera. They would do five or six shows at a clip, then take a lot of time off, so it was a good schedule for her. With the play "Father's Day" set to open in San Francisco in March, plus the additional work I was doing in television, Lee agreed to let me purchase the Porsche 911. His only requirement was that I let him arrange the deal with a Porsche dealer in Burbank where his clients leased a lot of vehicles. He got me a great deal! The Blue Collar Actor acquired toy number three! Man, was it some toy! Without a doubt, the best machine I've ever owned! It also looked really good when I would drive onto the Universal Studio lot, where I had made it a regular routine to always gift Scotty, the gate guard, with a bottle of very rare Scotch whisky on each holiday. That allowed me to drive onto the lot even when I wasn't working, and Scotty would always assign me a parking spot! Of course, my winning and pleasant personality also helped! But not as much as the Scotch!

    I continued to work before we left for San Francisco to do the play. I got cast in an episode of "Ironside", Raymond Burr's new series. Then Leo Penn cast me in a very good episode of "Switch", which starred Robert Wagner and

Eddie Albert. You might remember I had worked with Eddie on "Green Acres", where he didn't "cotton" to me, but he obviously didn't remember - I did. This time it went well.

I would go on to have a long and good friendship with Robert Wagner, "R.J." to his friends, which I'm proud to be one.

In March, we left for San Francisco with our clothes in the trunk of the Mercedes, and Rayne, the wonder dog, occupying the entire back seat. We wanted a couple of refresher run-throughs of "Father's Day" before opening at The Marines Memorial Theatre, a beautiful theatre of about 650 seats. Our cast was the same since the Parker Playhouse in Florida. Carole Cook, Barbara Rush, Laura Wallace, Tom Troupe, Paul Kent and me. San Francisco was a terrific town in those days, nothing like it is today. There were only a few places where you were better off avoiding - most of the city was a fun place to be. We had a run of sixteen weeks and the audiences loved the show. Always a good feeling for an actor when an audience gives off the vibe that they're really enjoying your work. I purchased two blue-colored sweatshirts with The American Conservatory Theatre blazoned across the back, and a small A.C.T. Emblem on the front left. As it turned out, these sweatshirts served us well when Laura and I finally took our European honeymoon.

After our run in San Francisco, we packed up and headed back to our little abode in Studio City. With no immediate work on the horizon, I checked with Alex, my agent, and informed him that I was thinking about taking Laura to Europe for our delayed honeymoon. He wasn't too happy about my plans to take about twenty-eight days for this trip, but I informed him that I didn't want to worry about our schedule. We weren't planning on doing any type of "tourist tour." We were planning on a "free-lance" visit and didn't want to be tied-down to an exact number of days. I began planning our trip. Fortunately, before I had made any airline reservations, or the reservations I wanted to lock-down for London, our planned first stop, I got cast in a big Movie-of-the-Week, "Once an Eagle", starring Sam Elliot and a huge cast. It was touted as an important MOW, and received a lot of press. While I was filming my role, a few days' work, I continued making our reservations, both with the airlines and the small hotel we would be staying at in London. I had devised a good wardrobe plan for us. We would wear nice jeans and buy a couple of corduroy jackets, sport-coat style. I'd packed a couple of shirts that I could wear with a tie. Laura would pack a dress for any restaurant that wouldn't allow a lady to wear jeans, and we'd take our A.C.T. sweatshirts that I bought in San Francisco.

Our deal with each other was if you pack it to wear it, you had to carry it! This way, we were limited to one suitcase each, small enough to carry by hand. Laura would take one shoulder bag, and the same for me. We were off!

Chapter Twenty-Two

London, our first stop was great. Didn't rain much at all, which was a good thing because we didn't bring a Bumbershoot – English for umbrella. Stayed in a nice little B&B. On our second night in London we were attending a play (I don't recall the name), and as we were seated, Bill Murray (the writer, not the actor) and an actress we knew from L.A., Sandy, Bill's "main-squeeze", came and sat down right in front of us! Now what in the world are the chances of that? Our first trip ever out of the States, and the second night abroad I see a writer and director I know from L.A.! I had done a play for Bill at The Melrose Theatre. It was about the Kitty Genovese murder in New York City, entitled "Witnesses". Where all these people in her neighborhood heard her screaming for help while she was being stabbed to death, and the assailant, scumbag, murderer, kept coming back, and repeatedly stabbed Kitty to death. Not one neighbor called the police for this poor girl! It was quite a powerful courtroom drama based on the attitude of the neighbors. I played the young prosecuting attorney. Bill wrote the play and directed it. And here he was sitting right in front of me in a London West Side theatre! Bill likes to say that he heard this very southern voice call out, "Hey,

Bill!" Obviously we got together after the show. Bill and Sandy were headed to Rome to meet with Martin Balsam, a fine actor most should remember from his being attacked and killed on the steps by Tony Perkins in Alfred Hitchcock's "Psycho". But Marty had an incredible career. Bill suggested we meet them in Rome, and after I told him we were "free-lancing," traveling without reservations, he gave us the name of a place where we could get a room. So, our trip to Rome was now arranged.

After seven days in London, we went to Paris. What a beautiful city. We made sure to avoid any of the places that catered to wealthy Europeans and Americans, so we found this little pension (pronounced pensione in Italy) on the West Bank that was within walking distance to The Louvre. We spent two days there, and it wasn't anywhere near enough time to see all the beautiful and incredible art work. The place is just incredible!

We found the French people, the working class people, to be very friendly and helpful. Laura could speak a little French, but if you made the effort, they appreciated it and would gladly help you. We had a wonderful time in Paris and almost every corner is a postcard! We left by train – we had purchased Eurail Passes for train travel - and were going to Lucerne on the advice of some people in London. This is where wearing our A.C.T. sweatshirts really paid off! We got on the train to Lucerne. It was fairly crowded and we couldn't find two seats together. I might add that the trains in Europe, for the most part, are pretty luxurious, nice size comfortable seats and big windows. They also travel at a high rate of speed. While searching for a couple of seats together, and without knowing, we wandered into a private car as the train was leaving the station. I couldn't read the notice in French that the car was a private car. It was for a group of hair dressers returning to Lucerne from a huge convention in Paris. As I peered into one of the compartments, where there were a number of seats, just three people were sitting in the compartment. I asked if we could sit there? A very nice man, upon looking us over, invited us in, and obviously observing our blue sweat shirts, asked us if we were members of the "Conservatory Theatre". I explained we were American actors that had just finished working at "The American Conservatory Theatre" in San Francisco, and that this was our honeymoon trip to Paris and Lucerne.

  That broke the ice in an incredible fashion. The man and his wife were Rene and Fineta Kaufman. Rene was a well-known hair dresser and stylist, and they were returning home to Lucerne after this huge convention in Paris. Rene was French and spoke English, French and Italian. His wife,

Fineta, was Italian and she spoke Italian and French, but not a word of English. So Rene was the interpreter. We were now joined by various people from the other compartments in this private car. Pretty soon we had wine, cheese, food and treats, and the compartment had turned into a party room! Rene and Fineta invited us to their home in Lucerne for dinner and to meet their kids. Rene also wanted to give Laura the newest hair style cut from Paris, and invited us to his shop in Lucerne.

    Once we arrived in Lucerne, we said our goodbyes to all the people we had been partying with from Paris, collected the address of Rene's business for Laura's scheduled haircut, found a quaint little hotel in the "old" section of Lucerne, and crashed for the night. Bright and early the next morning, we had breakfast at a nice little café, did a bit of sightseeing and headed over to Rene's Hair Salon for Laura's hair appointment. . Once we were inside and greeted by Rene, he went to work on Laura's hair which was shoulder-length. When Rene started his scissors flying on Laura's hair, I could only think of Edward Scissorhands and had to excuse myself. I went outside the shop and waited until I assumed the worst was over, then slowly returned. Rene had given her the greatest "Jean Seberg look" you could imagine. She looked great! And she kept that short hair look for quite a while.

She did confide to me that she had to take a deep breath after first seeing the "look", but she did love it. That evening we had dinner with Rene and Fineta and met their kids, whose names escape me, but we had a wonderful time.

After asking us about our travel plans, I explained that we were not on any set travel schedule. We intended to visit Italy, Amsterdam and the French Rivera. They invited us to join them on their vacation in the south of Italy, the Italian Rivera, where some of Fineta's family resided. We immediately accepted, changed our travel plans to coincide with their plans, and agreed we would meet them in the south of Italy.

With the change of plans, our next stop was Amsterdam where we observed marijuana growing out of many planters and "waving" in the breeze on the decks of boats in the canal. We walked through the "Red Light" district with me glancing at the various "wares" on display, a little sightseeing which was a treat for us both - especially for me since I'd never enjoyed any "exotic" foreign locations on any of the films I had done.

We left Amsterdam and headed to Rome where we were scheduled to meet my friend and writer, Bill Murray – remember, we had seen Bill and his girlfriend Sandy at the London theatre. We checked into the small hotel that Bill had recommended, got in touch with them and we all had dinner that night with Bill, Sandy, another friend of theirs (I can't recall the name) and the actor, Martin Balsam. Dinner that night extended into the wee hours of the morning and was an absolute treat, with Marty constantly entertaining us with his stories of working for this Italian director in a film, and the director spoke no English! The following four days we spent visiting all the sites, and I took a turn in the Roman spot to spew out the "Friends, Romans, Countrymen, lend me your ears" speech to no one in particular. As an actor, I just wanted to do it – so I did! From Rome, we went to Florence, and we got caught up in a communist street demonstration and riot which we escaped unscathed. We were not so lucky with the mosquitoes that had invaded the city because the waterways were so low, they made comfortable sleep impossible. We were not saddened to vacate Florence for the south of Italy, the "Italian Rivera", where we met the relatives of Rene and Fineta Kaufman.

After another train ride from Florence over to the "Italian Rivera", I have to add that the Italian trains were not quite as comfortable as the other European trains.

I don't remember the name of the little city where we met up again with Rene and Fineta. It was as though we had never been apart. We had such a wonderful relationship with these people, regardless of how short our time together had been. We met Fineta's cousin and his family. His name was Arturo and he had been a resistance fighter during World War II. He would hide out in the mountains during the day and fight the Germans. At night he would sneak back down into the village where different people would hide him for the night. Then he would go back up into the mountains early in the morning darkness to fight the Germans again. He was a fascinating man. He had built his house with his own hands, where we all stayed with him and his family. We spent two wonderful days and nights with them, including bathing in the cold water that came from the "shower room" constructed outside the house. Talk about enjoying life experiences for an actor – baby, this was it! Listening to Arturo's stories, you could never make that stuff up!

We were saddened to leave these new found friends, and we stayed in touch with Rene and Fineta for years after our trip.

From there we made a quick trip to Monte Carlo on the French Rivera. Even though it was incredibly beautiful, and also incredibly rich, it didn't excite us after leaving the Italians in the mountains! We did have a little luck in the casino, but the gambling atmosphere was extremely subdued, so one night was enough for us.

We had a wonderful breakfast on our little terrace overlooking the magnificent yachts, did a bit of looking around, called it a day, and left the following morning to return to London, where we would catch a flight out of Heathrow and take the long journey back to Los Angeles. We had spent twenty-eight days in Europe enjoying experiences we had never imagined. It was a great trip, and certainly a fitting honeymoon!

Back home in Studio City after clearing customs in New York, which took us forever (I can't imagine what that process is like today), we took a day to adjust from the jet lag, whatever that is, maybe another word for "tired." We reunited with Rayne, the wonder dog, and settled into our routine. Within days, my agent called me about an audition for James Franciscus's new show, "Hunter". I got the part, my third show with James. Then Laura decided she'd like to have our dining room painted. I went out, gathered up the paint and drop cloths (they were really made out of plastic so why we called them drop "cloths" is another mystery to me). I was busy painting our dining room, when out of the blue I received one of those strange calls from Alex, my agent, which I would occasionally get from him. He told me he had just received a call from the office of Quinn-Martin Productions, and they wanted to know if I'd be interested in the recurring role as the D.A. on their hit series "The Streets of San Francisco". Alex proceeded to tell me that I'd have to stay in San Francisco during the time I was on the show, and that I wouldn't be available for any other shows while I was doing "Streets". So he didn't know if I would be interested or not! I had to shake the phone receiver a couple of times to see if I was hearing him correctly! Was I interested in a recurring role on "The Streets of San Francisco"? Was I interested in working with Karl Malden? Here I was painting our dining room, and my agent is asking me if I'm interested in doing a recurring role on a hit TV series!!! Well of course, I was not only interested, but when did I have to leave? I went to work on "The Streets of San Francisco". When I was hired to recur as Jerry Billings, the D.A., I was replacing John Kerr. He had been doing the role of the D.A. for a few seasons, but he left due to some "creative differences". I had no idea at the time that Karl Malden was the man responsible for getting me the job. I had been hired to do a guest shot on the show in the previous season and I had worked with both Karl and Michael Douglas in that episode. Michael had announced that he was also leaving the show to produce the film version of "One Flew Over The Cuckoo's Nest," a play that his father, Kirk Douglas, had starred in on Broadway and had owned the movie rights for over ten years. Richard Hatch, a young hot actor, was coming in to take over Michael's role. The Quinn-Martin company was anxious to keep Karl happy, and now, with a new guy coming in, Karl was going to need to work at least five days a week, since Michael's character and storyline would no longer take a couple of days a week, until the new guy could be established. So the production company wanted to bring in a new D.A. that was capable of taking up some of the slack in the show and allow Karl to have a day or two off in a grinding season of shows. Lead actors work 10 to 12 hours a day on a series, and when it was a hit series in those days, you did 26 episodes a season. They went to Karl and asked him if he had any suggestions for the new D.A. Karl had remembered me from my appearance on the show in the previous season, and my character was an attorney whose partner was killed by an ex-convict, so Karl suggested they bring me back as a D.A. who left his private practice to join the D.A.'s office. Karl never said anything about this to me. I learned it later from someone in the production office after I had been on the show for a while. I learned a great deal from Karl. He was always looking out for me. If we were crossing the street in a shot, he'd take my arm and pull me closer to him and say, "Stay close, that way you'll always be more in the shot". He really looked out for me - even with the make-up people. He taught me that you always worked for the "good of the scene, the good of the story." He was just terrific to work with, and if you could leave your ego home, you would always learn something from working with him.

I'll only write one "funny" story here, which says a lot about our "working" relationship. You may remember that Karl's character, Mike Stone, always wore a tan raincoat. One afternoon, we were doing a shot outside and it was quite warm. Karl had, of course, established his raincoat as always, and my character was just in a suit. I noticed Karl was perspiring a bit, so I commented about him being a little warm in the raincoat. Karl just nodded and gave a little, um huh….and said no more. We didn't finish the shot that day, and had to return early the next morning. Now I don't know if any of you have ever spent any time in San Francisco in the late summer, but someone once wrote that "the coldest winter I ever felt was the summer I spent in San Francisco". Translation – it's a bit brisk in the early mornings in San Francisco. We were finishing filming the shot of the previous day in the early morning. It was, to be kind, a little "chilly", and I was kind of shaking while trying to stay warm. Karl, in his tan raincoat which had been established in the scene, just looked over at me, and commenting on my previous statement about him being a little warm, said, "Better to have it and not need it, than to need it and not have it".

I got the message! I'm thankful that quite a few years ago I took the time to write him a letter expressing my thanks for all he taught me, and his kindness toward me during the time I worked with him.

During my short seasons on "Streets" before it was cancelled, I met Kenneth Gilbert, another director who was filming one of my episodes, and we remained lifelong friends until his death in 2019. I was greatly saddened by his passing away and regret that I was unable to attend his memorial. I'm still in touch with Ken's family. In between my episodes on "Streets", I managed to book a shot on "The Rockford Files" and worked with James Garner, another real gentleman in the business. I also did a repeat on "Barnaby Jones". Quinn-Martin Productions really liked me, and this was right before finding out that Laura was pregnant! That was a happy surprise! Prior to finishing up on "Streets", I was hired to play a "movie star" in Barbie Benton's fantasy on - what else? "Fantasy Island". I had a chance to work with Ricardo Montalban, and spend a little time with Barbie Benton, many a man's fantasy at the time, and enjoyed some interesting conversation. Barbie was the first young lady that opened a conversation with me by asking if I'd ever had my toes sucked? I had to reply that I had never had that experience, to which she replied, "You should try it, it's very sensual". It was a fun show to do and I loved being a "movie star" in the script. The only time in my entire career I was ever a "movie star".

Chapter Twenty-Three

That July, our daughter, Cheyenne Elizabeth Rhodes, entered the world and has owned my heart ever since. I was there when she entered the world. Laura had planned for, and together we had practiced, both the Lamaze and Leboyer natural birth method. Easy for the father – not so easy for the mother, but I was there to both help, and lend support. Using the Leboyer method, the baby is birthed into a warm tub of water, with the father (if present and I was) taking the baby and supporting the infant in his hands. As I took her, Cheyenne's big dark eyes locked onto mine, and I was a goner! She captured my heart on that day and has never let it go. Today, she is a fine young woman who has presented me with two grandsons as of this writing, and we remain as close as ever. I'm very proud of her and the work she does with the deaf, and the community that she comes in contact with at The American School for the Deaf.

We spent a brief period of time at home with Laura and Cheyenne, arranging the baptizing at St. Charles, where my dear friend, Frank Christi, was Cheyenne's Godfather, a title that Frank loved! Laura was still the "Opel Girl" for the Buick Motor Company and got offered a gig in Seattle at the big auto show, and she wanted to do it. So, we gathered up all our needed belongings in the clothes department, packed up the now needed baby equipment and took off from Studio City to Seattle. Laura was breastfeeding at the time, so my job was to bring Cheyenne down to the Auto Show Coliseum where she would take a break and feed Cheyenne, then I'd head back to the hotel. We did that for the week of the Auto show, then we returned to our home in Studio City. During that period I was out of film work for about eight months, one of the longest periods without work I'd experienced in quite a while. I managed to direct a play at The Melrose Theatre during that time. It was a strange little play entitled "The Parade", and had to do with a man's obsession about a young lady that he observes during a parade. When she rebuffs his advances, he kills her during the parade. I told you it was a strange little play! I used some strobe lights and directed it so that the killing sequence appeared to be in slow motion. It was fairly well-received, and I enjoyed working with this young lady, whose first name was Chris. She was known as the "loves milk girl", which she modeled for and appeared on billboards all over the country with a little milk "mustache" on her lovely face.

    After my eight month layoff, I was reunited with Richard Hatch from "Streets" for a "Battlestar Galactica" episode, in which I played the role of Brace. I never thought I was particularly good in that role, but to this day it's one of the most requested pictures I'm asked to sign at the Celebrity Conventions. Afterwards, I quickly went into a "Quincy" episode, and then Laura and I were cast as a husband and wife in an episode of "Hart to Hart" where I once again joined my good friend Robert Wagner and we met his co-star, Stephanie Powers. The episode was directed by Leo Penn, and we were on location in Tucson, Arizona, so it was a very enjoyable experience. Soon after, I did a "Lou Grant" episode which was my second of that series with Ed Asner.

    It was around this time that cocaine was extremely prevalent in Hollywood. It was a time when the pay-per-view Heavyweight Championship fights were shown in movie theatres and came with a heavy price ticket. The Indy 500 race was also shown in the theatres as a pay-per-view event in those days, and a lot of people were snorting coke - the drug, not the soda. It reached a point where I could hardly attend any large party, and not find a mound of cocaine sitting on a glass table top. Now, I'm not dispensing any judgment here, I just didn't care to indulge, and I made the decision to remove myself from that environment and temptation. Laura and I were starting to discuss the possibility of moving out of L.A. to the mountains.

    By Christmas, Laura and I had discussed putting our

house in Studio City up for sale and purchasing some land in a place called Bear Valley Springs up north just outside of Tehachapi, CA. . It was a gated community and a number of fairly well know people, including some actors, made their homes there. With Christmas coming I wanted my mom and Herman, my step-dad, to meet Cheyenne, so I flew them out to California again, and as usual, we had a grand time. I always enjoyed taking my mom around and showing her this part of the world where her son lived and worked. We were doing some shopping one day at this little open-air shopping mall in the Valley - just me and mom - and I ran into Earl Holliman. He was working on a series entitled "Police Woman" that starred Angie Dickinson. I introduced him to my mom, and she was so shocked, surprised and excited to meet Earl Holliman, I thought she was going to shake his arm completely off! I finally was able to pry his hand loose from mom's, gave him a Merry Christmas greeting (you could do that in those days with no fear of a rebuttal), and departed. Mom continued to talk about meeting Earl all the way back to the house. She couldn't get over that her son knew Earl Holliman! Hey, I was on TV, but I was her son. She had just met Earl Holliman! A few nights later we were invited to a Christmas party at the home of Shirley Jones and Marty Engels. They lived a short walk from us so we didn't need to take a car. We walked over and rang the bell. Shirley answered the door and I introduced my mom, to which Shirley replied, "Hello Edith, I'm Shirley Engels, welcome, please come on in." Shirley told us to put our coats on the bed in one of the bedrooms, so we all walked back to the bedroom to deposit our coats. As we were putting our coats on the bed, my mom leaned over to me and said, "That woman looks enough like Shirley Jones to be her sister." I said, "Mom, that is Shirley Jones." Mom had this puzzled expression on her face, and said, "She said her name was Shirley Eagles". Without laughing too much, I explained to Mom that Shirley was married to a man named Marty Engels, and that she was using her married name. Mom said, well she thought she sure looked like Shirley Jones, and that was the end of it. Once again we had a great time at Christmas with my mom, more thanks for her sending me the money to bail my butt out in California all those years ago.

    Right after the holidays, we put our house on the market. We had made our decision to move to the mountains of Tehachapi. We made a few trips up there to visit the community of Bear Valley Springs to shop for a piece of land where we would build a house. Seemed like a good idea at the time.

    After getting Mom and my step-dad on their way back

to North Carolina, we set about finding a real estate agent to sell our house in Studio City. Once we had it on the market we made another trip to Bear Valley Springs, located just outside Tehachapi, to get serious about purchasing a piece of land to build what we would call our "dream house". I had my eye on a very nice seven acre parcel up around 5700 feet. The lower valley rested at 3200 feet above sea level. Naturally the seven acres was in the mountains and therefore not all level, but it had some magnificent views. Once I had announced our plans to move, using the "too many drugs here" rationale, and stating it was no place to bring up our daughter – I'm not sure if that was really my legitimate reason or not, but it's the one I used - my agents, both the theatrical and commercial ones, advised me against the move. It was too far out of town. I wouldn't be able to attend auditions on short notice. The travel would become too much, etc., etc. They were all reasonable reasons, but I just wasn't listening. Even Lee, my business manager, advised me against the move. As I remember, Laura was not 100% for the move either, but she went along with me.

    Prior to showing the house, I had heard about my dad again from one of his lady friends in Baltimore, and made the decision to take our daughter, Cheyenne, to meet her granddad. Even though it was a costly trip, I thought it was important for Dad and Cheyenne to meet each other. The meeting went well. Cheyenne and Dad really hit it off, and it was like she knew exactly who he was. The pictures we took certainly displayed an immediate bond. In retrospect, I'm glad I could get past my feelings about my dad, and bring my daughter to meet her granddad. It was the only time she ever saw him, but she still remembers it to this day.

The first year we were in the house in the mountains, Dad was hospitalized and I had to make another trip to Baltimore. Shortly after I returned to California, Dad died during my birthday month of June. I took care of all of the arrangements.

We found a buyer for the house in Studio City very quickly - the real estate market was just starting to explode in Southern California - and I got more than three times what I had paid for the house when I bought it six years ago. The two guys that bought it from me painted every room white, including the natural brick wall I had constructed around the fireplace. They did nothing else and then they sold it for almost twice what they paid me! Hey, we live and hopefully we learn! I also sold two of my "toys." I sold the Ranger 26-foot sailboat. I made out very well on that, since the oil shortage of the mid and late-70's had driven the price up, and oil was used in fiberglass boats, so I sold it for about a thousand dollars more than I paid for it. The other "toy" I sold was my beloved Porsche 911. I had a similar situation with the Porsche as with the sailboat, I was able to sell it for more than I paid for it. The Deutschemark had gotten very strong against the Dollar during the years I had the car, so the price of German cars had greatly increased. I sold it for almost three thousand dollars more than I paid for it. Here's a funny little fact – that same model Porsche 911 today, in decent condition, will sell for almost as much as I paid for it in 1974! So against all advice, we packed our household belongings and furniture in a moving van, which we followed in our Mercedes, and left Studio City for the mountains of Tehachapi and Bear Valley Springs.

Chapter Twenty-Four
Mountain Move Mistake

We lived in a rented one-bedroom A-frame house while we waited for our "dream home" to be built on the seven acre parcel of land we had purchased up at 5700 feet. Within a reasonable amount of time, the house was finished. We got our furniture out of storage and moved in. Laura wasted no time getting firmly involved in the community, and organized an amateur theatrical group and went on to direct and guide a couple of shows. One was damn good and received sold-out attendance for an entire week. Before moving, Laura and I had done a "Hart to Hart" as a husband and wife, and we got called for an episode of "Father Murphy" playing another husband and wife, and directed by my friend Leo Penn. The series starred Merlin Olson as Father Murphy, the same Merlin Olson that played for the L.A. Rams with Roman Gabriel, and owned the Auto Dealership that enticed me to buy the Porsche 911!

I continued to get called for a few auditions in L.A., but the two-hour drive, four-hour round trip there and back, got old very quick. I then made another career misstep. I told my agent I wasn't too keen on driving down to L.A. for these auditions, and I asked him to see if he would try just "booking" me for jobs. Alex made an effort to do that, but I just wasn't as much in demand as I thought I would be when I left Studio City. In the South, where I came from - remember that tobacco farm - they would have referred to the move with the term, "he got a little too big for his britches". At the time we were doing okay, and when I moved out of Studio City, and away from having lunches at Universal Studios, I wasn't aware of how the saying, "out of sight, out of mind" would work to my detriment. I had been working fairly regularly for about fourteen years, and as foolish as I was, I thought I'd just keep on working whether I was around or not. I did not realize how big a mistake it really was. As I wrote before, "It seemed like a good idea at the time".

I have always been able to adapt in my life and this was no different.

I liked horses, and Laura wanted to learn to ride, so I bought two quarter horses, built a corral down on a flat piece of the property and got into "cowboying!" I did some team penning events, and Laura learned how to ride and entered some local western horse and rider shows. There were a few actors that lived up there, most notably Chuck Connors of "The Rifleman" fame, and Jack Palance. I met Chuck one afternoon down at our General Store, which was on the gated property. Now Chuck was a pretty private guy, not prone to being outgoing because he had been in the public eye for many years, but I had my daughter Cheyenne with me and she was always a "charmer". We said hello. Chuck knew I was an actor, which surprised me, and for some unexplained reason, we became really good friends. Within a short two-year period of time, he starred in an award winning documentary "The American Cowboy," which I created and directed. Friends of mine - three brothers - Pat Anthony, Angelo Arvonio, Bobby Arvon, and their father, Angelo, Sr., all excellent musicians, did the music score to enhance the film, and they did an excellent job. Chuck and I were invited to the Cannes Film Festival with the film, and since we played golf, we were invited to be Guest Celebrities at The Cannes Film Festival Golf Tournament. I accompanied Chuck on a number of his convention appearances, and he was always coming up to the house for dinner. He loved to hold Cheyenne in one of his big hands, and also have her do her "word cards" for him. We had enrolled her in a Montessori pre-school up there and she was like a little sponge, learning everything. Chuck would bring friends up to the house to let her show-off.

  We filmed "The American Cowboy" on a 28,000 acre cattle ranch in Springer, Oklahoma, owned by A.C. Pletcher (everybody called him "Ace"), and he produced the film for me, but mainly because Chuck Connors was in it! Ace flew all of us from LAX in California to Oklahoma in his private plane, and put us up while we filmed the documentary. With this drought for acting roles I was going through, I adapted a screenplay, which I based on an original screenplay entitled "Dark Sun, Silent Shadow", which you can probably tell by the title was written in the early 60's. I did a lot of rewriting and changes to the script (with the original author's permission after payment of a nominal fee) plus changed the title to "Herk". It was the story of an over-the-hill, heavy-drinking rodeo cowboy on his last legs with the Rodeo in New York City at Madison Square Garden, and his relationship with a little ten-year-old deaf Mexican shoeshine kid, and eventually, the kid's mother. Chuck was going to star in it, and I was going to direct it. Chuck liked the script so much, he said it was going to be his "swan song". Unfortunately, trying to arrange the financing for that project, wound up costing me our dream home in the mountains.

However before that series of errors took place, my drought ended and I was hired, without auditioning, for a major mini-series. It was the first television show that Gregory Peck ever did, with a star-studded cast including Stacy Keach, and it filmed on location in Fayetteville,

Arkansas. It was entitled "The Blue and The Gray", and it was a biggie directed by Andrew V. McLaglen. I had a great time on that location and made some good friends, many of them on the high-side of wealthy, including a banker that owned his own bank! After a few weeks work I returned to Bear Valley Springs in the mountains of California. On one of my few audition trips to L.A. I met a guy, Rob Case, that was married to a lady, Elaine Roth, who had her own direct response marketing company. It was appropriately called D.R.M. They made these commercials, the ones that list a, "call 1-800-xxxxxxx" number to order certain items via direct response marketing.

    I had suffered some disappointing series rejections, including a recurring role on "Gunsmoke" because they thought my look was too similar to Dennis Weaver, who played Chester and had left the show. Then I was tested to replace Wayne Rogers on another hit series, "Mash," but it was decided I looked "too much" like Alan Alda's character, so an acting friend, Mike Farrell, nailed that job – which turned into a career. Since I was back in the drought as far as any offers for acting jobs were concerned, Rob asked me if I'd be interested in directing some of the DRM commercials for them. I started directing these DRM commercials with names like "The Talking Bible", "Rock and Roll Hits of the 50's

& 60's", "The Fish Popper", "Jiangsu Knives" and others with equally "catchy" and forgettable names – but hey, it was work! During this time, I was making every effort to secure the funding so I could film "Herk" starring Chuck. I made scouting trips to Bakersfield, California, where I had changed the location from New York City to an unknown town, where the rodeo was appearing. Needless to say this was all costly. My overhead was spiraling a bit out of control. Horses are fun to own, but they require food, horseshoes, and the occasional Vet check, all costly items. Combined with the Montessori school for Cheyenne, plus my mortgage payments due to going over budget building our "dream home", the Bear Valley Springs Association Dues, the membership fees for the country club and the golf course membership, added all together with no acting jobs coming in, and I was acquiring debt faster than a speeding plastic dish going down an icy hill! Which I did on one occasion with my daughter in the mountains!

The DRM commercials paid for some food, but didn't make a dent in my debt. I also made an effort to keep Laura in the dark about our financial situation, which was not a wise thing to do.

With all this literally coming down around my ankles, I was invited to a special screening of "The Blue and The Gray" being shown in Fayetteville, Arkansas, where we had filmed it, for a two-night presentation in a movie theatre, just like a premiere.

Of course I attended with the idea I could pitch my "Herk" film to a few of the wealthy people I had met. This resulted in two additional trips to talk about and pitch the film, but returned no results. I did receive a couple of those, "I'm willing to do some of the money if you get most of the budget" promises, but in the film world, those "promises" are always empty. Time continued to move forward, the acting drought also continued, and my "nest egg" was rapidly becoming all nest and no eggs! In addition to the discouraging work news I was dealing with, I was hit with the tragic news that my good friend, my Best Man, Cheyenne's Godfather, Frank Christi, had been shot and killed! Murdered by two low-life burglars that had been hired to kill him! Frank was shot in his carport at his home in the Hollywood Hills! I made plans to attend his memorial down in Hollywood. Laura decided it was best for her to stay home with Cheyenne and we agreed to keep the tragic news of Frank's death from her. Couldn't see any sense to try and explain a murder to a four year old. It was the most depressing trip I ever made down to L.A. The drive seemed to take forever. I left early enough to be at the memorial in plenty of time. I was scheduled to speak. In the past, I had driven at some foolish speed in the Mercedes down the mountain roads, with almost no traffic until I had to get over on the Interstate, but one conversation with my former mechanic, when I owned various sports cars, changed my attitude. His name, believe it or not, was Al Axelrod. I was bragging a bit about the road handling abilities of my Mercedes 280E at super speeds, I'll just admit to over 100 m.p.h. Al simply replied that it didn't make any difference about the handling characteristics of the car. If I blew a tire at those speeds, I would become a memory. That realization made me adjust my speed on all the future trips between the mountains and L.A. regardless of the lack of traffic on the road.

    I arrived safely at the memorial for Frank, was greeted by a number of friends, and met Frank's son, whom I never knew existed. He came over and introduced himself, and he wanted to return the Dunhill gold lighter I had given to Frank as my Best Man. It was engraved "FC the best man - love L&J." I still have the lighter to this day. After I started into the theatre where the memorial was to take place, I was greeted by another important person in my life, Jean Marie! I was surprised to see her. We sat together and listened to the different people relay their stories about Frank, and I got up to say my piece and of course, I lost it! I did manage to keep control of my emotions, and somehow struggled through to the end, injecting as much humor as possible into this somber affair. When it was all over, Jean and I decided to have a late lunch at Marina Del Rey, which obviously turned into an early dinner as we reminisced about all the fun times we shared together and had with Frank. I don't know if it was the emotions of the day, old flames still burning, or any other excuse I can come up with, but regardless, we wound up in each other's arms until late in the evening before heading our separate ways. I made the two-hour drive back to Bear Valley Springs very much alone, missing my friend all the way.

    I had one other shot with a money guy that expressed interest in the film "Herk" which Chuck and I wanted to do. This guy sent his son and a friend by private plane to Bakersfield to meet Chuck and me, and take a look at the locations I had arranged for the filming. More money spent on that day, while convincing the son I had everything in place that I had claimed for the film. When leaving, the son told us that he would recommend to his father that they finance the film. They left in the private plane, and Chuck and I drove back to Bear Valley Springs discussing our thoughts about if this guy was real or not? As it turned out, he was not! I was still experiencing my drought, which, for film and series work would last about six years. I continued to try and hold on, but not really believing we could sustain our lifestyle up in the mountains. I was in L.A. directing some more "pocket money" commercials for Rob and Elaine's DRM company, when I received an invitation to play in The Duke of Edinburgh's Cup, a celebrity golf tournament for charity, hosted by Prince Philip in aid of The Duke of Edinburgh's Award. The tournament would be played between the celebrities of the United States and Great Britain. It was an all-expenses paid invitation for me and a guest. Completely ironic at the time, since I was an out of work actor. However, one of the committee members had been involved with the Cannes Film Festival celebrity tournament that I had participated in with Chuck Connors, and "The Streets of San Francisco" was a big television hit in Great Britain! Remember, I was the D.A. Jerry Billings on "Streets", and I had been in The Cannes Film Festival tournament, so to the committee member, I was a United States celebrity! I had a couple of months to think about accepting the invitation, and I wanted to discuss it with Laura. Our discussion also included making decisions about the immediate future. With my financial well running completely dry, I needed to make some hard choices. Returning back to Hollywood was out of the question, real estate prices had soared into the stratosphere and I had quickly become a forgotten actor, even though I had Celebrity Status in Great Britain, attested to by my invitation to Buckingham Palace! Laura suggested that we could stay with her parents in Bayside Hills, Queens, just a short LIRR train ride out of the city if we wanted to go to New York and regroup. She was disappointed to leave the home in the mountains of Bear Valley Springs, but returning to her roots certainly softened the blow. Laura didn't believe it was a good idea to leave Cheyenne and go traipsing off with me to a golf tournament in England while we would soon be preparing to move. I had a few weeks before my birthday and about a month before attending the celebrity tournament in London, so I spent my time arranging storage dates for our furniture in California. I proceeded to sell our horses and all the tack, including a beautiful saddle I had acquired while filming "The American Cowboy" in Oklahoma. A bit strange to write this, but I was so busy preparing the arrangements for Cheyenne and Laura to go to New York, trying to see if I had any chance of selling the house, and getting ready to go across the Pond and be a celebrity for a week associated with Buckingham Palace, I had no time to be depressed or saddened. Laura had called her parents and asked about us coming to stay for a while – they were thrilled! At least her mother was thrilled to get her daughter,

Laura, and her granddaughter, Cheyenne. As for me, I don't think she was all that thrilled!

Chapter Twenty-Five
Buckingham Palace and Return

I accepted the invitation to The Duke of Edinburgh's Cup Celebrity Golf Tournament which took place on July 21 – 24, 1983. Now once Rob Case, the guy that I directed the DRM commercials for, discovered that Laura had no intention of going as my guest, he pleaded with me to take him. I tried explaining that if I took a male guest he would be required to at least play in the practice round. Since Rob didn't play golf I didn't see how I could invite him as my guest. Rob insisted that he would take lessons, and learn how to play well enough to participate in the practice round. He said he would cover all of our expenses. I explained that the invitation covered all the expenses, but Rob insisted he would pay for any and all incidental expenses like tips, extra food and drink, everything, if I'd take him as my guest! I liked Rob, and he was duly impressed with actors, stars, etc., especially if he could get the chance to hobnob with them. He would certainly have ample opportunity to rub shoulders with an array of stars. The United States team of celebrities included Telly Savalas, Glen Campbell, Richard Crenna, Ernest Borgnine, Steve Forest, Hal Linden, Fred MacMurray, Robert Stack, David Doyle, Greg Morris and yours truly!

The Great Britain celebrities included Henry Cooper (British Heavyweight Champ), Eric Sykes and Roger Waters (of the Pink Floyd Band).

Everything was absolutely first-class. We were flown out of LAX on British Airways and arrived at Heathrow Airport in London where each celebrity and their guest was met by these lovely young ladies, all dressed in beautiful orange jumpsuits and each driving a Rolls-Royce Sedan to chauffeur us to our hotel, The Grosvenor House in the heart of Mayfair, London. From the time we checked in until the celebration at the close of the tournament, our schedules were filled with black-tie parties and entertainment events. During our first evening's entertainment event, Glen Campbell performed, as did Hal Linden, who is quite a clarinet player in addition to possessing a marvelous singing voice. The very talented song writer, Sammy Cahn, managed to compose an original song that contained every celebrity's name. Imagine this Blue Collar Actor being immortalized in song by Sammy Cahn! We attended a number of functions prior to the day of the first practice round, which was followed by the Celebrity-Guest round, in which individuals paid an enormous fee to play a round of golf with one of the celebrities. I don't recall the exact amount of the fee, but it exceeded two hundred pounds! After all, it was for the Duke's charity! I will also add that the English golfers play a fine round of golf and take the game quite seriously! I was very happy to be playing to my 14 handicap. Our celebrity stars that could really play the game were Glen Campbell (he was a scratch golfer), and both Robert Stack and Steve Forrest, who managed to hold their own. After we had completed our required "party circuit," and the day before the practice round we were all invited to a cocktail party at Buckingham Palace, hosted by Prince Philip. It was black-tie as well, and we were once again driven by our lovely chauffeurs in the Rolls-Royces to the Palace. I was certainly traveling in "high cotton" to use a Southern phrase. Of course, even back then there were major security measures, including metal detectors scanning the underside of the cars as we were driven in, and metal detectors arrayed before the entrance into Buckingham Palace.

  Prince Philip was a most gracious host, making it a point to personally greet and visit with each guest. It was not a quick handshake and out visit, he took the time to engage each guest, myself included, in conversation, and as expected he was fluent on a myriad of topics. There are two funny memories from that evening in Buckingham Palace, or "Buck House" as some English subjects refer to it. One naturally involves my guest, Rob Case. Quite early in the evening during our cocktails and finger sandwiches, Rob managed to slip one of the engraved bronze or pewter small ashtrays from one of the tables into his pocket. Rob was quite pleased with this confiscation, and opened his jacket pocket to show a couple of us the souvenir he had acquired. Imagine his surprise, when we advised him about the metal detectors we had passed through to enter the Palace, and once again we would have to pass through on our exit. Rob spent the rest of the evening trying to find a proper time when he could return the ashtray to a table!

This next item is not as funny, but it demonstrates a very real side of Ernie Borgnine, at least to me. I worked with Ernie, and enjoyed his down-to-earth friendship. He approached me during this affair, and asked me in dead seriousness, "Jordy, have you been to the bathroom yet?" I said that I had not. Ernie said, "You got to go – they have gold toilet seats and handles in there".

It was a wonderful evening, and so far from my uncle's tobacco farm and any illusions, or expectations I ever imagined I might someday encounter. Afterward, we enjoyed three days of competitive golf, and I'm unhappy to report that we got creamed! Only a couple of our U.S. celebrities won their matches, including Glen Campbell, who as I mentioned before, was an excellent golfer. A few others did "halve" their matches. I believe we lost by seven to four. We were given a beautiful golf bag, some golf shirts, two sweaters and some very nice pewter memorial engraved small plates and two coins, which took the sting out of Rob having to return the ashtray in the Palace. I made some lifelong friends in London and would visit them again. Two of the friends were Ian Brill, who had the clothing manufacturing concern which furnished the shirts and sweaters, and Michael Winters, an entertainer along with his brother Bernie, that performed as Michael and Bernie Winters, and were as popular in the UK as Martin and Lewis were in the States. Michael became a writer, and did very well writing about sports personalities and trainers. He moved to the States and resided in Florida.

    We checked out of the Grosvenor House, were driven to Heathrow Airport in our Rolls-Royce vehicles, and boarded the British Airways flight for the long trip back to Los Angeles. I spent the night at Rob and Elaine's condo before making the two-hour drive back to Bear Valley Springs the following day. I now had to face the dreaded task of organizing everything for Laura and Cheyenne to move to New York, leaving me to close the house, put it on the market, get all the furniture into storage and join them once it was all complete. I had returned from this marvelous time in London, as a celebrity, without any idea of when, or if, I would work again. I understand that is a constant fear of us actors, that we may never get another job!

I was able to get Laura and Cheyenne packed and taken down to L.A. for their flight to New York, with the agreement that I would follow as soon as I could get everything arranged in California. Off they went. It was getting close to the start of school and Laura wanted to get Cheyenne enrolled in kindergarten so she would have the days free to try to find some work. I was hoping to get to New York by September provided I could get the house cleaned out, get all the furniture into storage and pack up some of the clothes and toys for Cheyenne so I could ship them separately. In addition, I had to arrange to leave Rayne, our wonder dog, with a friend who had agreed to keep him, and take care of him until we could find a place and then have him transported to New York. Rayne had stayed with this friend before and they got along great. The friend's name was Dave, he worked in construction and had taken a fall off a roof, which left him with a crippled leg and on disability. So being home all the time, he loved the company of Rayne. Regardless, it was hard as hell leaving my dog behind, even harder than leaving the house, or giving up the life we had lived for the past years. There was no time to dwell on my emotions. I had too much work to do, and Rayne was keeping me company, but he knew some heavy stuff was going down, especially when the storage movers showed up to clean out the house. It took me a month, but I got everything done. I left Rayne with Dave, and, controlling my tears, climbed back in the Mercedes with the one suitcase I was taking to New York and headed out of Bear Valley Springs for the last time. The final thing I had to do before getting my flight to New York was to turn in the Mercedes. It was on a lease, and the lease was up, so all I needed to do was cover some charges for the mileage overage and turn in the key. I had arranged with Rob, my Buckingham Palace guest, to meet me at the leasing company and give me a ride to LAX for my plane to New York, where I'd be moving in with my in-laws to join my wife and daughter in Bayside Hills, Queens, in New York. It had been a very emotional two months and I was nowhere near close to seeing any end to the situation I had created. The happiest thing I could look forward to was seeing my daughter and my wife, and making a herculean effort to clean up the pile of shit that I had brought down on us.

Written By Jordan Rhodes

Chapter Twenty-Six
New York – Second Tour

Arriving at LaGuardia Airport in New York, I honestly felt like the loser of all time. I was out of work, didn't have a clue about finding any work, about finding an agent, and I was preparing to move in with my in-laws! Yeah, I felt like a gold plated loser. I knew I had to keep it together. If I came apart, my whole family could come apart. So just suck it up boy, now let's see what you're really made of!

Arriving at the house of my in-laws, Mary and Joseph Wallace, I discovered two things immediately. Laura was very happy to be living back in New York, and my daughter, Cheyenne, was a little unhappy and, I'm sure, pretty confused. However, I'm happy to say, she was glad to see me! Laura had already found a job in production with a commercial production company. The boss was a man whose last name I don't remember. His first name was Bud, and I remember he was considered a "powerhouse" in the commercial production world. His second-in-command was Michael Saltzer, who would go on to create his own company, "MacGuffin Films", and hire Laura away from Bud's company, as his production manager. Laura became so good at her job that she earned the nickname of the

"Velvet Hammer" among the agencies and crew people she worked with and hired. That first weekend after I had moved into the upstairs attic living space, which contained a bed for Cheyenne, a double bed for me and Laura, and a half-bath, with the full bath being downstairs, I discovered some of the unhappiness of my daughter. I had asked her to tell me the time while I was shaving and she didn't respond. When I asked her again she said, "I don't know daddy, I can't tell time anymore." This shocked the hell out of me. When Cheyenne left California, where she had been attending the Montessori kindergarten, she could tell time, count to well over a hundred, knew the alphabet and had a very impressive vocabulary of words. Remember "Uncle" Chuck Connors always showing her skills off to anyone he encountered?? Well, I needed to find out why my daughter could no longer tell time. I asked her what the problem was, and she told me there were so many kids in her kindergarten class the teacher couldn't spend any time with her. The following Monday morning I went with Cheyenne to school, P.S. 31 in Bayside. I noticed she had on the rattiest damn coat I had seen since my days on the tobacco farm, which she was embarrassed to wear. I asked her where did she get that coat, and she said "Nana" – that was Laura's mother, Mary - told her she had to wear it. There was no need to spend money on another coat when this "hand-me-down" was fine. I accomplished three things on that Monday. First, I met with her teacher at P.S. 31, and Cheyenne was right - the class had twenty-two students in it. The Montessori school that Cheyenne attended in Bear Valley Springs had eight students. When I asked her teacher why her skills were not being kept up, the teacher said she simply didn't have enough time to work with all the kids and had to concentrate on the kids with less skills. By the end of that day I was already looking for another school for Cheyenne.

    Second, I found a Catholic school, St. Kevins, and starting making arrangements to enroll Cheyenne.

    Third – and the thing Cheyenne enjoyed the most, I bought her a new coat! I picked her up after school and we walked to Bayside for some shopping. I let her chose the coat and her pick was a dark purple one with a gold zipper, and to highlight how important this was to her, she was five at the time and she still remembers it to this day! She gave me the description of the coat from her memory, not mine, and she says it was the "coolest winter coat" she ever had. She also reminded me that I bought her a stone-washed pair of jeans with hearts on the back pocket. To make my daughter happy was my goal and I achieved it! Mother Mary was not happy, but I didn't give a damn! I was not going to have my daughter embarrassed about her coat, or any clothes she was wearing. These were the types of issues that I always had with Mother Mary, not a bad person, just tight with a dollar. So suffice it to say, my mother-in-law never cared for me, not even when I was doing well, and most certainly not at this point in my life.

However, things were about to change. A couple of friends from California had moved back to New York City. Elizabeth Allen had been hired on a daytime drama, commonly referred to as a "soap opera", and, since she had some great Broadway credits in addition to her film and television credits, she had a leading role. Another friend, Don Chastain, was also working in the soap opera world, both acting, and, eventually, writing for them. I learned from my friend Leo Penn that his son, Sean Penn, had also moved to New York City to try for some theatre work and experience. I called Leo and asked him to have Sean call me when he had a chance. Another good friend, Art Wolff, from summer stock many years before, was now an up-and-coming director in New York, and I knew he was casting a new off-Broadway play entitled, "Heartland". I knew about the play, because he had called me in California about doing the male lead, but at that time I had no idea I would be returning to New York, and told him I couldn't make the trip to do the play for off-Broadway money. Of course, if I'd known then that my "bottom" was going to fall out I would have taken the play! I knew there was a very good role in the play for the son, and I wanted to get Sean an audition. Sean called me that evening, at my in-laws, of course, and we talked for a bit. I told him about the play and said I was going to try to get him an audition. I hung up and called Art and asked him to read Sean for the role of the son. Now you need to understand that Sean Penn was not the "Sean Penn" you are all familiar with today, the two time Oscar winner, but at this time he was trying to get his acting career started. Art agreed to have him come in the following day for an audition. I called Sean and gave him the info, and told him to let me know how the audition went. The next evening I received a call from Sean, and he was distraught. He told me that he didn't do well, that he was too nervous and felt that he messed it up. I told him to hang up and I'd call him back. I called Art and he confirmed what Sean had told me, his exact words were, "He seems like a nice kid, but I don't think he's right, he didn't impress me." I called in a favor and asked Art to have him come back the next day and audition again. Art said no, that wouldn't work. I asked him who he was auditioning tomorrow, and he told me he was reading the women for the mother's role. I leaned on him as a friend, and suggested he have Sean come in and read with all the actresses that were auditioning for the mother. I explained it would be better than having the women read with the stage manager and I ended it by using the age old "do it for me as a friend" refrain. Art agreed to do it. I called Sean and told him he was going to get another chance to audition with all the actresses tomorrow. He was overjoyed! That following evening I received a call from Art, when I answered the phone all I heard was this: "Thank you, thank you, thank you. The kid was sensational!" Sean did the role – got a huge agent that saw him in the part – got a big role in a major film – the rest is history! Now everyone knows who Sean Penn is! The tag on this story comes just a little later.

    Laura had a good friend, Doug Marlon, a former actor that took up writing with amazing success and was now the head writer on the very popular soap opera, "Guiding Light". I was back to making the rounds in New York and contacted the New York office of my commercial agent, Cunningham. They put me back on the books for auditions. I also started contacting theatrical agents with limited success. I managed to find two - The Ann Wright Agency and The Brett Adams Agency - that I could "free-lance" with, but neither would sign me at that time. Laura also suggested I make an appointment with an agent she knew very well, Honey Rader.

I arranged an appointment with her agency and, as it happened, Honey interviewed me and asked me if I was open to doing daytime drama, i.e., soap operas. Of course I was open to any acting work, and Honey Rader was THE agent for daytime drama, she handled actors, writers, directors and producers. She was the agent for Laura's friend Doug Marlon, and was responsible for submitting him for a writing gig in the daytime drama world, where he rose to his current position of head writer on "Guiding Light". Once again in my life, that little Angel, or the Fates, must have sensed I had suffered enough for the time being, having lost all of my material items, including the house in the mountains which I was unable to sell, so it reverted back to the bank that held the mortgage. Regardless of the Angel's reasoning, I was smiled upon once again. An actor from Hollywood had submitted a reel of his work, which highlighted a scene from an episode of "Hart to Hart" where I was one of the Guest Stars. This actor's agent sent the clip to the producers of "The Guiding Light" for a new continuing role on the show. The producers didn't hire the young actor; however, the show was just preparing a story line where Morgan, one of the young hot female leads on the daytime drama, was going to be kidnapped and would be rescued by a new character, Detective Hank Mitchell. The producers liked me for the Detective role! They saw this other actor's clip, which included me, yet didn't offer him the part he wanted, but liked me for the Detective! Had to be the Angel! Now, the producers didn't know if I was a "West Coast" or "East Coast" actor, and the role wouldn't justify spending the money to bring an actor from the West Coast and having to supply living expenses for the run of the role in the story line. Who did they call to find out if Jordan Rhodes was West Coast or East Coast? Honey Rader! The agent I had just interviewed with a week ago! They called Honey, and she told them I was currently living in New York.

In the meantime, Doug Marlon, the head writer and friend of my wife, heard that the producers were considering me for the role of Hank Mitchell, and he made his recommendation that they offer me the role. Ah, but there's more! I had auditioned for a play, "To Kill a Mockingbird", for the lead role of Atticus Finch, the role Gregory Peck had done so well in the film. The play was for the Tennessee Repertory Theatre company, obviously in Tennessee. I had just been offered the role, but I hadn't accepted it yet, because I didn't know if I wanted to leave my daughter without her dad again for over a month. Oh, this gets even better. The Angel must have been working overtime. I received a phone call from Honey Rader at my in-laws house where we were still staying while seeking our own apartment, and Honey said, "I have a call for you for Guiding Light. I need you to go over to CBS tomorrow for this role of a police detective, Hank Mitchell. It would be $400 a day." Now when I was working in Hollywood, my agent had gotten me up to the rate of $1,000 a day, so that was my so-called "quote". I gave this info to Honey, but she replied she didn't believe they would go that high for my first time in daytime drama. I persisted and requested that she try to get me my "rate". Honey reluctantly agreed to go back and ask them for more money. Okay, this needs further explanation for the reader to fully understand this actor's discussion with the agent regarding this "call" and not consider him to be a complete asshole, when he's out of work and considering doing a play out of town, that would pay Equity minimum, about $379 a week for five week's work. In my defense, Honey had not told me I had an "offer" of a job. She said, "She had a call for me for Guiding Light." When Honey called me back, she said they had agreed to go as high as $600 a day with a three-day a week guarantee. I decided okay, I'd go on the audition, and if they offered me the job, I'd see if I could get the rate up. I asked Honey for the particulars. She told me which CBS studio location to go to, and ask for wardrobe for a suit fitting. I told Honey I had a suit. She replied, "Well you'll need more than one, this role is working for a few months." I couldn't believe what I was hearing! I stammered around a bit trying not to sound like a damn fool, and asked about the part, what was it again, and when was I actually starting? Fumble, fumble, fumble. Honey told me I'd get all the details and the first week's scripts once I went over to CBS, but she didn't think I'd start work until next week!

Obviously I turned down the "To Kill a Mockingbird" play, which wound up enabling AEA-Equity to use their "penalty rule", a Break-in-Service rule that would eventually enable Equity to steal my earned pension credits. However, I was not aware of that "penalty rule" at the time, and even if I had been aware, I would not have turned down a $600 a day job, guaranteed three days a week on a soap opera for six months, for a five week job in a play for less than $500 a week! My continuing bone-to-pick-with-AEA.

Laura was now firmly involved in the production world of commercials, working as the Production Manager for Michael Saltzer's McGuffin Films. She was making more money than she ever made as an actress, her first Christmas bonus was $25,000! I was working on "Guiding Light" and back to making a living doing what I absolutely loved doing, even though soap operas was not one of my favorite acting platforms. But I was indeed thankful, and happily gave one hundred percent effort, as I've always done and continue to do!

We found our own apartment just three blocks from St. Kevins, the Catholic Grade School that Cheyenne was attending. In very little time her skills all came back, and she loved the new school, her new friends and teachers. She now wore a school uniform which I totally support – no kids monetary standing can be judged by the latest fad of clothing they wear. Later on we would discover that Cheyenne had dyslexia which she obviously inherited from me, since I had it as a kid, but I never discovered it until we got help for Cheyenne. No one knew anything about it when I was a kid, so I suffered some cruel comments. We were able to find the proper help and professionals to deal with Cheyenne's dyslexia, and I'm proud to add that my daughter has gone on to achieve a number of degrees including a Ph.D, Masters, three Associates degrees, and a B.A. Plus she is Board Certified in American Sign Language. I've always admitted that she inherited her brains from her mother, but her stunning good looks from me.

Chapter Twenty-Seven

After I finished my run on "Guiding Light," having worked with some very good actors, I did a few other daytime dramas. I had a short role on "One Life to Live", a little longer one on "All My Children" where I played Nina's doctor (which fans seem to remember), and I had a good run on "Ryan's Hope". I was back in New York working as an actor after starting my professional career here over twenty-five years before! After my daytime drama work, I landed a role on "Law and Order", which almost every New York actor had done at least once! I made another misstep here. I asked the agent (freelance again, not signed) to seek guest star billing for my role on "Law and Order", and they turned me down flat!

It had been some time since I had achieved that billing status in Hollywood and I wasn't thought of in guest star terms in New York, just a Blue Collar Actor, so I declined any billing, which obviously was another misstep, because it must have pissed off somebody. They asked my reason for declining billing (by the way, I was not, nor have I been, the only actor ever to decline billing). I explained my reasoning thus: If someone that knew my work saw me on the show but didn't remember my name in the guest star credits upfront, and didn't see my credit with the end credits, they might assume they just missed my name up front, instead of me receiving a lesser credit. It appeared reasonable to me, maybe for future work? But it obviously hurt someone's feelings, and was taken as an affront - an insult - to the show – which was never my intention. However, I've never worked another Dick Wolf show, and he has a bunch! Brought back memories of my Jack Webb misstep!

Shortly after I finished "Law and Order", I made an appointment to have a chat with Brett Adams at his Agency. I had been free-lancing through his agency and I wanted to ask him to take me on as a signed client. I went in and met with Brett, who always treated me well without any attitude, and I asked him to sign me. Brett explained that his talent list was pretty full, and the other agents in his office could only allocate so much time to each signed client, but he said he would give it some serious thought and give me a decision in a couple of weeks. I thanked him for the time and left. Two days later I received a phone call from Sean Penn asking me if I could come out to L.A. to see him about a film he was preparing.

I went out and met with Sean and one of the producers, Don Phillips. Sean told me he was getting ready to direct his first film, which he had written, entitled "The

Indian Runner". He wanted to know if I would consider doing a role in the film, and he wanted me to meet David Morse who was doing one of the starring roles in the film. I told Sean that of course I'd do any role he wanted me to do. David Morse showed up and joined the meeting, we three just talked a bit, getting acquainted, all small talk, then David had to leave and he asked Sean if he could see him outside the office. While Sean joined David out in the hall, Don and I talked a little about New York, how did I like being back in the Big Apple, more small talk, then Sean came back in the office and said he would like to offer me the role of Randall in the film.

Of course I said, "Great, I'd love to do it." Then Don asked me who my agent was. I said I was working out of the Brett Adams Agency but wasn't signed. Don then said, "Why do you want to give the agent ten percent if you're not signed?"

I looked over at Sean and said, "Is this guy going to screw me if I don't go through an agent?" Sean laughed and replied no, you'll get the same money without an agent as with one. I told Don we'd do it without an agent. I shook hands with Don, and Sean and I hugged, then Sean told me that David Morse had asked him out in the hall "to give me the role, because I would make the character real, whereas the other actor they were considering might campy it up, due to his type".

In short order I was on a plane back to New York, told Laura I got this role in Sean's film, and in a few weeks I was on my way to Nebraska to do the fifth role in "The Indian Runner". I was hired for twelve weeks at a great weekly salary to work with David Morse, Viggo Mortensen, Valeria Golino, Patricia Arquette (I had written quiz questions for her uncle Cliff Arquette on "Hollywood Squares" a lifetime ago), Charles Bronson (for my second time) and Sandy Dennis. Unfortunately this would be Sandy's last film, as she passed away shortly after. I had a wonderful reunion with Charlie. He had suffered a great deal of tragedy in his life since we had filmed "Mr. Majestyk" seventeen years ago. His wife, Jill Ireland, had died from cancer, and he'd lost two of his sons, one to a drug overdose and one committed suicide. I had left him a brief "welcoming note" at the front desk of the Hotel where we were all staying, and Charlie let me know how much he appreciated it.

I had a great time working for Sean, he's just as good a director as he is an actor. He allows his actors to try a number of approaches, then he uses the best one for the scene. Not only did I enjoy working with everyone on the film, but, in addition to Sean, I've kept in touch with David and Viggo. It's been fun to see how both their careers just soared after "The Indian Runner". I finished my role on the film and returned to New York, only to be called back to Nebraska a week later to do a new scene Sean had written, where I got to work with his mom, Eileen Ryan (Penn). Eileen and I had worked together in a brief scene when I did the "Bonanza" episode with Pamela Franklin. I worked about two more weeks on "Runner," then I decided to go from Nebraska to North Carolina to check in on my mom, which I did often since my step-dad, Herman, had passed away a couple of years before. Now, since I didn't have to pay ten percent of my weekly earnings to an agent (remember, Brett Adams had told me he wanted to "think" about signing me before I got the call from Sean), I had set aside the 10% each week. When I got to North Carolina to see mom, in addition to treating her to whatever she wanted, and Mom never asked for anything, I bought her a new color TV among a couple of other goodies, and a little "teacup" poodle dog she had always wanted from a decent breeder. Then I treated myself to a used 1988 Black Ford Thunderbird, using part of that 10% agent's fee I didn't have to pay, and I always referred to the Thunderbird as my "Agent's Car." I drove it back to New York in a terrible snowstorm.

    Back in New York, Laura wanted a house. She was

making good money, and I was pretty flushed at the time, though trying to be a little more sensible than my "heydays" in Hollywood, after all "The Indian Runner" was just one film, no need to go crazy. The production company that she worked for had leased her a car, so she didn't have to take the subway and LIRR Train after working late, which she always did when they were shooting a commercial. We found a nice old house in the Manor Oaks section of New Hyde Park on Long Island. It was a three-bedroom, with two full baths, eat-in kitchen, a formal dining room, a living room with a fireplace, and was situated on a corner lot. We got a decent loan (pretty amazing after my disaster in the California mountains) and we bought it. The only sad part about us finding the house was the terrible news we received, when I called Dave out in Bear Valley Springs about making the arrangements to have our dog Rayne, the wonder dog, shipped to us. Dave told me Rayne had passed away peacefully in his sleep a few days ago and he was dreading calling me, so he kept putting it off. It seems Rayne's heart just gave out on him. Dave was obviously very upset, he insisted that he had taken care of Rayne the way we would have wanted, and he wouldn't accept any money for it. It was very sad news and we had to tell Cheyenne in as positive a way as possible – even if we didn't believe the sugar-coating we put on it ourselves.

After pulling ourselves together, we went to work on the house. We set about pulling up carpet, sanding hardwood floors, painting most of the rooms and updating one of the bathrooms. By the time we were completely moved in, Cheyenne was almost ready to start high school, and we had made arrangements for her to attend St. Mary's in Manhasset, Long Island. They had a school bus that would pick her up right on the corner at our house.

My commercial agent, Cunningham, was getting me out for auditions and I booked a national commercial for a loan company. Then I broke into doing some voice-over commercials for RC Cola, Kodak, Country Music Television (CMT), The Nashville Network (TNN), plus a few more. I wasn't getting any TV jobs or film roles during this slow period, going through another one of those "will I ever work again" fears, when I met a guy that had a small production company out on the Island. I mentioned my "American Cowboy" documentary, and told him I had directed some DRM commercials in L.A. He asked if he could see the documentary. I got it to him, and he asked me if I'd be interested in directing some small business films for his company. I told him, "Absolutely," and this Blue Collar Actor started directing low budget business films for various agencies, culminating with me writing, directing and producing "The One Hundred Year Anniversary Film" for the New York Subway Company. This business film was shown in the lobby of The Subway Company on 6th Avenue right off 42nd Street for an entire year. During this time, Laura introduced me to Doug McAward, and he had a company with Herb Lobell called Lobell & McAward up in Connecticut. Herb was a well-known cinematographer in the commercial field, but was semi-retired by the time I met him. I had done a couple of local commercials for Doug, then one day an interesting situation occurred. Doug had just booked a national commercial for the Ally and Gargano Agency, what was called an "A" commercial. He was getting ready to start the prep work when his director came down with a disease called "elephantiasis." His left arm had swollen up from his shoulder to his fingers, and obviously he couldn't work. Doug didn't want to lose the job, it was a national, so Doug called Herb and asked him if he would be willing to shoot a commercial with me as the director. Doug offered Herb a combined split of the DP and Director's salary, and Herb and I would split our combined salaries. Herb agreed that he'd be happy to work with me. Now, remember that Doug hadn't even checked to see if I was available, but he was making the arrangements. Doug grabbed one of my

"director's reel." In those days, that was a video with a few commercial and business films on it. He jumped into his Jeep up in Connecticut and drove down to the Ally and Gargano advertising agency on Madison Avenue in New York City.
He went in and met with the agency people and explained the situation with the director they had approved, then proceeded to show them my "director's reel" and added, "If Jordan directs this, Herb Lobell will be the cinematographer, he'll DP the commercial." That sealed the deal. The agency went for it. Doug then called me, and I was available.
I directed my first, and only (since I never got another chance) class "A" commercial. I would like to add it was the easiest commercial I ever filmed, because I had so many assistants and crew, unlike the lower budget class "B" spots and business films I was accustomed to directing.

  After the commercial was finished, which took about a week to do the rough cut, mix the dialogue and sound, then complete the finishing touches, I got invited to the premiere of "The Indian Runner" out in Los Angeles. Now, this was not one of the big splashy premieres like the "Marooned" premiere I had attended earlier in my career, but I had a much bigger role in Sean's film. I was really excited about attending this premiere showing of the film, and fully expected Laura to accompany me to the screening.

I mistakenly thought she would be as excited as I was. However, some of the people she had been associating with in the local musical theatrical world on Long Island had planned an old school reunion, and they were going to present Laura with a little award. This event could have easily been moved back a week or two, but Laura didn't want to hear it, so she refused to go with me to Hollywood for the premiere. Our relationship was not on the most solid ground at that time anyway, and her refusal to go with me to the premiere stung me much more than I let on. I went to Los Angeles for the premiere, stayed with my director friend, Ken Gilbert, and his family, and I called my ex-wife Jan and asked her if she'd like to go with me to the premiere. She said she would love to, and we went to the premiere . It was interesting to see the film for the first time, and observe the audience's reaction to my character and his lines, which provoked some unexpected nervous laughter. After the screening, I took Jan to the party where the atmosphere was typical "Hollywood" – everybody's glad-handing everyone, and dishing out compliments galore. I introduced Jan to most of the cast that was there, and we certainly had a good time. I was making my way over to see Sean, who was seated in a corner and had motioned me to come over. You can imagine how the noise level was in this room with everyone talking, drinking, laughing and having a high energy time. As I got over to Sean, he reached up and pulled me down so he could talk privately in my ear, and took me by surprise when he said, "I never forgot what you did for me in New York helping me get the play – just wanted to say thanks." We hugged each other, and I thanked him for giving me the role. Later, when I was taking Jan back to her apartment, she asked me what was that thing with Sean all about, and I told her the story. As I said before, it was a grand evening!

    I certainly felt good on the flight back to New York, and I had gotten over my "hurt feelings" about Laura not going to the premiere with me. I have often wondered what might have happened that night if I made any overtures to my ex-wife, Jan, but I didn't, and I behaved myself.

Chapter Twenty-Eight

Once back in New York, I continued to seek out agent representation and briefly found a new agent, The Bob Barry Agency, who assigned one of his assistants that was just starting out, to "handle me". I was with him a short time and he arraigned an appointment with this management firm owned and operated by two young ladies. After meeting me they immediately got me an audition for a new pilot series that was presold for thirteen weeks and would film in Canada. It was a series developed and written by Stephan J. Cannell, the very talented creator of "The Rockford Files", starring James Garner, one of the truly good guys in the business, and I had the pleasure of doing his series a few years before. I was flown out to Los Angeles and had my appointment to be tested for this regular role in the new series, the name escapes me at this time, perhaps because I didn't get the job!

But I was dressed right for the character. It was supposed to be a Texan P.I. that worked with the series lead to chase the bad guys. I went to a friend of mine over at Universal in the costume department (thankfully old Scottie the gate guard remembered me and let me drive on the lot) and he fitted me out with a conservative western suit, shirt, tie, and hat. I already had my own boots, so, if nothing else, I sure as hell looked the part! The next day I was scheduled for my test. I remember as I drove into the parking garage at Cannell's office and was parking, I saw Doug McClure, he had worked on "The Virginian" series for years, coming out of the building, and he, too, was dressed in western garb, so I knew he had just tested for the same role. My audition went okay, and I was prompted to make a comment that broke Stephen up as I was finished with the test/audition. I walked back into the room from the studio where I had just done the test, and when Stephen asked me, "What do you think?" I replied, "I don't know Stephen, I think I did it a hell of a lot better in the living room this morning." He laughed, I shook hands with him and all the executives in the room, then headed down to the garage.

By the way, Doug didn't get the part, either. The following day I returned my borrowed wardrobe back to my friend at Universal Studios, and the next day I was on a plane to get the hell out of Dodge and return to New York. I really didn't care a whole lot for Hollywood these twenty-some-odd years later.

Back home in Manor Oaks, New Hyde Park, I took a little time to lick my wounds over another missed opportunity to be a regular on a series, even if, in that case, it was short lived – the series was canceled after one season. I decided to drive down to North Carolina to check on my mom again, since she had recently moved from Sanford to Fairmont in a house right next to her sister-in law, Elvita Harden. Elvita had granted mom the land and I helped her get this beautiful double-wide manufactured home, and had it set up on a brick foundation. Mom loved it and the home had all the latest conveniences, plus three bedrooms, two full baths, a washer and dryer, a living room, a den and a formal dining room. It was nothing like what I expected a mobile home to be, plus it was what my mom wanted. Enough said!

    Cheyenne had some after-school activities, and the production company where Laura was working had a slow period, so she could arrange to meet Cheyenne at home after the school activities, so I was cleared to take a week. I'd always leave very early in the morning and make the drive to North Carolina in about eleven hours, have a few days with mom and then return. I had been at mom's new house in Fairmont for a couple of days when she called me to the phone and told me I had a call. I answered the call and it was Leo Penn! I couldn't believe it and I asked him where he was, and he told me, "I'm in Wilmington, North Carolina". I asked him what was he doing in Wilmington and he told me he was directing the "Matlock" series at Screen Gems Studio.

I didn't know there was a film studio in Wilmington. Leo asked how far I was from Wilmington. I told him Fairmont was only a little over an hour away, and he asked me if I could come to see him, he said, "I've got something I want to talk to you about". I told him I'd drive down the following day. When I left the next morning, I told mom I'd be back sometime that evening, and I drove down to Wilmington to see Leo. He had left a pass for me to get on the lot and go to his office. After we exchanged a hug and all the "how's the family" greetings, Leo said he had a role he wanted to talk to me about in the series. He brought me in to meet the supervising producer, Jeff Peters, and we talked a little about what I'd been doing - how did I like living in New York as opposed to Los Angeles? Then Leo told Jeff he liked me for a part in this "Matlock" episode he was getting ready to film. Leo told Jeff I didn't need to read because I had worked for him a number of times, and that I had recently finished a film with his son, Sean, and he knew I could do the role. They wanted to discuss this away from me, so Leo asked me to wait in his office. I went back to Leo's office and waited, I had no idea what was going on. Pretty soon, I found out. Leo came back to his office and told me that Jeff didn't want me to do this role. Jeff had showed Leo another "Matlock" script that they wanted Leo to direct a couple of shows later, and wanted to know if I'd be interested in recurring as this new character, police Lt. Harmon Andrews. The actor that had been doing the recurring role of the police detective when the series filmed in L.A. didn't want to move to North Carolina when the show moved and continue the role, so they needed to replace him. If I was interested in doing the role, Leo and Jeff were going to discuss it with Andy, who was also an executive producer on his series, and give me a shot at it if Andy approved. Leo and I finished up visiting, and Leo promised to call me as soon as everything had been discussed. I headed back to Fairmont to spend a couple more days with mom, before making the trip back home to New Hyde Park and Manor Oaks. Laura had been asking me about getting another dog since we had lost Rayne, and now had a place where we could keep a dog. So I found a breeder of Miniature Schnauzers close to Raleigh, not too far off the beaten path for my return trip to New Hyde Park. After getting an approval from Laura on the phone, I went to the breeder and fell in love with a little black and silver Mini Schnauzer, got all his papers signed with his vet approval, bought the little guy, and purchased a carrying case, some food, a water bottle, bowl, collar and leash, loaded him into the Thunderbird, and we were off. A twelve-hour journey, including a few stops for him on the way to his new home in

New Hyde Park. We really bonded on that trip; he stuck to me like glue every time I took him out of the car. I named him Harley.

We arrived at the house late that night so Cheyenne didn't get a chance to meet Harley until the following morning. Of course, she loved him right away, and it also helped to soften her hurt a little for the loss of Rayne. And this made dad a big hero! A bit exhausted from the long trip, but still a hero! Cheyenne absolutely loved animals, and still does to this day. In our house in Manor Oaks, she had two cats, one turtle, one rabbit, a ferret, and now Harley the Schnauzer. Later, a cockatiel would join our animal kingdom. Oh, and just for the animal lovers out there, Harley and the ferret got along great! We actually discovered their friendship by accident when the ferret, his name was Bandit, somehow got out of his cage one evening, and while we were all downstairs in the living room we heard this running and small thumping upstairs.

I went up to see what was causing the commotion and saw Harley and Bandit chasing each other all over the upstairs – wrestling with each other – then they'd both drop down on the floor, nose to nose, take a long breather, then go at it again! They would always remain friends! As for the cats, they just tolerated Harley, but didn't take to Bandit at all. The rabbit lived in a cage until he got so big that Laura was actually a little afraid to feed him, so I convinced Cheyenne to give him away to this little traveling circus that took all kinds of animals around to the schools so the kids could meet and greet them. Cheyenne thought it was perfect that her rabbit went into "show biz".

    Laura started directing some local musicals out on Long Island, and her younger brother, Kevin, an extremely talented dancer and choreographer, would stage all the dance numbers. Laura was doing this in addition to her production managing duties at MacGuffin Films. She became so good at it, that eventually she moved into this field entirely. During this venture she became very involved with this crowd of actors, singers and dancers. She started having some very late nights directing the shows, plus working during the day in her production job, and we weren't seeing a lot of each other. Then I got the call from "Matlock". Andy had approved me for the Lt. Harmon Andrews role for the episode that Leo and Jeff discussed with me. I packed up and took off for Wilmington, North Carolina, which didn't exactly increase the amount of time Laura and I would spend with each other. We'd been married eighteen years at this point, when I left to start "Matlock". My character introduction on "Matlock" had a really good scene with Andy's character, and

Lt. Harmon Andrews was featured heavily in the episode. Everybody liked my work, so Lt. Harmon Andrews appeared on "Matlock" for three seasons. I was able to get back up to New Hyde Park between some of the episodes, but the long distance was certainly putting a strain on the marriage. As we moved into twenty years of marriage, we were staying together to try and keep some stability for Cheyenne, but honestly I don't know how successful we were. Kids always pick up much more than adults believe they do. Also, I was so damn protective of Cheyenne, I can remember blowing up pretty good one night when Laura brought her home from a rehearsal and everybody in the car was smoking with the windows up. It was cold weather, and Cheyenne was ill from all the smoke. Laura had promised to quit smoking when she discovered she was pregnant, and to her credit, she did. She never smoked during the pregnancy or the entire time she was breastfeeding. It was only when we moved back to New York, that she started smoking again. However, after that blow-up, she never subjected Cheyenne to the smoke filled car again.

    As I was finishing up my run on "Matlock", Cheyenne was starting to apply to colleges, and she had visited me a number of times in Wilmington when I was doing the series, and she discovered UNCW. She had visited me on film and television sets her entire life, so she was never star-struck, because she grew up around all these "stars" I worked with. I remember her friends freaking out once when they came to the house, went up to her room and she had all these pictures signed to her from Sean Penn and Madonna (they were married at the time). Her friends couldn't believe it! Visiting me in Wilmington, she got interested in UNCW, and decided she wanted to apply. Laura and I discussed it, and I told her if Cheyenne got accepted, she could go to UNCW as an in-state student, saving a lot of tuition money, because I had established residency in the state, plus I was a native North Carolinian. I also had a little "juice" with some of the people at UNCW because I had become sort of a "big fish" in a little "pond", doing the "Matlock" series, plus a couple of plays at the professional theatre in Wilmington - Thalian Hall. Later, after I was off the series, I did a shot on "Dawson's Creek". It was now the new series in town. Then I did a film with my friend Joe Don Baker, along with Louis Gossett, entitled, "Last Dance with Olivia". I hadn't seen Joe Don in years, and since I was doing a small role I hadn't had the chance to meet him yet.

    I was standing outside my trailer on my first day on the set and Joe Don was walking across the lot. I called out to him, "Hey, Joe Don." He stopped and turned, took a minute, then he said almost as a question, "Jordan? What the heck are you doing here?" I told him I now lived in Wilmington and had just finished a run on the "Matlock" series, then I told him I was doing the hospital scene with him and Lou Gossett. Once again, a nice reunion. I had never worked with Lou Gossett, but he was an absolute gentleman.

    I had met another gentleman, Carl Venters, who owned a radio station in Wilmington, during a remote broadcast his rock and roll station was doing at the Harley dealership as I was finishing up the "Matlock" series. We got to talking and I asked him if he'd ever had any kind of an entertainment-type talk show on his station. He replied he had never given it much thought, but after hearing me give him an idea I had for this type of show, he gave me a card and told me to call him sometime and maybe we could set up an appointment to discuss my idea. Well, a couple of things happened that day. I had made a contact with a radio station owner, and I became very interested in Harley motorcycles.

    "Matlock" had ended, at least for me. You see, Andy had fallen "out of love" with me. He had completely misunderstood the time that Leo, when he was directing an episode, would spend talking to me. Andy must have thought that I was trying to monopolize Leo's time in order to get more work on the show. Andy didn't know that Leo and I had been friends for years, and the bulk of our conversations were always family-related. I would ask him about Eileen, his wife and my daughter's Godmother, his sons, Sean, Chris and Michael – and he'd ask me about Laura and Cheyenne. But Andy thought I was hustling Leo for more work. That last season, well at least the last season for me, I was interviewed in the make-up trailer one afternoon, and the reporter made it a front page story on the Entertainment Page of the Wilmington News, featuring me, Lt. Harmon Andrews. It didn't sit well with Andy, I was getting too much attention, and I'll be the first to admit, I was very well liked by the crew, which is something I've always prided myself on. I've always gotten along with the crew, wardrobe and make-up personnel, they're important people on any show. Andy had also made a derogatory comment about Leo's heritage and I had called him on it, since I didn't believe it was funny. Combine those things, and Lt. Harmon Andrew was history on "Matlock".

    I called and made an appointment to meet with Carl Venters and talk to him about doing a Radio Entertainment Talk Show. However that meeting had to be put on hold as my mom went into the hospital. They discovered that she had a heart condition, and they recommended surgery. I regret that I didn't talk her into waiting due to her age, but she believed that if the doctor was telling her she needed the bypass surgery, she thought she should go forward with the operation. Unfortunately, there was a mistake made during the surgery as it was explained to me by the lead doctor who was terribly upset. They had to take mom back into surgery and the second time she suffered a stroke. I don't intend to dwell on the sadness of this happening to my mom, and I will forever blame myself for not talking her into waiting. Just like my dad, my mom passed away in June, my birth month. I've always thought that was strange that both my parents died in the month that their son was born, even though fifteen years apart. I'm thankful that I could give my mom the kind of send-off that I know she wanted. Even though I was filled with sadness, and still carry that guilt of not trying to talk her out of the surgery, I am thankful and happy that my mom enjoyed seeing her son in films, on television and in theatrical productions. She always got a big kick out of meeting the various stars I had the privilege of knowing and working with, and she enjoyed her bit of celebrity in the city where she lived, because people knew her son was a "movie and television actor". As long as I live, her grave site will never go without flowers – and the kind she loved!

Written By Jordan Rhodes

Chapter Twenty-Nine
Radio – Wilmington – Hurricane

Finally I had my meeting with Carl Venters, and getting an opportunity on WMFD in the world of radio was quite an adventure for this Blue Collar Actor. Because that is exactly how I approached the job. As an actor. Carl liked me, and he liked my background but he wasn't sure I could do radio. He approached it like a series, said he'd give me a tryout. Twelve weeks to see how I'd do. If it went well, then we'd go from there. Well it went well. I started with an engineer, a nice young lady that was also kinda like a "co-host"? Maybe? My first show was a morning show called "Daybreak with Jordan Rhodes". I did a lot of "Good Morning Stuff" – did some voices, copied a lot from Jonathan Winters, who I always thought that - prior to Robin Williams - he was the funniest and quickest wit on the planet. I had an aunt Mauddie, a Country Wilbur, and a Gabby Hayes type guy – fun entertainment to wake you up in the morning. Our weather guy was Lou Musser, and I had this small studio where I could use my chair with the rollers to roll over to the door, after knocking on my desk, I'd open the door and greet my "guests", who were all "me". One morning, after about four days, Lou was leaving his studio where he did the weather, and on a break he stopped at my studio, and asked me, "Where are you getting all these guests?" It blew him away when I told him, they were all ME! The station started moving my show's timeslot. I went from the 7 a.m. to 9 a.m. slot, "Daybreak with Jordan Rhodes" - to 10 a.m. to noon, "Mornings with Jordan Rhodes" – to noon to 2 p.m. "Lunchtime with Jordan Rhodes", and, finally, the primetime - drive-time slot, 5 p.m. to 7 p.m., as "The Jordan Rhodes Show", a full call-in talk-radio show. Along the way I knocked off two highly-rated syndicated shows, "The G. Gordon Liddy Show" and a legend in radio, "The Barry Farber Show". I was having an absolute ball! I liked everyone at the station. By the time I was given the primetime drive time slot, at 5 p.m. to 7 p.m., I had been taught to engineer and run my own board, so I was responsible for producing, engineering and handling my own "call-ins". Suddenly, around town, I was well known by my radio "voice". I received more perks than you're supposed to receive. I'd do reviews of the films coming into town, which got me passes to the movies. I'd do reviews of the plays, which got me comps to the shows. I was asked to participate in the local parades, which led to me riding a Harley owned by one of the owners of the local Harley-Davidson dealership – which led to me buying one of my first two Harley-Davidson motorcycles, and attending The

Myrtle Beach Bike Show each year.

Cheyenne had been accepted to UNCW and I told Laura I thought we should consider buying a house in Wilmington. I was doing well in radio, and I asked her to come and join me, but she wasn't having any of that. For all intents and purposes we were separated - just not "legally". We did decide that buying a house where Cheyenne could live while attending UNCW was a good idea and a wise investment. It didn't turn out that way, but that was the original idea! Well, the best laid plans of mice and men. Life is what happens to you as you plan other things (one of my favorites) and so on!

I found a four-bedroom house in a nice section fairly close to UNCW, and my plan was to have Cheyenne rent out two bedrooms to other female students, take one bedroom for herself, and - get this! Her dad would take over the entire downstairs, with his own bedroom, bathroom, kitchen and office – plus his own entrance! It also had a two-car garage. It was a good plan and worked really great, with the exception of a few minor problems with "roommates", which was to be expected. What was not expected was Hurricane Fran! Unbelievable wind, evacuation orders and fifty-six inches of water, that's four inches short of five feet my friend, deposited into the lower level of the house, which backed up onto the waterway!

    I made a lot of friends in the listening area during the hurricane, because I showed up at the radio station along with a couple of brave (or foolish - take your pick) souls, and we stayed on the air through the entire time of the hurricane siege. The television stations were down, because you can't listen or watch TV with batteries when the power is out! We didn't realize how much the people that were "hunkered down" were counting on us to keep them informed on their portable radios, and they considered us a lifeline! Without any idea of how many people might have been listening, I continued to inform and entertain – Hey, like I said earlier, I'm an Actor, a Blue Collar Actor, and I just kept on going and going and going, like that bunny! After a full night of staying on the air, a group of postal workers braved the storm and came to the back door of the station, bringing us plates of ham and eggs with hot coffee, and buttered toast! It was a grand surprise!

    Only later, after the storm was finally over, leaving tons of devastation in its wake, did we discover how much we had meant to the entire community by keeping them company on the airwaves! WMFD acquired many new fans after Hurricane Fran. She was no lady, and we were glad to see her go!

Hurricane Fran created major changes and adjustments in our life. After I returned to our house in Wrightsville Green, the name of our development, I discovered the damage that Fran had done. The fifty-six inches of water had ruined all of my belongings in the lower level, computer, television, file cabinet, shoes and most of my clothes. When FEMA finally showed up, I discovered that the entire lower level where I had been living was built illegally and no one was supposed to be living down there. The house was constructed with "flow-through vents" all along the baseboard to allow for flooding in the event of a high-water surge, or a hurricane! These vents had been illegally covered-over in order to install interior walls, and obviously the walls were crushed in by the surging force of the water.

The downstairs was destroyed. My customized Harley-Davidson Sportster, another "toy" I had treated myself too, had been totally submerged and it would have to be taken completely apart and cleaned in order to ever be ridden again.

The lower level of the house was posted as "unlivable" and would require approximately twelve thousand dollars of work to be put back to "code". In the meantime, once I had all the debris removed from the lower level, Cheyenne and her roommates could move back in, but I needed to find a new place to live. Cheyenne would continue attending UNCW for three years in Wilmington with me, and we were able to enjoy a lot of father-daughter time. But after two more hurricanes during those three years (Wilmington had become "Hurricane Alley"), and another big one, Hurricane Bonnie, Cheyenne decided she would finish up her Masters and Ph.D. degrees back up North.

    I was sorry to see her go, but she was now a young woman, more than capable of making her own decisions, and she was smart as a whip! I helped pack her up in the four-door Chrysler I had bought for my mom, which Cheyenne had now inherited, and she returned to New Hyde Park to enroll in another college. Fortunately, Cheyenne was awarded a couple of scholarships (I told you she was smart), so that was a big help. She moved back into the house in Manor Oaks with her mom, Laura (we were now officially "separated"), and her mother was thrilled to have her back home in New Hyde Park.

    I will not bore the reader with all the legal crappola of my lawsuit against the fat-assed realtor that made a fortune in Wilmington and the Beach areas by having the flow-through area of the lower levels of houses illegally "closed-in & built" so he could sell them as additional bedroom and bath listings. Suffice it to say, I won, but I had to settle in arbitration for a pittance. Also, I took such a huge loss on the Wrightsville Green house, with the help and support of FEMA, plus the years-old lawsuit, I was able to let it go back to the mortgage company. So, if you're keeping score, at this point in my life, I had acquired four houses – sold one, Laura currently occupied one, and the Blue Collar Actor had lost two!

    After Hurricane Fran, I was unable to move back into the Wrightsville Green house. I had inherited Mom's beautiful manufactured home in Fairmont, just a little under two hours from Wilmington. My radio show was doing well, management was very happy, and I was enjoying the work. But I had to find a place to live. I bought a nice-sized lot in a little section outside the city limits of Wilmington, called Castle Hayne. I hired a house-moving company and moved mom's house from Fairmont to Castle Hayne. I hired a brick mason company to construct a brick foundation once the house was placed on the land. I already had a front porch added to the house, which I did for mom when she first moved in, so it was moved with the house. With everything going on, it was less than three weeks before I was living in my own house – thanks to Mom. Blue Collar Actor house score now - plus one!

I enjoyed living in Wilmington, and I'd get to see Leo whenever he would come into town to direct an episode of a TV show. On one occasion he brought his wife, Eileen, my daughter's Godmother, and it was great to spend some time with her and Leo. I had made some good friends with people like Jim Bath. Jim was a local favorite and owned a place called the Ice House where music was always being played outside, for free! I met and became friends with Joe Gallison, a veteran of Broadway theatre, and a film actor that performed the role of Dr. Neil Curtis on "Days of Our Lives" for over twenty-five years before moving to Wilmington. Other actors had located there – Henry Darrow of the series "High Chaparral", also starring Linda Cristal, a lady I had worked with on "Mr. Majestyk". Dennis Hopper had bought a building on Main Street and spent some time in Wilmington, obviously I knew Dennis, and had worked with him in Sean's film "The Indian Runner". Linda Lavin, of "Alice" fame, bought a wonderfully restored house in the downtown area. I had known Linda since she married an actor friend of mine named Kip Niven. I also met and became friends with Pat Hingle, he lived out at Carolina Beach. Pat had starred in the first Broadway play I ever saw, "The Dark at the Top of The Stairs". We walked a SAG picket line together to get a company filming in Wilmington to pay union scale. Wilmington had become quite a film hub with the Screen Gems Studio busting at the seams with series, films, and movies-of-the-week being filmed on a continuing basis. Frank Capra, Jr., had become president of the studio, and Frank and I knew each other from the film, "Marooned", where he was an associate producer and I worked with Gregory Peck as Glenn "the E-con engineer". At one time or another, almost all of the newly arrived actors would do a play at Thalian Hall, one of the oldest continuing performing theatres in America. Edwin Booth had performed there, and so had the Barrymores. It is a famous theatre where I hold some type of dubious record. I performed my PAPA play there, and then, years later, after the play was filmed during a live performance, the filmed version was shown as part of the theatres "Film Series". All of that info is forthcoming.

There was a beautiful theatre in Myrtle Beach, about an hour and a half's drive from Wilmington, called The Palace. My friends, Robert (RJ) Wagner and his lovely and talented wife, Jill St. John, were coming in to perform "Love Letters" during a tour they were doing with the play. They had called me on my radio show, and I had done some on-air plugs for the play, so, of course, I drove down to see them, and the play. They gave a wonderful performance (you would expect nothing less from these two talented actors) of the

A.E. Gurney play, and it was a treat to visit with them before having to drive back to Wilmington.

Everything was going well for me, even though the separation from my daughter and Laura was not an ideal situation. But I was working, always a plus for any actor, especially this Blue Collar Actor. I had a very nice house to live in, the lawsuit and lost house were behind me, at least somewhat. I had upgraded my "underwater" Harley-Davidson Sportster to a beautiful black Road King, and was a member in good standing of the Carolina Coast H-D Motorcycle Club. We would have a breakfast run each Sunday morning, plus we would participate in the various parades being held throughout the year. And we would always make Myrtle Beach Bike Week. All in all, everything was pretty doggone good. But you know that saying, "Beware of the light at the end of the tunnel – it may be an oncoming train". One pleasant afternoon I was served with divorce proceedings from Laura. I had ample time to respond, however, the hearing was scheduled in New York and I had a two hour live call-in radio show five days a week. Interesting thing about working in radio, the only way you get the holidays off is if you pre-record a holiday show, and the listeners know it's a holiday, i.e., Christmas! Otherwise, if you're "on-the-air", then you're "on-the-air". The only way I could get all those days off for a divorce hearing would be to quit. I didn't want to quit! I'll spare the reader any anguish, if any was forthcoming – Laura got everything! The house, the furnishings, the paintings, a couple of pieces of art, she even got the clothes I had left in the house. Not that she kept them, just tossed them, along with a couple of unknown "collector's items" possibly worth some bucks – one of them being the first uncirculated plastic-sealed copy of "Playgirl" magazine with yours truly in a picture story spread! Yes – the light? It was an oncoming train!

Once the divorce was final, I found myself single for the first time in over twenty years. Even though I wasn't currently working in films or television, I was enjoying hosting my own radio talk show, and doing an occasional play at Thalian Hall. During this time, I met a very talented guitar playing entertainer, William "Paco" Strickland, a Flamenco guitarist who was truly gifted. He was dating a very pretty young lady that wasn't interested in me, except as a friend, no matter how hard I tried for something otherwise. I had a lot of fun with Paco on my radio show, always teasing in a good-humored way about his incredible luck with the young lady. Paco has, unfortunately, passed away, but I'm still considered a friend by the young lady.

In addition to the many friends I made in Wilmington,

one wound up having a large impact on my career. His name is Mike Sapp. Mike was the artistic director of the Odell Williamson Performance Art Center in Brunswick County, just forty-five minutes north of Wilmington. Mike used to buy advertising time on my radio show for the theatrical events he would bring into the Odell Williamson Theatre. He would bring in touring shows from Broadway, new shows trying out on the road, plus musical entertainers. One of these was the country-pop singer Lee Greenwood, known worldwide for his, "Proud to be an American" solo. I knew Lee from having worked on a music video for him with Joseph Torina. I had met Joe years before in New York City, and over the years we have become good friends. Joe is an incredibly talented editor, director and producer. Over the years he has worked in more arenas than I have time to list; but they include NBC Sports, numerous high-end infomercials and business films all done through his own company, TorinaMedia, headquartered in Florida. The music video we did for Lee was a good one, with dancing ladies and a few trained wild animals with spots. I don't remember, but they may have been ocelots, a small spotted animal that resembles a leopard. Unfortunately, the lady producer we were working for overstepped more than a few boundaries regarding budget, hiring too many friends for "over the top" salaries, so MCA Nashville, the company that hired us, rolled into Miami where we were filming and pulled the well-known "plug". Joe and I had returned to his condo in Clearwater Beach, Florida, for two days off when we received word that Lee's music video had been cancelled! Too bad, it would have been a good music video!

    One afternoon at the radio station before I was due to go on air, I was walking down the hallway and I ran into Roman Gabriel! The former quarterback of the Los Angeles Rams – yeah, the same guy that owned the Porsche dealership during my "hey-days" in Hollywood. We had met in Los Angeles. Roman even got me a field pass to one of the Rams games so I took a few pictures when photography was a hobby of mine. Roman asked me what I was doing in Wilmington. I told him about my radio show. Roman then said, "Jordan I need you to play in my celebrity golf tournaments I do for charity. I remember you used to play a good game of golf". I told Roman I hadn't played any golf for a few years. He told me to get my game back together, and that he needed me! Long story-short. I got my golf game back together and started playing in Roman's tournaments, which got me invited into other celebrity golf outings, and in one year, I played in nine celebrity golf tournaments! All for charity I'm proud to add! It had been a long time since

The Duke of Edinburgh's Cup Tournament in England, but I was certainly having a good time. As a single "celebrity", I was meeting a few ladies, and fortunately for me, only one "crazy" came into my life at the time. I met a great group of guys in these golf tournaments, mostly retired professional football players, including the captain, Roman Gabriel. Others were Billy Ray Barnes, Roland Moss, Chuck Ramsey, Milt Plum, Karl Noonan, Don Testerman, Leonard Black, and a few actors and singers like Don Cherry, Tommy Sands and Joe Gallison.

Having done a couple of plays in Wilmington, I had met a few of the local actors. One of them, Mick McGovern, had formed an acting class, and therefore had come into contact with a lot of young ladies hoping to land a role in one of the many films coming into the studio in Wilmington. . Mick made an introduction for me to meet one of these ladies, who was working in the make-up department at the Belk department store. Mick thought we might hit it off. Her name was Lynn Moore. At the time we met at Belk, I didn't think it went very well. Lynn was certainly not looking for a relationship, which she expressed on our first outing, which was a lunch date down on the waterfront. As it turned out, we had met briefly once before when I was doing a play at Thalian Hall, entitled, "Glengarry Glen

Ross", where I performed the Jack Lemmon role. She was dating a former actor and stage manager that had moved to Wilmington from New York City. Since she was with this other guy when we first met, it was just a brief "hello-enjoyed the show" conversation. Lynn did tell me later that when she was reading through the program and saw my credits, her thought was, "What in the hell is this guy doing in Wilmington?" After we started dating, she discovered my radio show because it turned out her mother was a big fan of "The Jordan Rhodes Show". I made a big hit with her mom, Miriam, by bringing flowers for her when I first picked up Lynn. Lynn lived at her mother's house with her mom and her brother, Cliff. After we both declared, "I'm not looking for any serious relationship," we began dating on a fairly regular basis. It took another hurricane to get us really "involved". Hurricane Bonnie came into town, the same hurricane that caused Cheyenne to say, "Enough of this crap, I'm out of here," and it knocked out the power in the development where Lynn lived with her mother. They didn't have any hot water, so I invited Lynn to take a bubble bath in my round tub at my house in Castle Hayne. She accepted and I must admit she did look great in a bubble bath. We were certainly more of an "item" after that evening. Lynn had a very interesting background. She had been a singer in

Nashville under the name of Linda Carol Moore, appearing on the "Porter Wagoner Show". Porter had a lot to do with discovering Dolly Parton. During this time, Lynn met some of the biggest names in the country music business, people like Johnny Cash, Waylon Jennings and Hank Williams, Jr., just to name a few, plus she had done a lot of theatre in Nashville, and she was on a pilot film for a series with Tom Selleck. The problem was that Lynn didn't like to sing country music. She wanted to sing and write jazz, and I guess Nashville wasn't the place to try to accomplish that. So, after a few disappointments and unpleasant events, she moved from Nashville to Wilmington to be with her family. Unfortunately, her dad passed away shortly after she returned, so as I previously stated she was now living with her mom and her brother, when I met her.

After we had become an "item" in Wilmington, some changes began to take place with my job at the radio station. WMFD was unable to renew the lease on the land which contained the broadcast tower. The lady that owned the land had repeatedly told the owners that she was not going to renew the lease, but they didn't believe her. After all, WMFD was the oldest station in Wilmington. Surely this lady would renew the lease. But they were wrong! She didn't renew the lease. No tower, no WMFD. The station had two other radio shows, a rock show and a smooth jazz show. Yes, a number of changes were taking place!

After almost two years, I asked Lynn Moore to marry me!

Chapter Thirty
Marriage and Becoming Hemingway

I took Lynn on a weekend trip to Pinehurst where I proposed marriage, and she accepted. I did the whole bit, down on one knee in the beautiful gazebo of the Pinehurst Hotel, after securing permission to perform this task there, with many of the employees peering out of the windows to witness the event. I didn't know at the time that we would be returning to the Pinehurst Hotel and performing A.E. Gurney's wonderful play "Love Letters", the same play my friends Jill St. John and Robert Wagner had performed at The Palace in Myrtle Beach.

A lot of changes were coming my way.

We started talking about our wedding. We anticipated that we would have our wedding in about a year. Lynn had a sister in New Orleans and we thought it would be fun to get married in the "Big Easy". I asked Joe Gallison to be my best man, and he graciously agreed. We asked Lynn's brother-in-law, Cliff, to walk Lynn down the aisle and "give her away" and he agreed. (Cliff was married to Lynn's sister Shirley, and so as not to confuse anyone about the two Cliffs in the family, Lynn's brother and Shirley's husband, everyone called Shirley's husband, C.W.). Shortly after we returned from

Pinehurst, I found out about the situation at the radio station concerning the Tower. The station owner and his son-in-law, who was the station manager, still thought they could convince the lady to renew the lease for the tower, but she wouldn't do it. Without a tower, there was no WMFD and no "Jordan Rhodes Show". Management asked me to stay on until they could resolve the station signal issue, and I was offered an evening show called "Smooth Jazz". I actually enjoy listening to smooth jazz music, but going from a live call-in interactive show to just doing commercial breaks and "lead-ins" to the smooth jazz music just didn't work for me. I did stick it out for a while, hoping they would find a way to get my talk show back on the air. In the meantime, I was asked to do a little role on "Dawson's Creek", which I didn't care much about doing, but I could use the money, so I did it.

    I wound up giving the station my notice a little bit before we were scheduling our marriage trip to New Orleans. First, we had to go down to meet and arrange everything with an Episcopal Priest and the church in Metairie just outside of New Orleans - the parish where C.W. and Shirley lived. We met with a great priest, Father Ralph Byrd, and he was much more interested in asking me what Andy Griffith was like than asking me any questions about my two previous marriages. We had to have the interview in order to meet the requirements of the Church. Father Byrd opened our "interview" like this: " Now Jordan and Lynn, marriage is not something to be entered into lightly, it takes a great deal of commitment and hard work. Are you both prepared to make that commitment?" We answered, "Yes, we are." Father Byrd: "Okay. Now, Jordan, what's Andy Griffith really like?" End of the marriage interview. I liked the guy! He was really laid back and even cracked a couple of jokes about what we could, and could not do on the altar during the ceremony, most of it prohibiting any nudity! Like I said, I liked the guy!

    My daughter, Cheyenne, came down and was a "Best Girl" along with my friend, Joe Gallison, who was the "Best Man". We had a fine wedding ceremony, attended by all the above plus Lynn's sisters, Shirley and Jackie, and their husbands, then we climbed into our stretch limo which drove us through the narrow streets of the French Quarter to our wedding reception, and consummated our marriage in the back seat of the limo on the way to the restaurant. We had a great wedding, and a great wedding reception. We spent our honeymoon in New Orleans walking around the French Quarter, and enjoying some terrific Cajun food before heading back to Wilmington.

    When we arrived back in Castle Hayne, I didn't have

any idea of what this Blue Collar Actor was going to do, and while I was giving it some thought, I received a call from Peter Lawrence - not the actor whose lines I took over in the biker flick, but an English writer and producer friend of mine from New York, now living in California. He told me that a group he was now working with had a small independent film about Ernest Hemingway, that they intended to film in Key West with very little money. They wanted me to play Hemingway. I was very flattered and told Peter I'd love to work with him on a film, but I didn't think I looked anything like Ernest Hemingway (Ha-ha. Just wait). Peter, in his inimitable English accent said into the phone, "Grow a fucking beard and look in the mirror lad, you have an uncanny resemblance to Hemingway." I told Peter to send me a script and I'd give it unquestionable consideration. Yet, as it so often goes in the acting profession, they couldn't get the money together for the small film, so the project died. I was thinking about returning to New York City, but the rents were outrageous. Even if I could find us an apartment we could "almost" afford, I would still have to first sell the house in Castle Hayne. On a whim, I called my friend, Mike Sapp, the artistic director of the Odell Williamson Performance Art Theatre, and invited myself to see him for lunch. I drove out to Brunswick County and we visited for a while. He knew I no longer had the talk radio show, and I told him I didn't really know what I was going to do. But I was thinking about returning to New York because I didn't want to hang around Wilmington waiting to do any of the small roles that might come my way. Mike was well aware of my "Blue Color Actor" background. My career had been talked about many times during my radio show. Mike said to me, "Why don't you create a show for yourself?" I responded with, "Create my own show? Who in the hell is going to come out to see me in my own show?" Mike replied, "Don't give me that modesty shit Jordan, a lot of theatres would book you in a show, because a lot of people know about you. Hell, I'd book you in my theatre if you had a show"!

    Driving back home, I started to think about the call I had received from Peter Lawrence about playing Hemingway. The more I thought about it, the more the idea appealed to me. I just needed to come up with a concept.

    Back at the house in Castle Hayne, there was a vintage auto show over by the park where the battleship, the USS North Carolina, had been docked for years. It was a major tourist attraction. Lynn went with me and during our walk around looking at the vintage cars, we met an older couple that traveled around in their motor home selling some collectable car-related items like cards, steering knobs, and large cloth dice to hang from a mirror. This couple had two Rottweilers - a male and a female. I had never come into close contact with a Rottweiler before, but for the most part I have always preferred large dogs, or small dogs with big dog attitudes, like Harley. Well, we spent a good part of the afternoon visiting with these two "Rotties". Lynn and I had been talking about getting a dog, and this meeting with the Rottweilers had certainly grabbed my interest. I started reading about the breed and the more I learned, including the "misunderstood breed" part (very similar to the reputation of pit bulls), the more I liked the breed. Lynn was excited, but a little concerned about the size of the dog. As we both had decided we didn't want to get a puppy, I was going to try to find a young adult male.

    I started my search by phone, and it took me across the country to breeders from California to Chicago to Texas and, eventually, to Silverhills Rottweilers in Apex, North Carolina, about two hours from where we lived. A young lady by the name of Cathy Rubens owned and operated the kennel. We had tried to adopt a rescue Rottie but didn't have any luck, so I was trying to "rescue" a young adult that would be sold from a reputable breeder. Enter Cathy, and a three year old retired show dog, named "Chips". Now the person that put me in touch with Cathy was in Chicago, but she knew about Chips, and she also warned me that she didn't know if Cathy was willing to let Chips go or not. We arranged to meet with Cathy, and to be "interviewed" as to why we wanted a Rottweiler. My reasons were sound and Cathy said she would let us "meet" Chips. I felt like we were being interviewed to adopt a child! We accompanied Cathy out to this large room where she kept some of her dogs inside these very large individual crates. Chips was in one. Lynn knelt down on the floor and Cathy opened the crate. Chips charged out straight for Lynn, bumped her gently, turned around and sat in her lap! The rest is history, and I will not bore you with the additional trips up to see Cathy again before being "allowed" to adopt this blue ribbon-winning retired show dog, whose pups sold for one thousand bucks each – yes, Chips had been bred once, but Cathy did want to find him a home, and she found it with us! We adopted Chips, whose Champion name was longer than my arm, and he became, "Mr. Chips" to us. I will not divulge what I paid to adopt "Mr. Chips", I will just say that it was not the price of his pups, it was more than reasonable, and if it had been five times more, it would have been worth every dime! "Mr. Chips" became the greatest dog either one of us ever had. He was absolutely perfect! I was told since he was a show dog and had never lived in a house continually, he might take a little time to be housebroken. He lifted his leg once in the house, I quickly took him into the backyard – no harsh words, just let him into the backyard. That was it! Mr. Chips was home, and we took him everywhere! I couldn't get in the car without him wanting the backseat. Simply a great dog!

Since my meeting with Mike Sapp and his suggestion that I create a show, I was thinking about Hemingway, but I needed a concept. One day, I remembered a short film I had seen years before. It was a French short film made in 1962 based on an American short story from 1891 entitled "An Occurrence at Owl Creek Bridge". It was set in the Civil War. A group of Union soldiers was hanging a Confederate soldier for some reason. He was pushed off the bridge, and, as he was falling through the air, the rope broke and he fell into the water were he freed his hands and was carried downstream by the current. He escaped the gunfire and ran back to his family. As he is seeing his family and hugging his wife and children, the film cuts back to him falling through the air - the rope doesn't break and he is hung. His life had flashed through his mind as he was falling to his death. I had my concept!

I would create a play that takes place on the last day of Hemingway's life, and just before he shoots himself, he will hear a voice that takes him back to his early life. He will then tell his story to the audience, and take them on a journey about his life from his earliest days as a writer, through all his incredible adventures and returning to the present time where he does end his life! Now, all I had to do was write it! I called a writer friend, Ken Vose. Ken is indeed a writer. He has written a number of books (even hired me to write a section on Porsches for his best-selling, "Dream Cars, Past and Present"). He wrote the book and the film "Greased Lighting" which starred Richard Pryor. I asked Ken if he would be interested in working with me on "spec" – meaning that you don't get paid until the show is sold or makes money - on a play concept I had for Ernest Hemingway. My title was, PAPA "the man, the myth, the legend" – A Tribute to Ernest Hemingway. Ken loved the idea and agreed to work with me. To this day, we have only had a handshake deal. How many people in the entertainment business can truthfully say that! We set to work. Ken lived in Pennsylvania and I lived in North Carolina. Our research and writing, plus rewriting took a year. I had a good idea of letting Lynn bridge the scenes by singing clips of songs. Ken had a brilliant idea - let Lynn play all five women in Hemingway's life! I asked Lynn if she'd be interested in playing all five women with these short intro scenes in the play. Lynn is an actress, so naturally she said,

"Of course, I'd be interested in playing the five women". Once the play was completed, I gained forty-three pounds and grew a beard, which Peter Lawrence had suggested. By this time of my life, my beard was white or gray, your choice, so I didn't need to "color" anything. I called Mike Sapp at Odell, and asked him if he would be interested in helping me stage the play and direct me on stage? Mike agreed and we started rehearsing the play every chance we had. I started putting together ideas I had for the set. My brother-in-law Cliff made me a very unusual prop I needed to give the illusion of PAPA turning his desk into his fishing boat. Another good friend, and extremely talented graphic artist, Mike Schnorr, designed and made various mounted animal heads to complete the Hemingway room look.

    During our rehearsals, one of the booking conventions was going to take place in Atlanta. Mike Sapp thought it would be important for us to have a presence at this convention because he explained that the "buyers" at these conventions book their shows early. So, even though we were in rehearsals, I put together some promo material, gathered up Hemingway's wardrobe and we signed up for the Atlanta convention. I believe it was a three-day affair, and sure enough, just as Mike had predicted, we got a booking! We did not have a finished show yet, but the subject matter was so appealing, The Hoover Library Theatre in Hoover, Alabama, booked us almost a year in advance. In addition, we received a lot of booking interest, and gave out our contact info to a number of theatres. It was certainly an indication that we could Book PAPA "the man, the myth, the legend".

We returned to our home in North Carolina excited about the prospects, and returned to rehearsing the show, and creating more ideas for the set.

After weeks of rehearsing we finally believed we should at least try a preview. Ken was an adjunct professor of writing at Wilkes-Barre College in Wilkes-Barre, Pennsylvania, and they have a theatre in The Darte Center for the Performing Arts. Ken approached them about having our "premiere" of PAPA "the man, the myth, the legend" at their theatre. Obviously for pay! In addition to being the creator and co-writer, plus the star of the play, I was also the producer, having used my money to put this show together. They agreed and even though it was called the "premiere" of the play, we considered it a "preview" so I could find out what did, and didn't work. I was nervous as a cat on the preverbal hot tin roof! Over fifty pages of dialogue pal, and this was a play – no starting and stopping, no "pick-ups", no "don't worry, we'll dub it in later" – there was no "later".

This wasn't film, this was professional theatre. I would be out there on stage with my ass hanging out and I had to swim, or I would surely as hell sink! Since the Darte Center had a legitimate theatre including a workshop where they built sets, they were supplying a number of set pieces including the desk, the gun cabinet, chairs, tables, and bookcases with books. So, all we had to pack into our four-door Lincoln Towncar were a few of the "special props", including the animal heads, our show wardrobe and personal props for the show. We had to put Mr. Chips into a kennel, which he was always absolutely great about, plus the people at the kennel immediately fell in love with the big dude! And we were off to Pennsylvania! This Blue Collar Actor was back in the acting profession!

Chapter Thirty-One

I had priced the show within the scale that Mike Sapp had suggested, and which would prevent any smaller theatre with under 500 seats from turning us down because of the cost. Eventually, once we had our complete set and we needed to haul it in a trailer, sometimes taking a lighting or sound technician with us, we would get our booking price beyond $7,500 for a single performance. We would also make a number of "package deals" for additional performances while at the same venue. Due to the "penalty rule" imposed on me by Equity (AEA), stripping me of all my earned pension credits since I had less than ten, and refusing to grant me any recourse, or invoke a waiver for any working professional actor still performing in any sister union, finding themselves being screwed over by this same asinine "penalty rule", that I was a victim of, I represented myself as just wearing a producer's hat, and never performed the play under Equity's jurisdiction in a single theatre. Later you will discover that we toured this play for over five years in numerous "Equity" houses, and never once would I sign an Equity contract. I also paid my co-star (and wife) Lynn Moore over double what an Equity touring contract would have required.

We performed a weekend at the Darte Center in Wilkes-Barre, received outstanding reviews, and, yes, I did make it through unscathed! Funny thing about making the reading of reviews a "regular ritual". If you do, you always have to accept the "pans" along with the "praise". A lesson for you young actors!

We returned back home to Castle Hayne, picked up Mr. Chips, many kisses all around, and went back to rehearse and "polish" a few spots. Mike allowed us to bring Mr. Chips to the rehearsals, and he was just super! He would stand in the wings and watch what we were doing. We always brought his crate along, which was so big, even folded down it took up the entire trunk in the Lincoln. And those cars have a large trunk! Once we started a run-through we'd put him in the crate backstage, where he'd just lay down until the run-through was over.

We had that "preview" at the Darte Center in Wilkes-Barre in May, and in August we had our "official opening" at Mike's theatre, the Odell Williamson Performance Art Theatre. It's a twelve-hundred seat house and it was packed! Everything worked perfectly with all the light cues and sound cues, and the Blue Collar Actor was functioning on all cylinders! Lynn was letter - and emotion - perfect, as always throughout the entire run of the play. She had written and recorded the theme song "Meet me in Memory", and it set the mood and opened the play every night. Tony Rivenbark, the wonderful artistic director for Thalian Hall in Wilmington, had come out to see the play, and met me briefly afterwards, congratulated me on the play, and told me he wanted to book PAPA into Thalian Hall. He said he'd have his booking manager call me to work out all the details. The reviews (here we go again, about reading those reviews) came out and they were sensational. One critic stated, "He could have been sitting in a New York theatre, the play was that good!"

Tony Rivenbark was good to his word, and we did perform PAPA at Thalian Hall. We went on to tour the play for over five years in a number of states, and we appeared at a couple more of the convention-booking shows, but we didn't see the need to attend any more of the conventions after the first couple of years. Word had gotten around, and we were getting calls about booking the play for a number of theatres. One really interesting call certainly got us excited. We had just finished another very successful production in Charlotte, North Carolina, at a beautiful theatre that was part of the Blumenthal Performing Arts Center, and had only been back home in Castle Hayne for a few days, when one afternoon we received a call. Lynn answered the phone, and it was for me. Lynn had asked, "Who was calling", and she handed me the phone saying, "It's Peter Entin from the Schubert Organization". I answered the phone and Peter introduced himself and told me they had heard that I had a very interesting play about the life of Ernest Hemingway. I confirmed that, and Peter asked me if I would send the play and any material related to the play up to him in New York. Of course I put together a copy of the play and the reviews we had received and mailed them the following day to Peter Entin, VP of Theatre Affairs at the Shubert Organization. Within a week, I received another call from Peter telling me that he and Dessie Moynihan had read the play and the accompanying material and that The Shubert Organization would like to meet with me and offer me one of their theatres for the play. He asked if I could come up to New York City? We didn't have a booking for the play for the next three months, so I made arrangements with a performing arts rental agency for a place to stay, and literally with our feet "off the ground", we flew to New York.

We met with Peter in his Schubert offices, and they arranged to show us three theatres, The Music Box, The Booth and The Cort. We were told we needed a general manager, so I contacted Leonard Soloway, a well-known and respected general manager. I liked The Booth theatre for PAPA. I thought it was a Hemingway theatre. We returned for our third meeting in three days with Peter, and he knew and liked our choice of general managers. Everything seemed too good to be true. And it was! The shoe finally dropped when Peter, very matter-of-factly asked, "Where are you getting your production money?" What? Who? How? Say again? I naively answered, "I thought your organization was financing the play." Peter replied, "Oh no, we don't finance plays, we just lease you the theatre." No need to say our bottom fell out! But it fell out! We spent another week wading through bullshit offers from potential "bullshit investors", but the truth of the matter was that no one was going to put up the needed funds to star this Blue Collar Actor in a Broadway play! We returned home, a little shell-shocked, but a hell of a lot wiser, having "dealt" with a few devious and dishonest "investors" interested in funding our play. It never happened and we returned home. We still had over two months before our next booking.

    Within three days after we returned from New York, I got another call. This time it was from Sean Penn. Sean asked me if I was currently touring in my play, and I told him no, we didn't have a booking for about two more months. Sean said, "Great, Jordan, I need you down here in Baton Rouge where I'm doing All the Kings Men, and I need you to help me out with this role. They tried to use a local actor, but he couldn't cut it, can you come down and help us out?" I asked Sean, when did he need me, and he answered, "Tomorrow." I told him I was living in Castle Hayne, North Carolina. He said, "Don't worry about it. I'll have the production office call you with all the details, and they'll get you on a plane."

The next day, I was in Baton Rouge. I met Sean in his trailer, he took me to meet the director, Steven Zaillian. Obviously, I still had my PAPA beard. Steven asked me if I would shave it, since I was playing a senator, Senator McMurphy, the guy trying to impeach the Governor, Sean's role, and so, of course, I shaved the beard. I was given my script and needed to be ready to go to work the following day on "All the Kings Men" with a star-studded cast including, Sean, Jude Law, Kate Winslet, Mark Ruffalo, Patricia Clarkson, James Gandolfini and Anthony Hopkins.

Within less than a week after I'd been kicked right in the old cajones by the Broadway theatre world, now this Blue Collar Actor was doing a huge film! Ain't the acting life strange? That night, Sean invited me to go out to dinner with him. I accompanied him, and we were joined by Mark Ruffalo, Kate Winslet, Patricia Clarkson, Jude Law and Tanya Balsam, whose father, Martin Balsam, I had dinner with in Rome a number of years before. After a glorious dinner with that group of "A" list actors, I went back to the hotel with Sean, and I called Lynn and simply told her, again, "I was traveling in high cotton." On my last day, I spent the evening with Sean and we were up until about 4 a.m. in his suite, and I was due to fly out at 9 a.m. Need I say that I was indeed hung-over? But it was another great experience for this Blue Collar Actor.

      Back home, Lynn and I had decided to relocate from Castle Hayne to a community right outside of Pinehurst, where I had proposed to Lynn. It was Seven Lakes, North Carolina. And it did indeed have seven lakes. We sold my inherited manufactured home, and I sold my Harley Road King - I wasn't finding much time to ride it anyway. We started packing up, and in the process I had to go through a lot of my mom's papers that I had not gone through since she passed away. They had remained in one of the cabinets, so you can image my shocked surprise when I found information about a baby she had when married to the Air force S.O.B., and he had demanded that she give it up for adoption! Here, at age 62, I'm discovering I have a brother! He lives in Wisconsin. I had always thought that my mom went to Madison, Wisconsin for a job, when the truth was that she went there away from all family and friends to have a baby. I could only imagine the emotions she was going through, basically doing what she needed to do, in order to keep her life together. I harbor no resentment for my Mother, I only sympathized with her incredible plight. My mom was great and she went through enough crap for three lifetimes! Who knows, maybe mom would be happy to know we found each other. I'm happy that I was able to do as much as I did for her, and only regret it wasn't more!

    My brother's name is Mark, and even though it's correct to refer to him as my half-brother, I chose to say he's my "brother". After all, my mother gave birth to him. Mark is married, lives in Wisconsin, has kids and grandkids and we keep in touch, though not often. I've made it a point to get him as many pictures and as much information about our mother as possible.

    We packed up our furniture and belongings, plus the crate and toys for Mr. Chips - he wasn't about to let us go without him. Once the movers starting taking everything out, and I was packing some of our things in a rented moving van, Mr. Chips came out, walked right up the ramp, and laid down inside the moving van, giving us that Rottweiler look that said, "You're not leaving me, pal!"

    We found a nice three-bedroom house with a big fenced-in backyard, a large garage, yet only a short walk to the biggest lake in the community. Naturally, I bought another "toy" – hey! I had given up my Harley, so I bought us a Pontoon boat. Mr. Chips loved it! We had also found a really great kennel where we could board Mr. Chips whenever we went out with the play, and we continued touring, until the performing centers and theatres were hit with the energy crunch. There were still many theatres that wanted to book us, but they couldn't afford to pay the booking price, and we couldn't afford to travel the show for the money they were offering. So, after a great five-year run, I decided to close the play down. When our theatre friends heard the news, all of them started telling me, "You got to film this play, man, you just got to film it. You have to film it during a performance, it's got to be preserved." Well, that was easy to say, but costly to do, and I had no idea where I could get that money.

    Enter what turned out to be one of my best friends, Jeff Swartz. I met Jeff while doing a TV interview show during the Azalea Festival back in Wilmington. Which by the way, was the first time I had ever been invited to be a celebrity in the Festival, even though I had lived in the area for years, recurred on the "Matlock" series for three seasons, had my own top rated talk show, did plays and films, but was never invited to appear in the Azalea Festival Parade until we moved away!

Anyway, I met Jeff at the Festival and for some reason he liked me right off the bat, and I liked him. I had no idea that he would wind up becoming such a great friend, and I certainly didn't know he was a billionaire, and would be the only one I've ever known! Jeff owned more real estate than any single individual on the East Coast, plus his own 500,000 square-foot warehouse where he sold everything from out of date Easter Peeps to Martha Stewart's fiber-optic Christmas trees. In addition, he owned several small shopping malls, gas stations and lived in a thirty two million dollar mansion with guest rooms for about twenty people, a three hundred seat banquet room, with full sized kitchen to serve it, more cars and collectibles than anybody could count, a few large-sized movie props, and animals (including a camel, horses, a couple of ponies and two ostriches). Jeff was always buying more since he was on the "A" List at Sotheby's Auction House. I could continue on, but I'm sure you get the picture by now. To top this all off, Jeff was one hell of a great guy and friend to me! He thought the world of Lynn, and loved to tease the hell out of me, by always telling everyone that I had been on the "Peyton Place" series, so I was a lot older than I looked! But he always introduced me as his friend, the actor!

Now, why am I telling you this? Because I had stated

that I didn't know where I could get the money to film PAPA "the man, the myth, the legend". Jeff knew I had been to New York and tried to get my play on Broadway, but he said he didn't know anything about that "business", and he wouldn't invest in something he wasn't familiar with. I respected him as a friend, and never asked him about investing in my film. During a traditional Thanksgiving dinner at his house, even though Jeff was Jewish, he celebrated Thanksgiving as the pilgrims. He had invited me for Thanksgiving, knowing that Lynn was in Florida with her sisters and her mother, and he didn't want me to be "alone on Thanksgiving". After a fine dinner his wife, Angel, prepared, we were having coffee and dessert, and he asked me how was I doing about trying to film my play? I told him I was contacting some sponsors to see if I could raise the money. Jeff asked me how much did I need?

    I told him the amount, and he responded with, "I can do that. Come on by the office tomorrow and I'll cut you a check".

    Thanks to Jeff, I had the money. I contacted Mike Sapp at Odell, and asked him if we could rehearse the play there, and do a filming of a live performance? Mike agreed but said he didn't know how quickly he could set up the pricing. I made a deal with him. Contact all his subscribers

and invite them to the filming as a special Thank You for their support over the years. No reserved seats (I didn't want anyone complaining about sitting next to one of six cameras I intended to use for the filming). It was on a first-come, first-served basis. We did one performance for camera rehearsal, and the following night we filmed the live performance before a packed house! A lot of friends showed up to support us. Even my good talented friend Joe Torina came up from Florida – Joe would become actively involved with the editing process, and be responsible for correcting a botched editing job, and helped the filmed version of PAPA achieve the quality it was filmed in with the six cameras.
I thank my friend Jeff Swartz for making it possible for me to film PAPA, and preserve the integrity of the play for generations to come. Thank you Jeff, we love you!

    Once the play was filmed, I set about tackling the job of editing all of the digital information contained on the files from all six cameras. I also decided it was time to shed the forty-three pounds I had put on for the role, and I don't need to tell anyone that it's much easier to gain the weight than it is to take it off! It took the better part of a year but I lost the weight! I spent over six months of editing to finally have a finished "rough cut" of the play. During that time, Lynn and I had a rollercoaster of emotions from the highs of me getting some film work, to the lows of family illness and death. I did a small indie film in Wilmington, a role with three scenes in a little film that never saw the light of day, and I can't remember the title. Then I was called by a producer, Michael Davis, who owned and operated Uptone Pictures, to do a faith-based film entitled "A Long Way Off", another slant on the prodigal son story, that starred Robert Davi. We filmed in the Raleigh/ Wake Forrest area of North Carolina. I played a likeable old professor that befriended the wayward son and his girlfriend.

Chapter Thirty-Two

The lows included the death of Lynn's brother, Cliff - he died from Agent Orange, which he got serving in VietNam, and having her step-dad, Ben, placed in an assisted living facility, leaving her mother, Miriam, living on her own.

I continued editing and polishing the PAPA film, and when it was completed, a number of friends suggested I submit it to a few film festivals. At first I resisted, claiming PAPA wasn't a film, but was a "filmed play". The friends countered by reminding me that the play version of "Death of a Salesman" was filmed, that the play version of "Barrymore" was filmed, and that the play version of "Long Day's Journey into Night" was filmed. Okay, okay...I submitted it to The New York International Independent Film Festival in New York – where else?? While I was waiting to hear about being accepted or not, I was contact by another producer who was doing a spooky horror film, scheduled to be filmed in the Blue Ridge Mountains of Floyd, Virginia. The film was entitled "House of Good and Evil" and the role was one of the co-starring roles - one of the "Evils". Rachel Marie Lewis and Christian Oliver were the two stars. You can score this as another "high" for the Blue Collar Actor. Then we were hit with a devastating "low". Mr. Chips was diagnosed with bone cancer in his front leg, and it had metastasized. We had to have him put down. That's a terrible term for anything you love so much. We hired a vet to come to the house in Seven Lakes. After one last trip down to the lake with Mr. Chips, and I swear you could see in his eyes that he knew it was time to leave us, we brought him back home, had him lay comfortably down in our laps, plying him with his favorite cookies, and the Vet put him to sleep. Outside it started raining – the Angels were crying. Lynn and I were a complete basket case for days! Losing Mr. Chips after over eight years of pure joy with him was so terrible, that the word "devastating" doesn't even come close to describing the feeling and emotions! Damn, damn, it was an incredible low! I published another poem about Mr. Chips and us.

We Three

Since he came into our lives,
      We've always been three
My wife Lynn, our dog Mr. Chips, and me.
We played, loved and had a lot of fun,
      Traveled near and traveled
Far, sometimes on a walk, other times in
      The car, My wife Lynn, our dog Mr. Chips
And me, we three.

At rest stops along the way, and the like
        Mr. Chips would be seen
As quite a sight. You see, a Rottie is he, a big
Powerful guy, a gentle giant that goes by,
        Gracefully he romps and bounds
He talks by making vocal sounds.
        It's always my wife Lynn, our dog
Mr. Chips and me,
        We three
And when it's late at night, well he's good to
        Have around
In November we were told that he wouldn't
        Be with us for much longer
An illness that drains his energy, removes the
        Glint from his eyes.
So now his talking will all become sighs,
        Always loved and never will he
Be forgotten.
        So we give him the meds, treat him
With kid gloves, still take him on trips, don't leave
        Him alone, because he knows when he's
With us, it's always home.
        You see, it was just meant to be,
My wife Lynn, our dog Mr. Chips and me,

We three.

After the loss of Mr. Chips, we received word that PAPA "the man, the myth, the legend" had been accepted into The New York International Independent Film Festival, and we needed to make arrangements to attend the Festival for the screenings and interview events scheduled in New York. The Festival was to be held at a large multiplex theatre on Second Avenue in Manhattan. We decided to go up to New York for a week. Lynn had never lived in New York and I decided while we were there I was going to look into some housing possibilities. I found one with a building that The Actors Fund owned, The Dorothy Ross Friedman Residence. It was a building for performing artists that offered reasonable rentals if you met the qualifications. We went over and put in an application.

The Film Festival was a terrific experience. We had a film in the Festival that starred us both, me playing Hemingway and Lynn playing all five women. My friend and co-writer, Ken Vose, came in from Pennsylvania for a screening, and Richmond Sheppard, the mime I had known years ago, and opened for his act when I was one of the folk-singing duos, "The Castaways", attended the screening! Lynn, Ken and I partied a bit during the Festival. After a wonderful week in New York, we headed back to Seven

Lakes. Lynn contacted her mother, Miriam, and after some discussion, it was decided that we would move in with Miriam to look after her in Wilmington. So we set upon preparing to leave Seven Lakes, and the many memories of Mr. Chips that we had enjoyed, and headed back to Wilmington.

As we were gathering boxes and packing up, I received a phone call from The Film Festival people, who had returned to Los Angeles, and I was asked if we planned on attending the awards ceremony to accept our award. I asked where was the awards show taking place, and get this….The New York International Independent Film Festival Awards Show was being held in HOLLYWOOD! Does that make any sense?

I thanked the young lady on the phone for the invitation, but politely declined, saying we couldn't make the trip out to Hollywood because we had prior commitments. Total bullshit! We had no commitments – not yet - but soon! Plus, I couldn't afford to go to Hollywood for an award.

We exchanged a couple of pleasantries, but before I hung up, I asked the young lady, "What award did we win?" She said, "Oh, you won the Best Historical Drama Feature Award for Best Film – Best Actor – Best Actress – Best Director!"

Were they kidding me??? I was speechless – which

isn't easy for me! While I was trying to pull myself together, the young lady said, "Don't worry, we'll mail your awards to you since you can't attend". I thanked her, hung up the phone, and told Lynn, "You're not going to believe this!" We both just won frigging awards for PAPA!

We moved in with Miriam in Wilmington after renting a storage unit and putting our furniture away. We were able to keep our clothes packed in wardrobe boxes in the garage at Miriam's. It was always a treat for me to be around Miriam, she was the only mother-in-law I ever had, that liked me! Once we were settled in and I had given all our contacts the new phone numbers, where we could be reached, I heard from the Actors Fund. We were told that we qualified for an apartment in the Dorothy Ross Friedman Residence, so we were put on the "waiting list". The contact we had met in New York at the Residence was Ellen Celnik, and she was really helpful while we kept on our "waiting coats".

Once back in Wilmington, I had to get on the "horn" and try to find some work for this Blue Collar Actor. Lynn's time was taken up by helping out her mom and driving her out to see Ben at the assisted living facility on a daily basis – Miriam never missed a day to go out and spend it with Ben. Her devotion was beyond belief! She never missed a day the entire time we lived with her!

I started contacting different small theatres that had inquired about PAPA but didn't have the budget to bring it in, and I suggested they hire us to do a performance of "Love Letters". It was the easiest show in the world to perform from a traveling actor's point of view. The set could be put together on site, lights were easy to arrange, and sometimes they had all that were needed. So we booked the show in a few places, after getting permission and paying the royalty, which, unfortunately, not all non-professional actors bother to do. As we were performing "Love Letters" at different venues, I contacted some film art houses and sent them some material we had put together about the PAPA filmed version. I booked a few of these theatres, and two of them, The Sunset in Southern Pines, and Thalian Hall in Wilmington, had previously booked the legitimate theatrical play of PAPA, and now where booking the filmed version for their "Film Series". I believe we hold the honor of being the only show to ever accomplish that at Thalian Hall. Perhaps it's also true of The Sunset. We took the filmed version of PAPA to a couple of colleges, Sandhills Community College in Pinehurst, North Carolina, and the University of Georgia in Athens, plus we screened it at art houses like The Cameo in Fayetteville, North Carolina. We always did an audience Q&A after each screening and the audiences appeared to appreciate that little extra added bonus! They enjoyed meeting the actors! Ah, the life of a Blue Collar Actor!

We had been on the waiting list for one of the performing artist's apartments for almost three years when I received a call from Ellen Celnik. She told me they had an apartment for us, and asked if I wanted to come up to "view" it. I told Ellen we'd take it! She said, "Are you sure you don't want look at it first, before you sign a lease?" I asked her, "When did she need me up there to sign the lease?" She wanted to know if I could manage it in a few days, and I said, "No problem." She ended the conversation by saying, "It's a small one-bedroom, but it has a great view!" Before the week was out I had made my flight reservations and arranged to stay at one of the performing arts studios for a night. I told Lynn we were moving to New York!

Chapter Thirty-Three

Return to New York – Present Tour

I signed the lease at The Dorothy Ross Friedman Residence, viewed the apartment on the 16th floor with a beautiful view of New York City and a view across the Hudson River to New Jersey. On my flight back to Wilmington, I was smiling like a happy Cheshire cat – I had just left OUR Manhattan apartment.

Back in Wilmington, we arranged for one of Miriam's granddaughters to move in and look after her, then we called movers for our furniture in storage, sold our car, rented a U-Haul truck, loaded up our clothing and belongings we had in Miriam's garage and drove off for New York City. I allowed for two stops overnight on the way to the Big Apple and we arrived on Sunday afternoon, May 14th, 2014, in front of our building on West Fifty-Seventh Street. As we were unloading, one of the tenants of the building, Brad, a really nice guy, offered to lend us a helping hand. Brad became the first of many friends we acquired in the building. It took us a few weeks to empty the boxes in the apartment, and divest ourselves of many items we not only didn't have the room for, but actually had no need of. It is wonderful on so many levels to be living in New York City again. My daughter, Cheyenne, lives in Connecticut, just a short train ride away, with my two grandsons, Chayton and Declyn. If nothing else, we are a family of names; Jordan-Cheyenne-Chayton-Declyn. We visit often, and they make trips into the City. My grandsons are crazy about Lynn, and she and Cheyenne get along great. I certainly enjoy supporting the various activities that my grandsons participate in, and they like having Papoo (that's me) and Mimi (that's Lynn) around. It's one of the special "highs". It's good that we can be so close to Cheyenne and the boys, since Cheyenne's mom, Laura, my second wife, passed away unexpectedly after a long illness. I couldn't leave this family section without expressing how proud I am of my daughter and all the good work she accomplishes at The American School for the Deaf. I consider Cheyenne the "best work" this Blue Collar Actor has ever done! Now, for my recent birthday, I'll only admit to being over sixty-five (well over). My daughter treated me to another physical experience to add to my resume which includes; racing motorcycles in the desert, riding motorcycles in general, competing on western horseback, doing some of my own stunts in film & TV and flying in small helicopters, again in film & TV. So, Cheyenne scheduled a skydiving adventure for us both! Yes, you read right, skydiving! My daughter had long heard me say, "I'd like to see if I had the nerve to jump out of a plane." She had already done it twice, and now Ole Dad was invited to go skydiving with his daughter and her fellow. No way I could back out! My wife paid to have it filmed, and on my birthday, I went skydiving with my daughter, doing a tandem jump out of a plane at 14,500 feet! You readers can view that event on YouTube under the title "Actor Jordan Rhodes Skydives!" Pretty amazing!

As Lynn and I are Guild Members of the various professional unions, we immediately began checking out the "boards" where the list of available auditions were displayed. I contacted Cunningham, which now was known in the business as CESD, and made an appointment for both myself and Lynn. Ken Slevin had been one of the lead agents when I left New York the last time, and now he was one of the top partners. I had a number of conversations with Ken prior to moving back to the City, and I thought I would be represented once again by the only commercial agent that ever represented me. I was wrong! Ken informed me that I would need to meet with each department head, and it would be their call whether or not they'd represent me. Everyone was very nice and spoke with me and Lynn, but each department, theatrical, commercial, and voice-over, turned us down. But the print department wanted to represent us.

After all my years in the business – I was now going to be a print model, once again! Lynn has booked more print work than I have, after all she is much prettier than I am, but we've booked a couple together. In my opinion, CESD made a mistake in not wanting to represent Lynn in the theatrical field. She booked 32 shows in 2019.

    Being back in New York, I'm always auditioning for new plays, the ones I see posted on the "board" at Actor's Equity, but I still haven't landed that legitimate agent to move me out "front and center". Just another plight of A Blue Collar Actor! Our theatrical booking agent, Robert Gewald, who had handled some of the bookings for PAPA "the man, the myth, the legend", has since retired, but I had long ago stopped touring the PAPA show. I did have a New York premiere screening of the filmed version at Theatre 80 St. Marks Place in the East Village, which was arranged because of the artistic vision and dedication of Theatre 80's owner, Lorcan Otway. We have become good friends. I've managed to have some short-term associations with a couple of agents here in New York, but nothing of any lasting quality. Currently, I have a booking agent that represents me for the celebrity nostalgia conventions which I have enjoyed doing over the past few years.

    Shortly after arriving back in New York, I was

contacted and asked to appear at the largest celebrity nostalgia convention in the Northeast, The Mid-Atlantic Nostalgia Convention in Maryland. You can Google that one! Many of my celebrity friends were there, including Robert Wagner, Stephanie Powers, Morgan Fairchild, Mark Lester from "Oliver", and Ed Begley, Jr. I was asked to do two panel discussions, one with the lovely Morgan Fairchild, and Ed Begley, Jr., and I substituted for Peter Marshall at the request of Cathy Rudolph, the author of Paul Lynde's biography. Cathy believed I was more than qualified since I had known Peter and Paul from my early years of writing for "The Hollywood Squares". Appearing at these shows gives me an opportunity to meet and greet fans, and I'm happy to autograph my pictures, and take pictures with them. I also enjoy the conversations with the fans at these conventions, plus appearing on the above mentioned panels to answer questions posed by the audience members. An actor friend that I've known for years, Joe Don Baker, told me he had figured out exactly what a "nostalgia celebrity" was. When I asked him what he thought it was, in my case, he answered, "An old actor with a lot of credits."

Coming in contact with old actor friends, and meeting new young ones, is another advantage of being in New York City. I've had an occasion to help one of those actor friends celebrate a birthday in his nineties. I was asked by the manager for Larry Storch, of "F-Troop" fame, if I'd read a letter written to Larry by one of his co-stars, James Hampton, whom I also know, at Larry's birthday celebration, being held at the Triad Theatre on West Seventy-Second Street. I was honored to do so.

In addition to the celebrity conventions, I make some appearances with a solo show, "Conversations of a Blue Collar Actor". I've directed a couple of staged readings of new plays by up and coming writers, and last year (2019) I did a little film for a very talented young female writer and director, entitled, "Last Breath of Spring". For this Blue Collar Actor, these are all "highs". But the highs are always accompanied by some lows. And some lows are lower than others!

After appearing at one of the conventions, I was contacted by an individual who claimed he represented a group of film investors that were looking to produce low-budget films. I was asked if I had any film projects that might interest them. Now being an actor, a writer and a director – of course I would have film projects! Unfortunately, this lowlife was nothing but a "troll" for a group of major scumbags that had a well-organized scam and rip-off scheme. They had an attorney that handled the escrow of funds and contracts, located in another state, plus they "rented" office space in a high rent district of Manhattan where they held their "meetings". The deal was simple. Their company, which they represented as having a multimillion-dollar film fund, would finance eighty percent of the film. The filmmakers (us) would put up the remaining twenty percent for the film, and go off and make the film. Well, my film partners and associates had our legal representatives go over all the contracts and agreements, and we signed off on the deal. I had written the screenplay, hired a number of name actors I knew, whose names I will not divulge, hired production people, located to North Carolina where I had many film contacts. We set up production offices, put our twenty percent of the budget into the escrow account, which was substantial, and went into pre-production for my first directorial feature film. Five weeks into pre-production, using some of our own funds, we requested the funds as agreed to in the contract from the escrow attorney, and we received a One Million Euro check via FedEx, which turned out to be bogus! I called the head of this group in the New York office and he assured me he'd have this misunderstanding resolved. He stated he would wire us the needed funds but it would take a couple of days. My team held on! Three days later we received an email confirming the wire transfer of

$1,000,000 US transferred from a Canadian bank to our bank in North Carolina. We went to the bank, and discovered the wire transfer was also bogus! I had to shut down the production. It was all an elaborate scam being run by a number of individuals that had been ripping off people for a long period of time. Dream shattered! To let the readers know, we filed a lawsuit, and actually won and were awarded a judgment of $2,717,000. Plus, since the scam artists used the mails and banks for the fraudulent funds, the FBI got involved and then the District Attorney of New York City. This group was indicted by a Grand Jury, arrested and arraigned, and are scheduled to go to court under all the criminal charges. As for our "awarded judgment", we have not collected a single dime, and since the courts don't force the defendants in a civil action to actually pay anything, we have to hire a collection bureau to attempt that. My answer to "The Truth about Legal Justice for Victims" – is simple. There isn't any!

Returning to our wonderful apartment in Manhattan, much wiser, and much poorer, we continued to seek work in our chosen field. We did a cabaret, Lynn did a small role in a pilot film and we are putting everything back on the "tracks". I have been introduced to a wonderful business consultant, Jeff Pearce (we have since become friends as well as "business associates"), and Jeff is putting together some incredible projects. The only good thing that came out of the "dealings" with the scumbag, scam, rip-off group was that I managed to meet my manager, Charles Lago.

My business consultant, Jeff, found a very savvy group of investors and producers that have approached me about doing my PAPA play on Broadway! Jeff has also found some people interested in the very same film project that the scumbags had derailed years ago. Everything was looking extremely promising, then China decided to infect the entire world with the Coronavirus, Covid-19! I live in Manhattan, so we are considered the epicenter, and therefore everything is currently on lockdown as I write this! All of these projects are on hold. For the PAPA project, it appears it will move forward as the Covid-19 crisis is conquered. Like so many others, Covid-19 put a complete stop to my work. Two celebrity conventions were canceled. Three of my presentations scheduled for Florida were "postponed", and a film Lynn was cast in was canceled. Everyone has been affected.

But, as that wonderful actress and entertainer, Elaine Stritch, stated, and I'll steal her line, "I'm Still Here!" My manager will have me out at book signings, so if you read this, or even if you don't, but want to come by and say hello, I'll be happy to see you! As for all the bull-shitters that constantly drift in and out of this business, screwing up people's lives, and upsetting good apple carts - and it's the profession I chose to spend my life in. I'd like to leave you all, regardless of your profession with an Ernest "Papa" Hemingway quote. Now it pertains to writers, but I believe we need to have it, or acquire it, in order to achieve success in any field of endeavor, and to avoid all the bull-shitters. Here's Papa's quote; "The most essential gift for a good writer is a built-in shit detector. This is the writer's radar and all good writers have it."

    I hope you've enjoyed my book.

-- Jordan Rhodes

Written By Jordan Rhodes

Acknowledgments & Notes

I want to express my gratitude to Leo Penn for putting my career on the map, for his friendship and support, and encouraging me to write this book. There are many friends and people to thank for their contributions during my career, and I'll list them in no specific order since each is equally important. I thank all the teachers that helped me discover that I had something to offer, these include; Karl Redcoff, Wendell K. Phillips, Leslie Irons, Paul Kent and Lee Strasberg even though he rejected me at The Actors Studio.

My thanks to the many directors including, Leo Penn, Kenneth Gilbert, E.W. Swackhammer, John Sturges, Jeffrey Hayden, Jud Taylor, Harry Falk, Charles Rome Smith, Tom Troupe, Andrew McLaglen, Lee Madden, Michael C. Sapp, Sean Penn, Phillip Pruneau, Leslie Irons and James Komack. A special thanks to my good friend and writing partner Ken Vose, for our journey writing the Hemingway play, and various projects we shared. Thanks to another very good and talented friend, Michael Schnorr, whose talent as a graphic artist made my book look good.

Thanks to the sketch artists, Audrey Faye Costa and Emil Gustave Keller for their talent.

There are so many actors that I've enjoyed working with, it would be impossible to list them all, but I thank them all for the pleasure, and the list includes; Karl Malden, Michael Douglas, Fess Parker, Robert Wagner, John Wayne, Paul Sand, Chuck Connors, Scott Brady, Tom Troupe, Carole Cook, Barbara Rush, Paul Kent, David Morse, Robert Pine, Art Kassel, Paul Koslo, Al Letteri, Don Stroud, Kent McCord, Martin Milner, Sam Elliott, Richard X. Slattery, Roger Smith, Darren McGavin, Lee J. Cobb, Buddy Ebsen, James Garner, Walter Brennan, Wally Cox, Dennis Hopper, Sean Penn, Lee Grant, David Canary, Michael Landon, Lorne Green, Viggo Mortensen, Sandy Dennis, Tyne Daly, Ernest Borgnine, Brenda Vacarro, Monte Markham and James Franciscus – to mention a few.

I owe a debt of gratitude to many people on the production and tech side of this industry where I've spent my entire adult life, and first is another good friend, and talented producer and film editor, Joe Torina, we've been down some good and bad roads, but his talent and friendship has remained. There are too many producers to thank but I need to single out a few like; Walter Mirish, Dan Curtis, Quinn Martin, Herm Saunders and David O'Connell. My appreciation to the cameramen, make-up artists, wardrobe people, drivers and technicians, who all contributed to help me do a better job. I have appreciated all of you, and you know who you are, so please accept my sincere thanks and forgive me for not being able to list all your names, but like everyone mentioned in this acknowledgement, I couldn't have done the work without your help.

For the ladies in my life, I'm going to borrow and paraphrase lines from Willie's song, and thank all the ladies that have traveled in and out of my life – I'm glad you came along and I'll dedicate Willie's song. Obviously this includes my former wives, Jan, and Laura, the mother of my daughter Cheyenne, who remains the love of my life, and believes I'm the world's greatest dad. I want to thank Lynn, my present wife of more than twenty years for her love and support, and continued belief that I can always, "pull a rabbit out of a hat".

I'm grateful to Jill St. John and Robert Wagner for writing the foreword to this book, and I greatly appreciate their friendship. This acknowledgement would not be complete without thanking so many friends whose stories are detailed in the book, and these include the Penn family, and the Gilbert family where I spent many wonderful Sunday evening dinners - My musician friends, Patrick Arvonio and brothers Angelo and Bobby, along with their Dad, who scored The American Cowboy film for me.

Obviously agents play an important part in any actors life, and more so in a Blue Collar Actors life. I traveled in and out a number of those agency doors both in New York and Hollywood but only a handful stand out. First on my thank you list is Ted Wilk, he really opened the door for some outstanding jobs for me, and Alex Brewis tried to fill his shoes. In New York the only one that pushed the envelope for me very early in the Soap Opera world was Honey Rader.

I want to thank the only entertainment attorney I've ever had, Rich Agins. He was always willing to offer me advice and help for any project I was working on. His legal advice and guidance was instrumental in the development of PAPA, the Hemingway play.

Of course no one can survive in this professional arena without falling into the occasional pit with the liars, cheaters, thieves and bull shitters. They come disguised as producers, financers, creators and even distributors, all with no talent, so they steal your money, and they all know who they are! Some are awaiting justice, and others have justice coming!

In closing, I'll offer some encouragement to the new group of young actors I continue to meet on both a personal, and work level. I never excelled at team sports, but I do remember one coach that always told us players, we never lost….we just ran out of time. So I hope you'll keep on trying and never quit, because quitters never win – and winners never quit.

-- Jordan Rhodes